Wealth, Poverty and Starvation

By the same author

Social Security: Beveridge and After (1968)
Foster Care: Theory and Practice (1970)
Motherless Families (with Paul Wilding) (1972)
Social Security and Society (1973)
Ideology and Social Welfare (with Paul Wilding) (1976 & 1986)
Socialism, Social Welfare and the Soviet Union (with Nick Manning) (1980)
Poverty and Inequality in Common Market Countries (with Roger Lawson) (1980)
The Impact of Social Policy (with Paul Wilding) (1984)

Part of the author's royalties will be paid to OXFAM

Wealth, Poverty and Starvation

A World Perspective

Vic George
Professor of Social Policy
University of Kent

WHEATSHEAF BOOKS · ENGLAND
ST. MARTIN'S PRESS · NEW YORK

First published 1988 by
Wheatsheaf Books Ltd,
66 Wood Lane End, Hemel Hempstead, Hertfordshire HP2 4RG
A division of
Simon & Schuster International Group

and in the USA by
St. Martin's Press Inc,
175 Fifth Avenue, New York NY 10010

Printed and bound in Great Britain by Billings & Sons Ltd, Worcester

---

British Library Cataloguing in Publication Data

George, Vic *1930*–
Wealth, poverty and starvation: a world
perspective
1. Income. Distribution. Inequalities.
Political aspects
I. Title
339.2
ISBN 0-7450-0070-3
ISBN 0-7450-0207-2 Pbk

Library of Congress Cataloging-in-Publication Data

George, Victor.
Wealth, poverty, and starvation: a world perspective/Vic
George.
p. cm.
Bibliography: p.
Includes index.
ISBN 0-312-01980-7 (St. Martin's Press): $45.00 (est.)
1. Income distribution. 2. Wealth. 3. Poor. 4. Economic
development. 5. Income distribution—Developing countries.
6. Wealth—Developing countries. 7. Poor—Developing
countries. 8. Developing countries—Economic conditions.
I. Title.
HC79.I5G47 1988
339.2′09172′4—dc19   88–4689
                                                              CIP

1 2 3 4 5   92 91 90 89 88

Contents

List of Tables

Introduction

Wealth, Poverty and Starvation reflects my concern at the grossly unequal distribution of income within and between countries, and my theoretical interest in the origins and uses of power at the international, national and group level. Apart from a few exceptions (Seabrook, 1985; Smith, 1977), the literature on inequality and poverty is divided into two groups: one which deals with these issues at the global level, and another which examines them as they operate within individual countries or groups of countries of similar socio-economic standing. The book is based on the premise that theoretical and policy debates on development and under-development at the world scale bear a very strong resemblance to theories and policies on poverty and inequality within countries. It therefore attempts the dual task of documenting the extent of poverty and inequality at the international and country level, and of assessing the usefulness of the theoretical literature that purports to explain both of these patterns of distribution.

Such a discussion necessitates the division of the world into groups of countries—the first, second and third world countries. Yet such a division clearly oversimplifies what is a far more complex situation. It runs the risk on one hand of giving the impression that conflicts of interests are between the various groups of countries only, and on the other of con-cealing or underplaying conflicts of interests within countries and between countries of the same group. Hopefully enough care has been taken in this book to avoid these dangers as much as it is possible without cautioning the reader *ad nauseam*.

The book begins with a detailed review of theories of development and underdevelopment—Chapter 1—and contrasts these with theories of poverty and inequality. Structuralist explanations of both underdevelopment and poverty fit the facts better than any other theory both on the country and the world level. Chapter 2 reviews post-war trends in economic growth and world inequalities as well as trends in the distribution of wealth and income within individual countries. It shows that these inequalities have proved very resistant to change, and that they will continue in similar ways in the future. Chapter 3 examines the extent of poverty within the affluent countries, and it shows that despite real progress over the years, poverty still exists on a substantial scale. It also examines the causes of poverty from a structuralist perspective and concludes that despite the affluence of these countries, poverty will persist in the foreseeable future.

Chapter 4 reviews the evidence on famine, starvation and subsistence poverty in the Third World. Despite the problems of data, it is shown that the degree of progress made is not only small but it varies considerably between countries. Economic growth by itself does not reduce poverty though it makes its alleviation more possible if governments embark on the right policies. But poverty in third world countries is the result of maldistribution of both internal and world resources. It is, therefore, far more prevalent and far more severe than in the affluent countries, and its alleviation is a much more daunting task. Chapter 5 reviews the various explanations and concludes that external factors are far more important than internal factors in explaining Third World poverty. Chapter 6 is a brief conclusion with a pessimistic forecast of trends in poverty and inequality in the immediate future. The current economic recession has not only reduced rates of economic growth but it has also, for the time being, weakened those political forces making for the reduction of inequality and poverty on a world and country scale.

In accordance with convention, I wish to acknowledge my debt to several of my colleagues who read individual chapters and made helpful comments—Paul Wilding, Nick Manning and Peter Taylor-Gooby. My thanks, too, to Ian Shirley with whom this book would have been written jointly had it not been for the geographical distance and the vagaries of the postal system between Britain and New Zealand. My thanks, too, to Margaret Joyce who typed several drafts of the book with good humour and efficiency. Errors of omission and commission are, of course, my responsibility alone.

Any book that attempts to document and explain inequality and poverty at both the global and the country level will inevitably suffer from problems of oversimplification and over-generalisation. Yet production and distribution issues can no longer be dealt with satisfactorily at the national level while ignoring the individual country's position within the world system. Thus despite its weaknesses, the book will hopefully help readers to gain a better understanding of the issues of poverty and inequality at both the world and country level. Above all, however, it is hoped that the book will make some contribution to strengthening the forces making for a less unequal distribution of resources and life chances both within and between countries.

1 Theories of development and underdevelopment

Theories of development and underdevelopment at the international level are very similar to explanations of wealth and poverty at the national level, and they can both be grouped under two main headings—individualistic and structural. Individualistic explanations attribute wealth and poverty primarily to the characteristics of the individual unit, whether this is a country or a person. Structural explanations, on the other hand, consider these conditions at both the national and international level as being primarily the result of structural factors, reflecting the balance of power between countries or groups of individuals or both. Though this chapter concentrates on explanations of wealth and poverty at the international level, it makes brief references to the corresponding theories at the national level which are examined in more detail in subsequent chapters. Before we do this, however, a brief account of the notion of development is necessary.

THE NOTION OF DEVELOPMENT

The notion of development is both normative and multidimensional, and it shares the essential contestability of all important notions in the social sciences. Being contestable means, in the words of the Brandt Report, that development 'never will be, and never can be, defined to universal satisfaction' (*The Brandt Report*, 1980, p. 48). Value judgements are inevitable in the way it is defined, and this in turn has significant implications for the type of policies necessary for its promotion (Baster, 1972).

Though universal agreement on the definition of development is not possible, it is feasible to highlight the most important approaches to it out of the long list of definitions that have
been adopted by different writers over the years (Elliott,
1971). Three such definitions have in fact dominated the literature during the post-war period, and have had varying degrees
of influence on the policies pursued by national governments
and by international bodies.

The literature of the 1950s equated development with
economic growth, in terms of either increases in the country's
national product or more specifically in terms of rises in
income per capita in a country. It was a definition that seemed
to make sense during a period when the efforts of most governments were inevitably directed at rebuilding their war-ravaged
economies. The United Nations reflected this mood by pro-
claiming the 1960s as the first development decade and classifying countries that achieved a 6 per cent growth in their
national incomes as achieving a satisfactory level of development. This emphasis on economic growth either ignored issues
of income-distribution and poverty or, at best, assumed that
as the economy of a country expanded everyone would benefit
more or less alike. In the language of economists, the fruits of
economic growth would 'trickle down' from the top to the
middle income groups as well as down to the poor.

The second definition of development emerged to replace
the first when it was realised that this 'trickle down' effect was
not usually taking place. It was, in fact, quite common for a
country's national income to grow quite substantially without
benefiting the poor sections of the country as much as the rich.
Absolute poverty could remain unaltered and even rise at
times of substantial economic growth. Out of this realisation,
development came to be defined in terms of poverty alleviation
and inequality reduction. Economic growth was still important
but, for development to take place, it had to be accompanied
by the achievement of these social objectives. Development
now became a synonym for social improvement, and could
only be measured by the extent to which the social objectives
were achieved. Seers's approach to the definition and measurement of development both highlighted and established this
new mood:

The questions to ask about a country's development are: What has been happening to poverty? What has been happening to unemployment? What has been happening to inequality? If all three of these have become less severe then beyond doubt this has been a period of development for the country concerned. If one or two of these central problems have been growing worse, especially if all three have, it would be strange to call the result 'development' even if per capita income has soared. (Seers, 1972)

Various names were given to this new approach to development—redistribution with growth, anti-poverty approach, the basic needs approach, and so on—and they were all taken up as guidelines for the development policies of the international agencies in the 1970s (Lisk, 1977). They were characterised by high idealism and a gross underestimation of the political obstacles to their implementation.

The third meaning of development emerged at about the same time as the second, but went beyond it to include not only 'basic needs' but emotional, spiritual and political needs as well. Writing from a Marxist perspective, Rodney saw development at the level of the individual as 'increased skill and capacity, greater freedom, creativity, self-discipline, responsibility and material well-being' (Rodney, 1972, p. 9). From a structuralist perspective, Todaro agrees with Courlet that the notion of development incorporates three core values: first, life-sustenance, i.e. the satisfaction of basic physiological needs; second, self-esteem; and third freedom 'from the social servitudes of men to nature, ignorance, other men, misery, institutions and dogmatic beliefs' (Todaro, 1977, p. 97). President Nyerere's definition of freedom also belongs to this approach of development: it includes not only political freedom but freedom from hunger, disease, ignorance and the like, as well as the right of individuals to live in dignity and equality with others (Nyerere, 1977).

The very broad nature of the third definition makes the notion of development very appealing but also very vague, and hence not amenable to any social scientific measurement. It is a goal towards which societies may strive but rarely, if ever, reach. It is no surprise, therefore, that both policy makers and social scientists have adopted the second definition. Development, therefore, refers to the multi-dimensional process whereby societies improve their living standards, reduce inequalities and abolish poverty among their members.

Social scientists showed very little interest in third world countries in general until the early 1950s. Anthropologists were the exception, but their concern was not with the development process but rather with the strange customs and practices that they observed among 'primitive' tribes or 'peasant' societies. The colonial status of third world countries obliterated their individuality and rendered them appendages to their imperial powers. Anthropological studies tended to reflect and reinforce this.

The situation changed considerably, however, in the early 1950s when several colonies gained or were about to gain independence. The West could no longer take it for granted that the newly independent countries would remain within its political orbit, particularly at a time when the Soviet Union was beginning to extend its influence and to show designs for future world domination. The West's response came in the form of the Truman doctrine—a vigorous attempt to strengthen and expand American influence in third world countries through both economic and military aid programmes. It was within this political climate that social scientists, with generous financial support from American agencies, began to take an active interest in the 'development problems' of underdeveloped countries.

Five main theories have since been advanced to explain the underdevelopment of third world countries: the modernisation thesis, the classical Marxist approach, the dependency thesis, the neo-Marxist approach, and the structuralist explanation. Though each of these theories attempts to explain inequalities between groups of countries, they can also be used to explain inequalities within countries and particularly between different regions of the same country. Inevitably they all suffer from the problem of overgeneralisation, for no two countries are alike in all respects; nor can all first and third world countries be treated as two homogeneous groups. The opposite approach, however, of treating every country as totally unique and rejecting all forms of theoretical generalisation, is equally unproductive. As Roxborough points out, theoretical generalisation is possible and in fact desirable but 'the process is a complex one' (Roxborough, 1979, p. x). At the present stage of our theoretical understanding of development issues, none of these theories can possibly be used to provide a detailed explanation of underdevelopment in each and every country. What these theories can do, however, is to provide their own distinctive conceptual framework for collecting and synthesising the relevant data necessary for explaining the underdevelopment process of different countries or different regions within countries. They also imply different and conflicting paths to development and they, therefore, have different implications for the policies to be pursued by both governments and international development bodies.

MODERNISATION THEORY

It was within this socio-political climate that the first theory of development—the modernisation theory—emerged during the 1950s, though its intellectual origins can be traced back to the writings of Spencer, Durkheim and Weber in the nineteenth and early twentieth centuries. Modernisation theorists saw development as an evolutionary process going through various stages and transforming all societies from traditional to modern. The number of stages varied from one writer to another: Hoselitz referred to two—traditional and modern; Lerner added an intermediary third—transitional. Parsons extended them to five; and so did Rostow with his well-publicised stages of traditional, pre take-off, take-off, the road to maturity and the society of mass consumption (Hoselitz, 1960; Lerner, 1964; Parsons, 1966; Rostow, 1962). Like all evolutionary theories, modernisation theory maintained that each successive stage is not only different from but superior to the one preceding it. Development is a cumulative improvement process, and this becomes abundantly clear when one compares either historically or contemporarily societies at the two extreme stages of development.

In more precise terms, modernisation means 'a "total" transformation of a traditional or pre-modern society into the types of technology and associated social organisation that characterise the "advanced", economically prosperous, and relatively politically stable nations of the Western World' (Moore, 1963,

p. 89). In other words, modernisation implies changes in the technological, economic, political and social systems of developing nations so that they become increasingly like the Western European and North American countries. The modern man (or woman) too, is a very different person from his traditional counterpart in the way he thinks and acts in the various aspects of his life. In traditional societies, claims the modernisation theory, behaviour is characterised by particularism, ascription, and functional diffuseness; in modern societies it is characterised by the exact opposites—universalism, achievement orientation and functional specificity (Hoselitz, 1960). In simpler language, government officials in modern societies, for example, deal with individuals impartially while in traditional societies they tend to favour their relatives, friends and suchlike (universalism versus particularism); people in modern societies are judged by their individual achievement and behaviour while in traditional societies they are judged by their family origin (achievement versus ascription); and relationships between individuals in modern societies are role-specific as, for example, between employer and employee while in traditional societies they are generalised as in the case of master and apprentice or lord and serf (functional specificity versus functional diffuseness). Thus the modernisation process involves the substitution of the traditional in favour of the modern types of both individual and collective behaviour, in all the various subsystems of society—work, politics, business, family, leisure, religion, and so on. It is the Westernisation of all humanity.

What, however, are the driving forces behind the modernisation process? Weber's work was used, and more often than not misused, to provide the answer to this very crucial question. Weber's basic argument was that the development of capitalism in Western Europe was due not only to the existence of the appropriate economic conditions but also to the existence of the appropriate value system, i.e. the Protestant Ethic which emphasised the values of hard work, savings and entrepreneurship. Some modernisation theorists tried to combine economic and attitudinal factors, others highlighted attitudes and values only but, above all, they all considered changes in attitudes and values as the most important prerequisite to the development process in third world countries. McClelland's writings represent the strongest advocacy of the importance of values and attitudes to development. Central to economic development in any society is the existence and general acceptance of 'the need for achievement' value. Third world countries do not possess this value to any great extent and it is, therefore, imperative that it should be vigorously propagated through the formal and informal processes if economic development is to take place. When the younger generation of third world countries is socialised with the 'need for achievement' value, economic development will take place even if the economic circumstances appear unfavourable. As he put it: 'Men with high achievement will find a way to economic achievement given fairly wide variations in opportunity and social structure' (McClelland, 1961, p. 105).

Rowstow's approach gives more emphasis to economic factors than McClelland's though it, too, makes entrepreneurship the most important factor for development. Economies can only go beyond the pre take-off stage if they can invest over 10 per cent of their national income, if they concentrate on one or two manufacturing sectors and, above all, if the spirit of entrepreneurship can flourish within a Western type political and social framework. Advanced industrial countries can assist in this process by providing some of the capital necessary for investment as well as some of the personnel necessary for the introduction of new techniques and ideas in industry, government, education, and elsewhere. Rostow's ideas of take-off received wide support in both developing and developed countries, for they promised benefits to all concerned as well as a programme to rival the Eastern European model of development. It was both a political and an economic model of development, and it became the capitalist manifesto for economic development during the 1960s.

The essence of the modernisation theory can also be found in the writings of economists supporting dualist explanations of underdevelopment. Such societies consist of a dynamic, expanding sector based on capitalist lines and covering the large urban areas of a country, and a stagnant, subsistence sector in the rural areas. Very little contact exists between these two sectors, with the result that the majority of the population, being rural, continues to live in poverty even when the modern urban sector expands. Thus the solution to the problem of underdevelopment lies in creating linkages between the two sectors, so that the modernising influences can spread from the urban sector to the rural areas. The implication clearly is that both the problem of underdevelopment and its solution are to be found in factors that are internal to the economy of a country (Lewis, 1955).

In essence all modernisation theorists saw development as the result of endogenous factors, i.e. factors which operated within the country, and are hence amenable to improvement particularly with help from rich countries and outside international agencies. In the same way that the industrialised countries of the West moved from the first to the last stage of development, so, too, would third world countries if they copied their example. The major policy implication of the modernisation thesis in all its variations was to Westernise all third world countries in every respect. Thus the 1960s witnessed a range of programmes in developing countries financed and directed mainly from outside, in a grand effort to modernise their education and health care systems, industry and agriculture, political and government systems and so on. Social scientists, with massive research funds from the USA and the World Bank, developed sophisticated but value-based matrices of social and economic indicators to measure the degrees of modernisation needed or achieved by the various aid programmes.

The academic dominance of the modernisation thesis lasted for over a decade until it was effectively challenged and replaced by the dependency thesis in the late 1960s. In retrospect, the modernisation thesis suffers from so many weaknesses that it now seems surprising that it dominated social science debates on development for so long. Nevertheless, a brief assessment is necessary, partly because of the influence it still has on the policies of international bodies, and partly because such an assessment will suggest the forms that later development theories assumed.

In the first place, the dichotomy between tradition and modernity is far too broad and vague to be of any meaning in the classification of countries. Thus India and Lesotho are classified as traditional while Greece and Sweden as modern, despite the fact that there are as many differences within the pairs as there are between the two pairs of countries.

Secondly, the claim that the forms of social behaviour between the two groups of countries are exact opposites is far from correct. It is an oversimplification of much more complex forms of behaviour that cannot be neatly packaged into two opposites. Thus, taking the twin variables of ascription versus achievement as an example of this, it is misleading to argue that in advanced industrial societies the road to individual economic success is through personal achievement only or even mainly. Working class people have fewer opportunities than middle class people, women are disadvantaged in relation to men, black people are discriminated against, and those with large wealth inheritances do not have to rely on personal achievement. Similar comments can be made in relation to ascription in developing societies. In other words, what we find is varying degrees of both ascription and achievement in all types of societies, the importance of each varying from one group in society to another.

Thirdly, the claim that there is a functional compatibility between the various subsystems of society, and that economic development is only compatible with certain types of the other subsystems is manifestly untrue. For example, the claim that economic development is only or mainly compatible with parliamentary democracy is empirically incorrect. Any cursory examination of the recent history of third world countries shows that authoritarian governments are no more unsuccessful in achieving economic development than parliamentary democracies. Similarly, the claim that the nuclear family system is either a prerequisite or at least optimally functional to economic development is unsubstantiated by historical and contemporary evidence. Historians are divided on the forms of family systems that prevailed prior to industrialisation in Europe (Anderson, 1980); while today different forms of family systems exist in industrial countries. Even if it were empirically true that the nuclear family is the norm in industrial societies, it would be a mistake of the first order in the social sciences to consider it as the cause of economic development. If anything, the causal relationship is in the exact opposite direction—economic development may be the cause or one of the causes of the restriction of the family unit.

Fourthly, the assumption that what proved necessary or useful to the advanced industrial countries of the West must also apply to developing countries has, on several occasions, proved a costly policy guideline. A case in point is education. Third world countries were actively encouraged to modernise their educational systems i.e. to expand them along European lines, whereas they would have been better off to use their resources to eradicate illiteracy before building universities, to provide school curricula suited to their specific needs and to emphasise their culture rather than that of their ex-colonial masters. Education is important to economic development but it must be the kind that is relevant to the needs of the country and, as Harrison points out, 'not the kind of education made up of academic irrelevances, alien concepts and sentiments, the kind that fills children's heads with dreams of the city and unfits them for their role in the village, the kind that brands the many as failures, so that the few can enjoy the excessive rewards of success' (Harrison, 1979, p. 327). Similar comments apply to health care and other government services.

Fifthly, many of the modernisation writers claim or imply that there is no conflict of interest between the affluent countries of the West and third world countries in terms of trade, manufacture, agriculture and so on, and that the development of one group of countries always facilitates and benefits that of the other. Without getting involved in the debate at this stage, it is worth simply making the point that the claim may be true in some instances but, as Chapter 5 shows, it is untrue in many more cases. The same comment applies even more strongly to the related claim that European countries industrialised without any outside help. It is a claim that ignores the vast contribution that colonies made as exporters of cheap raw materials and as importers of manufactured goods, as we shall see later in this chapter.

Finally, there is the vexed question of the importance of values and attitudes to economic development. It is an argument that has been used to explain the poverty of individuals as well as the poverty of whole nations. People are poor because they do not possess and hence are not motivated by entrepreneurial values; whole nations are poor because their cultures are empty of entrepreneurial values. Individuals and nations are poor because they are motivated by such values as apathy, pessimism, laziness, tradition, resignation, and so on. Thus it is imperative to change the value systems of the poor as individuals or as nations if they are to rid themselves of their poverty. It is a thesis of poverty best known as the 'culture of poverty', first popularised by Oscar Lewis in his work in Latin America in the 1960s (Lewis, 1966).

The first problem with the 'culture of poverty' thesis is that it uses values and concepts which are vague and almost impossible to define precisely for any scientific measurement. Such values as 'deferred gratification', 'apathy', or the 'needs achievement', or 'entrepreneurship', are just impossible to define in ways that can be validated by other researchers. The result is an even more vague exchange of views between the various contestants. Bearing this in mind, research among the shanty-town dwellers of several Latin American cities failed to corroborate the culture of poverty thesis. It showed that the poor as a group do not possess values that are different from those of the rest of the society in which they live, even though their behaviour may at times be different (George and Lawson, 1980, Chapter 1). Moreover, when poor people as individuals or communities behave in ways that appear fatalistic or anti-growth, this may reflect a realistic reaction to an insecure, threatening situation, bearing in mind their life experiences of deprivation.

Changing the structure rather than the assumed culture is the way forward for the abolition of poverty. Several studies of impoverished rural groups reviewed by Long led him to similar conclusions, i.e. that peasant culture was no impediment to development and on the contrary 'once a viable set of opportunities presented themselves, the peasants showed every willingness to increase production and become more involved in the market economy' (Long, 1977, p. 50). A similar position is taken by Barrington Moore in relation to Indian small farmers in the 1960s whose practices, thought to be the result of their values were impeding agricultural productivity. Calls by experts or government officials for farmers to change their attitudes and practices would be as unproductive now as in the past, for by themselves they had a hollow ring about them. Instead: 'It is necessary to change the situation confronting the people on the land if they are going to alter their behaviour. And if this has not yet happened, as by and large it has not, there are likely to be good political reasons' (Moore, 1969, p. 387).

These and other criticisms exposed the theoretical weaknesses of the modernisation theory, and led to its gradual demise as the dominant theoretical paradigm of development. Attempts to revise the theory in order to rid it of its most obvious weaknesses came to nothing, for the theory grossly overestimates internal factors and it almost neglects external factors to development; it is based on the principle of congruence of interests both internally and between nations; it overemphasises attitudinal factors and underestimates structural factors to development; and it is an overoptimistic evolutionary theory, downgrading the cultures of developing societies and idealising Western European culture in all its aspects. It is impossible to modify sufficiently these component parts of the theory without altering it beyond recognition (see Randall and Theobald, 1985, for a detailed discussion of this).

Despite its academic decline, the essentials of the theory still influence heavily the work of the main international bodies of development—the World Bank and the IMF in particular. Thus internal rather than external factors are still seen as being responsible for the poverty of developing countries, and these internal factors are perceived not as such structural issues as the maldistribution of wealth and land, but rather as behavioural and policy issues—rapid population growth, political instability, government pricing policies, agricultural policies, and so on. Thus one of the World Bank's reviews of the forces relevant to development concludes that 'while powerfully influenced by the international environment, the progress of developing countries depends even more on their own policies, and initiatives' (World Bank, 1980, p. 96). A similar view was taken in a recent report on poverty in Sub-Saharan countries (World Bank, 1981), a view which was found wanting by several African and other commentators on that subject (Ndegwa, *et al.* (eds), 1985). The policies recently adopted by the IMF in relation to the problems encountered by third world countries in meeting their debt repayments constitute an even more extreme form of the modernisation theory. The problem of third world indebtedness is seen in terms purely internal to third world countries, and the solutions proposed— reducing public expenditure, holding down wage rises and the like—have the general effect of protecting the interests of advanced industrial societies at the expense of the Third World, as we shall show in a later chapter.

DEPENDENCY THEORY

The severest and most effective criticism of the modernisation theory came from a group of scholars who subscribed to what has come to be known as the dependency theory. In fact, the criticism was so effective that the dependency theory replaced modernisation as the dominant paradigm in development debates, and retained that position all through the 1970s. Though dependency theorists have strong affinities to Marxism, most of them are not Marxists because their theoretical framework for development and underdevelopment is not based primarily on the production system of societies. Though the dependency school includes a large number of well-known social scientists, we shall concentrate here on the work of Frank, Wallerstein and Cardoso, for they represent the three main strands of thought within the dependency school.

The dependency theory was for a long time associated mainly with the work of A. G. Frank, though its origins are to be found in the Marxist writings of Baran in the late 1950s and in the structuralist writings of a group of Latin American economists working with ECLA (United Nations Economic Commission for Latin America) in Santiago in the early 1960s.

Baran's work was the first major break among contemporary Marxists from the orthodox Marxist view on economic development in the Third World. Unlike Marx who, as we shall see in the next section, saw all countries going through a series of stages until they reach the socialist stage, Baran saw third world countries as being stuck in their present stage of underdevelopment as a result of their structural exploitation by the industrialised countries. The Third World provided the rich countries both with raw materials and export markets at very favourable trade terms. There is no possibility in sight for economic progress in the Third World for, in Baran's words, 'economic development in underdeveloped countries is profoundly inimical to the dominant interests in the advanced capitalist countries' (Baran, 1957, p. 28).

A similar, though not as pessimistic, view was adopted by the ECLA economists, led by Prebisch, who rejected the traditional trade theory which maintained that international trade would gradually spread the economic benefits of industrialisation from the rich to the poor countries. Instead, they argued that the terms of trade between the industrialised world and Latin America had been moving against Latin America since the 1870s. The general conclusion was that international trade perpetuated and even strengthened the advantages of the First over the Third World. Unlike Baran, however, who argued that the only way forward for third world countries was through a political solution that changed their dependent status, the ECLA economists argued for deliberate economic policies that fostered 'import-substitution industrialisation', i.e. state economic policies that favoured national industrialisation and thus reduced the import of manufactured goods from industrial countries.

Frank's formulation of the dependency theory is based on the historical experience of Latin America and particularly of Brazil and Chile, though it has been used to cover all third world countries. Unlike the modernisation theorists who saw underdevelopment as the result of endogenous factors, and as a stage through which all countries go before they become developed, Frank argued that it was the result of exogenous factors, and it was a condition that the industrialised countries had never experienced. Underdevelopment is a condition imposed on the Third World by the industrialised countries in order to promote their own development. Thus underdevelopment in one group of countries is the result of development in another. Or, in Frank's words, 'Economic development and underdevelopment are the opposite faces of the same coin. Both are the necessary result and contemporary manifestation of internal contradictions in the world capitalist system' (Frank, 1967, p. 9).

This process of active underdevelopment began during the period of mercantile expansion of European countries in the sixteenth century, it was reinforced during the long period of colonialism and it has continued during the period of political independence by third world countries down to the present day. It is a structural situation through which developed and underdeveloped countries are inextricably linked in an unequal and exploitative relationship. It involves a triple form of related exploitation—economic, political and cultural—as a result of which Third World countries are mere 'satellites', serving the interests of the 'metropoles', i.e. countries in the capitalist industrialised world. This unequal and exploitative chain goes well beyond the international level into the internal system of stratification of every dependent country. The national metropolis exploits the regional towns, which in turn exploit the local centres and they in turn exploit the impoverished rural population. At any one time, the picture of the world consists of, according to Frank, 'a whole chain of metropolises and satellites, which runs from world metropoles down to the hacienda or rural merchant who are satellites of the local commercial metropolitan center but who in their turn have peasants as satellites' (Frank, 1967, pp. 146-7). Each in the chain extracts profit from the satellite below it, keeps some for itself, and passes the rest upwards until it reaches the primary metropolis of the industrial country—New York, London, Zurich, Frankfurt, Rome, and so on. These chain relationships are more than economic—they are also political and cultural—and they may vary slightly from one case to another though such differences 'do not obviate their essential similarity in that all of them, to one degree or another, rest on the exploitation of the satellite by the metropolis' (Frank, 1967, p. 17).

The driving force behind this unequal relationship between countries and within countries is economic and political power. Frank is not all that explicit as to how this structural maldistribution of power operates in detail, though he dwells at some length on the incorporation of national elites into the world capitalist system. Thus national elites are not independent—they are 'comprador' elites whose wealth and power rest on the approval they receive by their masters, the metropole elites. Similar comments apply to the power of elites at lower levels within any dependent country.

The implications of Frank's theory of dependency for under-developed countries are as far-reaching as they are depressing. In the first place, autonomous economic development in third world countries is impossible within the world capitalist system. It is, of course, possible for a certain degree of indus-trialisation to take place; but when this is foreign controlled, either directly or indirectly, the result is that, first, most of the profits are reaped by the comprador and metropole elites and, second, such industrialisation can easily be brought to an end by foreign capital if it considers it necessary.

Secondly, the stronger the economic, political and cultural links between metropole and satellite, the greater the degree of domination and exploitation; vice-versa, the weaker the links, the lesser the degree of exploitation. Thus, third world countries should try to reduce their dependence on rich countries if they want to maximise their chances of auton-omous development.

Thirdly, it follows from all this that the underdevelopment of third world countries cannot come about through peaceful, bourgeois reforms but through the revolt of the masses, perhaps along the lines of the Cuban revolution. Having closed all the avenues for gradual political change, Frank turns to national revolution and proclaims rather than argues that 'the long exploited people themselves are being taught and prepared to lead the way out of capitalism and underdevelop-ment (Frank, 1967, pp. 217-8).

Frank's ideas gained wide acceptance, and they were adopted by other scholars to explain underdevelopment in other parts of the third world and particularly in Africa by Amin (Amin, 1972, 1974, 1976). These writings, however, were so close to Frank's position that, for our purposes, they do not warrant separate discussion. Thus we turn to Wallerstein's work which represents a very substantial extension of the dependency theory. In Wallerstein's 'world systems' theory, the main focus of analysis becomes the world system rather than individual countries. In one of his earlier works he states clearly that he 'abandoned the idea altogether of taking either the sovereign state or that vaguer concept, the national society, as the unit of analysis. I decided that neither one was a social system and that one could only speak of social change in social systems. The only social system in this scheme was the world system' (Wallerstein, 1974, p. 7).

What happens in individual countries is therefore the result of events in the world capitalist system. Even revolutions are the result primarily of contradictions in the world capitalist system rather than of conflicts within individual countries. Events within a country may be of some importance, but in comparison to outside forces they are of such secondary significance that one can say that outside forces are always determinant over internal forces. For this reason, all countries in the world system today are capitalist. 'There are no socialist systems in the world economy', he insists, 'anymore than there are feudal systems because there is only one world system' (Wallerstein, 1977). For Wallerstein, as for Frank, the essential feature of capitalism is exchange, the sale of goods for private profit rather than the mode of production, i.e. who owns the means of production and the relationships around them. Clearly, circulation and production are related, but the former is determinant over the latter rather than vice-versa as is the case with Marxist theory. It is for this reason that both Frank and Wallerstein are referred to as 'circulationists' and it is also to be expected that Wallerstein considers all countries today as capitalist.

Countries within the world system are divided into three sub-systems, beginning with the inner ring of core countries and stretching out to the periphery with a small group of countries forming an intermediate tier which Wallerstein calls the semi-periphery. It is possible for a small number of countries to move from the periphery to the semi-periphery and even to the core group of countries though the latter is extremely difficult and rare. Wallerstein gives three reasons for this movement of countries from one capitalist sub-system to another: by invitation, as when a country in the periphery is chosen by a multinational company as a base for industrial production; through the 'self-reliant' strategy, as in the case of China; and a rather random process, the 'seizing the chance' strategy that may be open to some countries. Altogether, however, only a small number of countries will be able to change their position in the world system through these methods. The only way that third world countries can develop and prosper is through a world socialist revolution, for Wallerstein's world systems model does not allow for nationalist movements and country revolutions (Wallerstein, 1980). This is a view rejected not only by many other dependency theorists, but by Non-Marxists and by Marxists. Writing from a Marxist perspective, Navarro finds Wallerstein's World Systems Theory unacceptable and dangerous for, contrary to Wallerstein's views on world revolution, 'only a *national transition to socialism* is possible' (Navarro, 1982).

The concept of dependency refers to two related processes: first, the dependency of third world countries on the few advanced industrial societies and, second, the consequent conditioning of internal political forces so that, according to Frank, they are of very little significance or, according to Wallerstein, they are irrelevant to development. It is on this issue—the importance of internal relative to external forces—that the main disagreements within the dependency school exist. And it is on this issue that Cardoso's contribution is crucial. Unlike Wallerstein and Frank, Cardoso insists that the political forces within a country can be an important variable in its development. Thus the state, and the political struggles around the state, need to be analysed and understood before one can say whether development (and what kind of development) is possible within a country. External and internal forces interact and though external forces are all-important, there are occasions when the internal forces can be of sufficient strength to make development possible. In brief, the state in some third world countries is not always a mere passive institution that is 'mechanically conditioned by external dominance' (Cardoso and Faletto, 1979, p. 172). It can have its own dynamic, with the result that a certain type of development—'associated dependent development' is possible (Cardoso, 1973).

Dependency and development are not always mutually exclusive. How this type of development fares will depend on the strength of internal *vis-à-vis* the external forces. Thus working class political struggles can be of significance to the economic and social development of a country. It is not necessary for the working class to wait for the socialist revolution, national or international, before it can begin to improve its living standards. Cardoso's analysis places him closer to the neo-Marxist school of development than to the orthodox dependency theory. Before turning to the Marxist views on development, however, it is necessary to provide some appraisal of the main themes of the dependency theory.

The first main claim of dependency theory is that historical and contemporary evidence shows that development and underdevelopment are causally linked. Beginning with the mercantile period right through the colonial period and down to the post-independence years, third world countries have been oppressed and exploited by their colonial powers. This exploitative relationship accounts for both the development of the industrial countries and the underdevelopment of the third world countries. This exploitation has taken several forms and has assumed varying degrees of intensity ranging from plain plunder and looting, to the destruction of native industries, and to unfavourable trade terms.

Several dependency writers document in great detail the historical 'underdevelopment' of third world countries in Latin America, Asia and Africa. Rodney's account of the various ways in which African countries have been oppressed and exploited is typical of dependency literature on this issue: the expropriation of minerals and agricultural produce; the total neglect of industry and agriculture; the repatriation of profits; the payment of subsistence wages; the neglect of the social services; the cultural imperialism, which claimed that underdevelopment was due to the inferiority of African people rather than to 'the organised viciousness of the capitalist/colonialist system' (Rodney, 1972, p. 240).

The fact that colonial powers exploit their colonies is neither new nor unexpected. Many writers from several colonies documented all this long before the dependency theory. Writing at the beginning of this century of the situation in India, Rai described in detail the drain of wealth from India to Britain as well as the destruction of local industries to make room for British imports. Rai concludes that in 'less than seventy five years (from 1757 to 1829) India was reduced from the position of a manufacturing country to that of a supplier of raw materials' (Rai, 1917, p. 132). There have, of course, been those who have argued that the flow of resources from the colonies to the imperial country is nothing more than a recompense for the civilising influences of the latter over the former. Vera Anstey has, for example, argued that the drain of wealth from India to Britain was not enough to recompense Britain for the civilising influence of its administrators on Indian society, the defence of India by the British army and navy and the introduction of new ideas and techniques by British industrialists, businessmen and technicians (Anstey, 1936). From this point of view, empires benefit more the colonies than the imperial power! The overwhelming evidence, however, supports the first claim of the dependency theory, i.e. that development and underdevelopment are causally linked.

The same conclusion applies to the second claim of the dependency theory even though it is qualified in various ways. This is the claim that the world is divided into metropolitan and peripheral countries, that in each peripheral country the same subdivision applies and that a long chain of exploitation exists linking the village of a third world country to the banking quarters of the cities in metropolitan countries. Marxists have criticised Frank's reliance on trade relationships rather than production relationships for explaining exploitation, and they have been unhappy with his use of pyramidal spatial relationships instead of class relationships to account for underdevelopment, but they do not reject the essence of his argument. Thus Roxborough is critical of Frank's view that every group on the chain, apart from the top, is both exploited and exploiting, and also feels that 'the notion of a single pyramid of exploitation, oppression and poverty is a pathetic oversimplification' (Roxborough, 1979, p. 90). Several other writers have found the division of the world into two or even three groups of countries to be too simplistic, even though they do not reject the notion of a hierarchical structure. Lall, for example, concludes his criticism of Frank by suggesting that a better way of conceptualising international relationships is to view the world as a hierarchical, pyramid shaped structure with the USA at the apex and a number of successively expanding layers beneath it (Lall, 1975).

Long has made similar criticisms in relation to the national metropole-periphery chain. From his research in the highland region of Peru, he argues that many villagers have direct commercial contacts with the capital Lima without going through regional metropoles (Long, 1977, pp. 90–91). A more general criticism is that multinational companies have many bases and headquarters, and it is not always possible to distinguish the metropolitan from the peripheral centres. All these criticisms contain an element of truth, but they do not challenge the essence of the dependency argument—they merely assert that the dependency theory overemphasises the uniformities and underestimates the complexities of the structural pattern of exploitation.

The third strand of the dependency theory is its claim that national elites are incapable of independent political and economic development, with the result that third world countries are condemned to indefinite impoverishment. On the empirical side, many have pointed out that several third world countries have developed substantially during the past thirty years or so—the newly industrialising countries mainly in Latin America and South East Asia—and that the development is not ephemeral, as we shall see in the next section. Cardoso has also shown the same situation prevailing in some Latin American countries and he has, as pointed out earlier, argued in favour of the notion of 'associated dependent development', thus rejecting the view that 'the internal or national socio-economic situation is mechanically conditioned by external dominance' (Cardoso and Faletto, 1979, p. 173).

Similar theoretical criticism has come from other political scientists, who feel that the Frankian approach to dependency marginalises the political, i.e. that 'the character of governments, parties, bureaucracies, elections, militaries, and the substantial variations between countries, as well as within the same country at different periods of time, all tend to be treated as appendages of the world capitalist system and therefore peripheral to the analysis of change in UDCs' (Randall and Theobald, 1985, p. 115). Ley's most recent study of the Kenyan industrial elite and Evans's study of Brazil lend support to the criticism that national elites can acquire some degree of independence over the years from the power of international capital and thus exert an independent influence on the country's development (cited in Randall and Theobald, 1985, pp. 168 and 118).

The fourth claim of the dependency theory, i.e. that a socialist revolution is the only way out of underdevelopment, follows naturally from the marginalisation of the political forces within a country. It is a view which may have been influenced by the Cuban revolution, but twenty years since the emergence of the dependency theory, there does not seem to be any evidence that the masses in third world countries are anywhere near to a socialist revolution. There have, of course, been numerous coups and counter-coups but these are nothing more than indications of the economic and political fragmentation and instability prevalent in so many third world countries.

In conclusion, the dependency theory provided a much-needed corrective to the western oriented modernisation theory of development. Its central premise that development and underdevelopment are both largely the result of the same process—the exploitation of Third World countries over several centuries—is largely correct. Its main weakness has been the marginalisation of internal political factors and hence its blanket pessimism concerning the prospects of future development in all third world countries. The group of writers around the Cardoso position form a bridge between the early *dependistas* and the neo-Marxists to whom we shall now turn.

MARXIST THEORIES

Marx and Engels wrote very little that referred explicitly to the underdevelopment of third world countries. From their scanty references to underdevelopment and from their general theories of social change, however, they envisaged that all countries, irrespective of their state of industrialisation at the time when they were writing, would sooner or later be transformed into capitalist and eventually into socialist societies. The march of industrialisation would engulf all countries and they would all travel the same road eventually, along the five stages of their evolutionary model—from slavery to feudalism, capitalism, socialism and finally communism.

The main driving force for social change in this evolutionary development is always the conflict engendered in the mode of production in the country's economic structure. Clearly, ideology, religious beliefs, political and historical factors, as well as other elements of the country's superstructure, have some influence on the speed of social change but they are not determinant. It is the intensity of conflict within the economic structure of society that always determines in the end the onward march from one stage to the next.

Under capitalism, the conflict is between the two main contending classes in the economic structure—capital and labour—and it is this class conflict that will eventually lead to the peaceful or violent overthrow of the capitalist system and usher in a socialist society. Capitalist development thus performs two seemingly contradictory functions: on one hand it exploits the working class and it leads to the accumulation of profit in a few private hands; and on the other it politicises the working class through class struggle, so that it eventually overthrows the very same political and economic system that was the source of its exploitation. Thus, despite its destructive and dehumanising effects, capitalism has an overall progressive effect as the progenitor of socialism.

This overall progressive role of capitalism was as applicable in third world countries as in Europe. Capitalist industrialisation possesses the same logic wherever it may take place. The imperialist powers of Europe were creating capitalist conditions in their colonies through their attempts to industrialise them and were, therefore, creating an industrial proletariat that would eventually perform the same political role as its counterparts in Europe. No country could isolate itself from the spread of capitalism, for it was productively a superior system to feudalism. Thus the growth of capitalism in Europe will 'compel all nations, on pain of extinction, to adopt the bourgeois mode of production', claimed Marx and Engels (Marx and Engels, Communist Manifesto). Capitalism would spread to the whole world and would have very similar short-term and long-term economic as well as political effects. The experience of European countries was thus very relevant in understanding the future development of third world countries, for the latter would mirror the former. In an often quoted passage, Marx claimed that 'The country that is more developed industrially only shows, to the less developed, the image of its own future' (Marx, Capital, Vol. I, 1976, p. 91).

Though Marx's references to Ireland seem to suggest that colonial rule might thwart development, his more detailed discussion of British rule in India leaves no room for doubt that he saw colonial industrialisation as a very potent force for destroying peasant traditions and religious practices, for creating a modern railway system, for spreading literacy, for increasing economic growth and, above all, for creating the necessary industrial conditions for the growth and politicisation of an industrial working class. The fact that this regenerating role of British rule in India was both unwitting and repressive did not alter its character, Marx argued. It could not, in fact, have been performed in any other way for it was an unavoidable feature of the contradictory nature of capitalist development, whether performed by a colonial power or by a national government. In one of his dispatches to the New York Daily Tribune, Marx wrote: 'England has to fulfil a double mission in India: one destructive, the other regenerating—the assimilation of old Asiatic society, and the laying of the material foundations of Western society in Asia' (quoted in Warren, 1980, pp. 41–42).

In brief then, Marx saw colonialism as both a negative and a positive force for development. It destroyed customs, beliefs, social relationships and the like, but it created the right conditions for industrialisation and hence for economic and political change. Underdevelopment, therefore, is the result of insufficient rather than excessive colonial penetration as the dependency theory claims.

Marx's views on development remained unchallenged for several decades, largely because Marxist debates focussed on Europe and particularly on western European countries. The first major modification of Marx's views on development in the Third World came in Lenin's discussion of development in Russia and of imperialism. In his arguments with the Narodniks, who considered capitalism to be unnecessary for the development of socialism, Lenin adopted the orthodox Marxist view that capitalist growth, despite its destructive and dehumanising effects, was a necessary step towards socialism.

He maintained that capitalist development was taking place in Russia at the end of the nineteenth century, but at a slower pace than in Western European countries because of the survival of pre-capitalist structures and cultures amidst capitalist development, the adverse effects of industrial competition with the more advanced economies of Western Europe and the political weakness as well as economic inability of the Russian middle classes to raise the necessary capital internally for industrial development (Lenin, 1956).

There is clear acknowledgement here that Marx's views on economic development were overoptimistic, even in politically independent underdeveloped countries. They were even more so in relation to the colonies, according to Lenin's views on imperialism. For Lenin, imperialism was the most advanced stage of capitalism, characterised by the dominance of monopolies and colonisation. Capitalism in the form of international monopolies penetrated the colonies where higher profits could be made than in the mother country, and which could be used partly to buy off the working class at home by conceding to its demands for better living standards. The capitalist penetration of colonies was thus beneficial to the long-term interests of capital and to the short-term interests of the working class in Western European countries, but it operated at the expense of third world countries. Political independence was thus a necessary prerequisite to capitalist economic development in the colonies (Lenin, 1966). Once a colony became independent capitalist development was possible, but it would proceed at a slow pace because it would face very similar problems to those encountered in Russia at the end of the nineteenth century. In brief, though Lenin accepted the progressive nature of capitalism, he was far more aware of the problems involved and, therefore, he was far less optimistic than Marx and Engels about the prospects of economic development in independent let alone colonial countries.

As we saw in the previous section, Lenin's qualifications of the progressive nature of capitalism thesis paled into insignificance compared with the onslaught from dependency theorists, who rejected totally the whole thesis that capitalism is a progressive force in developing countries, be they politically independent or not. Perhaps as a result of this, there are very few Marxists today who adhere to the authordox Marxist explanation of development but one who does is Warren, whose views came as a reaction to the dependency theory. They are a powerful reaffirmation of Marx's original thesis and a rejection of the Leninist and dependency views. His arguments are worth quoting in full because they provide the clearest and most comprehensive statement of Marx's views on development. He summarises them as follows:

1. Empirical evidence suggests that the prospects for successful capitalist development in many underdeveloped countries are quite favourable.
2. The period since the end of the Second World War has witnessed a major surge in capitalist social relations and productive forces in the Third world.
3. Direct colonialism . . . acted as a powerful engine of progressive social change, advancing capitalist development far more rapidly than was conceivable in any other way.
4. In so far as there are obstacles to this development, they originate not in current relationships between imperialism and the Third World, but in the internal contradictions of the Third World itself.
5. The overall, net effect of the policy of 'imperialist' countries and the general economic relationships of these countries with the under-developed countries actually favours the industrialisation and general economic development of the latter.
6. Within a context of growing economic interdependence, the ties of 'dependence' (or subordination) binding the Third World and the imperialist world have been and are being markedly loosened with the rise of indigenous capitalisms. (Warren, 1980, pp. 9–10)

For Warren, as for Marx, political independence loosens the dependency ties and opens the way to industrialisation. Any obstacles to industrialisation are to be found largely within individual third world countries rather than in international relationships.

Though many of the criticisms levied at the orthodox Marxist thesis will emerge later in this chapter, it is worth summarising them here for the sake of clarity. Its first and obvious weakness is that of all evolutionary theories, i.e. the claim that all countries go through the same stages of economic and social development, irrespective of their historical, cultural, political, religious or other circumstances. There is no evidence to sustain the claim that, say, Tanzania or

Afghanistan will eventually arrive at a situation when their economies, political systems, stratification systems, family systems, religious practices, and so on will be similar to those of Britain or the USA today. The convergence thesis is just as unacceptable, empirically speaking, whether it refers to the post-industrial society of Bell and others or to the communist society of Marx.

Secondly, because of this emphasis on the grand sweep of history, the orthodox Marxist view of development underplays the importance of internal political factors. Thus Warren notes but brushes aside the importance of government policies in third world countries as a relevant factor to development from the long-term point of view. 'The squandering of many of the benefits of third world post-war economic development due to major policy blunders has failed to halt the gathering momentum of capitalist advance and associated material progress' (Warren, 1980, p. 253).

Thirdly, the evidence that Warren provides does not substantiate the claim that development has been taking place in all or most of the underdeveloped countries, if development is defined as a rise in living standards, reductions of social inequalities and abolition of poverty. We shall look at these issues in detail in subsequent chapters but suffice it to say here that the orthodox Marxist theory of development cannot explain the mounting international debt of so many third world countries, nor the continuing famines and impoverishment of so many millions of people. To see such failures as mere epiphenomena on the long road to socialism is hardly convincing. Equally unconvincing, to say the least, is Warren's appeal to Marxists that, despite all such problems, they 'must accept the view that the epochal imperialist sweep was indeed a titanic step towards human unity' (Warren, 1980, p. 137).

In brief, the claims of the orthodox Marxist thesis are just as unreal and unacceptable as those of the dependency thesis for, as Booth rightly observes, Warren's line of argument 'takes us from the indiscriminate pessimism of the dependency view of the world to a barely less misleading generalised optimism. Worse, it distracts attention from some of the most deplorable aspects of the contemporary situation, and hence from the exploration of the underlying causes' (Booth, 1985). The entry of neo-Marxists in this debate is an attempt to carve out a theoretical position that steers clear of both generalised over-optimism and overpessimism for third world development.

The first main contribution of the neo-Marxist position came in Laclau's critique of Frank's views on capitalism and hence of the distribution of power in third world countries. Laclau insisted that Frank's definition of capitalism in terms of production for profit for the market—the circulationist definition—meant that capitalism has existed from the beginnings of civilisation and hence every country has long been, to a greater or lesser extent, ready for a proletarian revolution. This was clearly an untenable position. If capitalism, however, was defined in Marx's terms, i.e. a mode of production where 'free' labour is used by employers to produce for profit, then capitalism could not have existed in the sixteenth century in Europe, let alone in the colonies of the Third World.

Moreover, the introduction of a capitalist mode of production does not necessarily wipe out pre-capitalist, feudal relationships. It is quite possible for feudal or semi-feudal relations to co-exist with capitalist relations in a country for quite some time—an argument that is similar to Lenin's views on the position in Tsarist Russia. All this is not merely idle theorising. It has clear political implications for it suggests first, that no two third world countries are totally alike in terms of their internal political forces and, second, that in most third world countries the bourgeoisie has to share power with the landowning semi-feudal class. In other words, there is no unitary upper class in third world countries and, at the same time, of course, there is no unitary exploited class (Laclau, 1971).

Laclau's work was based on an historical analysis of the situation in Latin America but it had, of course, implications for countries elsewhere. Indeed, Alavi's work takes the debate a step further, for he argued that no single hegemonic class dominated the state in Pakistan. He identified three dominant classes in post-colonial Pakistan—the landowners, the national bourgeoisie and the metropolitan bourgeoisie—with conflicts in their short-term interests though, of course, united in the preservation of the capitalist system. This means that no one class dominates the state and, hence, the state possesses considerable autonomy, particularly in view of the fact that it also possesses a highly developed state apparatus that was inherited from the colonial days (Alavi, 1979). Government policies, therefore, do not always serve the interests of any one class but are, at times, used to the benefit of sections of the state apparatus.

The fragmentation of the upper class is matched by a similar fragmentation of the oppositional class. The orthodox Marxist position was that the industrial proletariat was the legitimate oppositional class and the vanguard of the socialist revolution. From Lenin onwards, however, there was a tendency to upgrade the peasantry as the revolutionary class and to downgrade the industrial proletariat because of its partial incorporation into the capitalist system, earning it the description 'the aristocracy of labour' (Arrighi and Saul, 1968). Mao in China and Guevara in Latin America certainly relied heavily on the peasantry for their revolutionary activities.

Dependency theorists tended to refer to the 'masses', the *'lumpenproletariat'*, the 'wretched of the earth' and such like phrases as the revolutionary class. It was certainly a downgrading of the industrial proletariat and, to some extent, of the peasantry. Mingled in all this has been a prolonged and intense debate on definitional issues around all three groups or classes—industrial proletariat, peasantry and the lumpenproletariat. What seems to be emerging out of all this debate is a tendency to define the industrial proletariat more broadly, to ascribe to it the vanguard role in the revolutionary process and, above all, to insist that what is equally important is the kind of political relationship that it has with the peasantry and the millions of the urban underemployed. As Roxborough puts it 'the political behaviour of any class, group or category is not an inherent function of the class itself but rather a result of its interaction with other classes in the context of the overall political system' (Roxborough, 1979, p. 87).

If neither the dominant nor the dominated class is unitary, and if their composition varies from one third world country to another, then the nature of the state and the possibilities for socialist change are matters for detailed analysis of the economic and political situation prevailing in individual countries. This is a far cry from both the dependency and the orthodox Marxist position. It also has implications for the degree to which any one third world country is dominated by the advanced industrial countries and by international capital. We have already referred to this in the critique of the dependency theory. Neo-Marxists accept that international capital both exploits third world countries in a variety of ways and also distorts the development of class relations. But studies of individual third world countries—Kenya, Nigeria, Brazil and others—suggest that national bourgeoisies in some countries are beginning to acquire a certain degree of independence from international capital, and are therefore not mere servants to it. They possess a certain degree of autonomy with the result that economic development is possible even though its pace and character will inevitably be greatly influenced by international factors. In other third world countries, however, the national bourgeoisie is still very much a 'comprador' bourgeoisie, as the *dependistas* argued. Only meticulously detailed studies of individual countries can show the pattern of the balance of power between external and internal factors, as well as the nature of the state.

The strength of the neo-Marxist position lies in its emphasis on empirical studies within the theoretical framework of the mode of production. It avoids unwarranted generalisations, and it tries to show how the internal class dynamics of a country affect the nature of its development process. Its weaknesses are firstly an excessive emphasis on the notion of class in countries where classes, in Marxist terms, are only just emerging. The relevance of ethnicity, tribe, religion, and such like groupings to the politics of third world countries is still very significant and they cannot be subsumed under the notion of class without the latter losing its usefulness. There are numerous examples of countries where ethnicity and religion—South Africa and Nigeria are just two such examples—have played a greater part at times in their internal strife (peaceful and violent) than class. The second main weakness of the neo-Marxist approach is the great diversity of various strands of thought that it incorporates. The disagreements around such important theoretical concepts as upper class, working class, the peasantry, the state and so on make it almost impossible to speak of a unified neo-Marxist approach, in terms of the conclusions reached on the prospects of future economic development in third world countries. This weakness applies just as much to the non-Marxist structural approach to which we now turn.

NON-MARXIST STRUCTURALIST APPROACH

The writings of left-wing, non-Marxist structuralist social scientists on development in third world countries are not only as disparate as those of the neo-Marxists but they overlap in many ways. Some of the writers of this group featured before the dependency thesis, and in some ways contributed to its emergence, while others belong to the post-1970 period and have been influenced by dependency and Marxist writings. Most of them have worked as consultants or researchers for international bodies—the ILO, the World Bank and the United Nations—and they have substantial first hand experience of third world countries. Though there is no unified body of theory that is acceptable to all these writers, there is a core of ideas which Todaro identified as follows:

> This approach (i.e. the structuralist-internationalist models) views under-development in terms of international and domestic power relationships, institutional and structural economic rigidities, and the resulting prolifer-ation of dual economies and dual societies both within and among nations. Structuralist theories tend to emphasise external and internal 'institutional' constraints on economic development. Emphasis is placed on policies needed to eradicate poverty, to provide more diversified employment opportunities and to reduce income inequalities. (Todaro, 1977, p. 51)

It is also true to say that over the years there has been a shift of emphasis within this broad school of thought from a predomi-nantly economic to a political economy approach. Whereas in the 1950s and early 1960s the emphasis was predominantly on economic factors, on economic explanations and on economic growth, the mid-1960s witnessed an extension to cover politi-cal and historical factors, to incorporate political explanations and to dwell on development as much as on economic growth. Blomstrom and Hettne correctly conclude that the contem-porary versions of structuralism 'emphasise the importance of *both* domestic and international structures, as well as the importance of considering the history of the underdeveloped countries' (Blomstrom and Hettne, 1984, p. 171).

Most of the writers in this ill-defined group accept the importance of historical factors, particularly the period of colonisation, as crucial in our understanding of the development and underdevelopment of nations. Their approach is not very different from that of the *dependistas* on this issue. This is best exemplified in Griffin's early work on Latin America and by Harrison's recent and more general discussion of issues of development and underdevelopment. Griffin emphasises not only the expropriation of raw materials from the colonies but also the usurping of their land, the destruction of their industries, and the general subjugation of their economies and cultures. In words which have a Frankian ring about them, he wrote in 1969:

> Underdevelopment as it is encountered today in Spanish America and elsewhere is a product of history. It is not the primeval condition of man, nor is it merely a way of describing the economic status of a 'traditional' society. Underdevelopment is part of a process: indeed, it is part of the same process which produced development. Thus an interpretation of underdevelopment must begin with a study of the past. (Griffin, 1969, p. 49)

Harrison, using evidence from the work of others on third world countries in general, describes as follows the same process of colonial exploitation that has laid the foundations for the current division of the world into industrially affluent and peripheral impoverished countries.

> Colonial powers laid the foundation of the present division of the world into industrial nations on the one hand, and hewers of wood and drawers of water on the other. They wiped out indigenous industry and forced the colonies to buy their manufactures. They undermined the self-sufficiency of the Third World and transformed it into a source of raw materials for western industry. Sometimes they forced locals to grow the desired crops—as the French did with cotton in the Sahel or the Dutch with sugar in Indonesia. Sometimes they bought land or just seized it to set up plantations, drafting in cheap labour to work them. In this way, the colonial powers created the world economic order that still prevails today, of industrial centre and primary producing periphery, prosperous metropolis and poverty-stricken satellites. (Harrison, 1979, p. 45)

The second area of general agreement among this group is that political independence has not brought to an end the direct and indirect economic domination of third world countries by the advanced industrial societies. Trade relationships between the two sets of countries have continued to be disadvantageous to the Third World. We shall be discussing this at length in a later chapter and we shall therefore be brief here. Myrdal's work is perhaps the earliest expression of this position. The neo-classical view of development, that dominated the 1950s, and which was implicitly part of the modernisation thesis, held that trade between countries raised the economic level of all countries and also helped to reduce income inequalities between them, particularly when countries specialised in the sale of goods that they could produce more cheaply than other countries. Myrdal's argument, stemming from his research in Asian countries, was that free trade and the free movement of capital between unequal nations, as well as between unequal regions within a country, has exactly the opposite effect—it exacerbates inequalities. It does so because the strong industries or the strong countries or the strong regions within a country attract more capital, skilled labour and business than their weak counterparts and, if need be, they can also protect their position more successfully. In Myrdal's words the 'backwash effects' outweigh the 'spread effects'.

> Contrary to what the equilibrium theory of international trade would seem to suggest, the play of the market forces does not work toward equality in the remunerations to factors of production and, consequently, incomes. If left to take its own course, economic development is a process of circular and cumulative causation which tends to award its favors to those who are already well endowed and even to thwart the efforts of those who happen to live in regions that are lagging behind. (Myrdal, 1956, p. 47)

This is a structural process resulting from the free play of international market forces, but when trade protectionist policies of industrial countries against certain types of imports from developing countries are also introduced, the result is both a structural and an intentional process of exploitation of underdeveloped countries.

Several other writers in this group adopt the same positions.

Todaro also adds that free competition for the products of third world countries has been undermined by the large international companies which buy and sell goods; that in recent years terms of trade between the two groups of countries have become even more unfavourable to the developing countries; and that within developing countries foreign elites have benefited disproportionately to other groups. In his own words 'the principal benefits of world trade have accrued disproportionately to rich nations and within poor nations disproportionately to foreign residents and wealthy nationals' (Todaro, 1977, p. 314).

The third area of agreement concerns the distribution of power within third world countries. There is general agreement that too much power is in the hands of small economic and political elites and that too little power is exercised by the mass of impoverished people. Elliott, for example, presents third world societies as rigidly stratified where 'a relatively small group control much of the production and all the fiscal distribution in such a way that their interests and their level of living are not seriously threatened' (Elliott, 1975, p. 13). Inevitably, upward mobility is limited and where concessions are granted to the poor, the motive is to deradicalise and thus preserve the existing *status quo*. Such concessions are not at present widespread because the poor are still politically weak and inarticulate, with the result that the ruling groups 'have little incentive to undertake the structural changes and the budgetary cost of the kind of direct intervention that is usually required to secure equity of access for the excluded' (Elliott, 1975, p. 391).

This general line of thinking is evident, and given more precision, in Griffin's writings, particularly after his work on poverty in Asia in association with an ILO team of researchers. Having argued and shown that economic growth in Asia has benefited the rich and has almost bypassed certain impoverished groups of the rural population, he outlines three reasons for this process: the unequal social structure; the bias of governments in favour of the upper classes; and the bias of the free market in favour of the same classes. The corollary, therefore, is that poverty can be eradicated only by changing the structure of those societies and not merely by minor reforms or by simply increasing economic growth (Griffin, 1978, p. 160).

The fourth area of agreement is that if there is one reform that is pivotal to the improvement in third world countries, it is land reform. One finds calls for reforms in all aspects of life—income, education, health, environment, etc.—but land reform is given top priority because it affects directly the living standards of most people in third world societies. On the one hand, the present unequal pattern of land tenure accounts for the impoverishment of masses of people and, on the other, it holds back increased productivity, particularly of the small farmers. Thus Myrdal argues that almost all the difficulties that have to be overcome in order to apply more advanced forms of technology in agriculture have a 'root cause' in the system of unequal land ownership. Griffin, Harrison and others also make this point, and, again, they realise the immense political obstacles to such a major reform. However, without such a reform, Myrdal insists that 'there is little basis for a hope that all the other institutional reforms—such as community development, agricultural extension, and credit co-operation—will not continue to become perverted to serve the interests of the better-offs' (Myrdal, 1970, p. 401). Others have also argued that without this major reform, the rural exodus to the towns will continue unabated with the result that urban unemployment and poverty will rise as industry and trade find it impossible to expand fast enough to absorb the continual stream of migrants.

The fifth area of general agreement is that, despite various qualifications, certain aspects of the behaviour of the poor are not always conducive to their betterment. The example most often cited is population growth. It is generally accepted that high birth rates have a structural explanation, but it is nevertheless argued that a reduction is a necessary, though not a sufficient, condition for an improvement in the living standards of the poor. It is also acknowledged that industrialisation will reduce birth rates but, on the whole, it is felt that this process is too slow. Harrison perhaps expresses these fears too dramatically when he concludes his discussion on population as follows: 'If man does not conquer the population problem, nature will step in and do it for him. And everywhere it will be the poorest families who bear the brunt of the attack' (Harrison, 1979, p. 260). Similarly, writers of this group will stress the positive aspects of education, not only in terms of technical skills but also as a medium of change in attitudes towards health issues, the position of women, and so on. Also whilst this group considers the attitudes and values of the poor as important to development, it does not see them either as the most important factor or as always relevant to economic development. Structure rather than culture is the determinant variable in our understanding of poverty and in the policies that are necessary for its abolition.

The sixth common feature in the writings of this group is their long-term, reluctant and vague optimism that the living standards of the poor in third world countries will improve gradually, haltingly and unevenly. This is always dominated, however, by a stronger feeling of pessimism for the immediate prospects of developing countries. Elliott makes an almost unanswerable case of how the system excludes poor people from the benefits of economic growth, but he couples this with the qualification that the system possesses some degree of flexibility and plasticity and hence some hope for improvement. He concludes his book by emphasising the importance of public participation in government planning as the best way forward. It is 'through the enablement of the excluded (most immediately through their leadership and bourgeois allies) to see for themselves the nature of the system in which they are caught and the ways in which that system can be used for their ultimate advantage' (Elliott, 1975, p. 399). Myrdal, too, is equally pessimistic of any major structural changes that will improve the lot of poor people in the short run but again improvements can come about 'in the rather long run' when mass education and public participation in elections and elsewhere have their desired effects (Myrdal, 1970, p. 428). Griffin, too, recognises that profound changes will be resisted by the powerful groups—both within the country and at the international level—because they impinge upon their interests. But he points out that certain changes may be unopposed by the dominant groups because they may be seen 'as a necessary concession to popular demands and as a legitimate exercise of national sovereignty' (Griffin, 1969, p. 281). In other words, it is through these minor reforms that the future may hold some hope for improvement in the condition of the poor in the very long run.

Finally, a similar position is taken in relation to the future prospects of living standards in developing countries *vis à vis* those of the rich industrial societies. It is generally accepted that for most developing countries the gap will remain the same and for some it may even widen. For a few, however, there are some possibilities that the gap will narrow though not close as far as one can see in the future. There are no agreed criteria that can enable one to decide what the future of a developing country is likely to be. In general, however, it is argued that there is an interacting relationship between high rates of economic growth and lesser inequalities in society. On one hand high rates of economic growth make reduction of inequalities politically more feasible, and on the other a more equal distribution of resources within a country is a positive factor for high rates of national economic growth. Thus the interests of the poor and of poor nations are best served by policies that promote both greater equality and greater economic growth. Griffin puts it well when he concludes that: 'undoubtedly the key to greater prosperity for the poor is a combination of greater equality and faster growth' (Griffin, 1979, p. 158).

A comparison between the neo-Marxist and the left structuralist perspective reveals that they are very similar in many ways. In essence, they both agree that the dominance of advanced industrial societies is of crucial importance to the prospects of development in third world countries. They disagree, perhaps, on the degree to which the former group of countries dominates and exploits the latter. Within this framework of world exploitation, some third world countries may still achieve high rates of economic growth and thus raise the living standards of their people. At the present state of our knowledge, only individual country studies rather than generalised development theories can help us understand both the ways in which the internal forces of a country interact with the outside world processes and, through that understanding, the prospects of growth and development in individual third world countries.

At the superficial level of comparison, it appears that Marxist theories rely heavily on class analysis whilst structuralist perspectives accept the importance of race, religion and such factors in addition to class. In reality, however, Marxist analyses do not discount the importance of non-class factors but they try, against all odds at times, to see them within a class framework. Structuralist perspectives do not deny the possibility of a relationship between class and other factors, but they do not make class the dominant factor at all times. The differences between the two perspectives are thus matters of detail, perhaps important detail, at times. This difference in their theoretical perspectives is reflected in their estimation of the possibilities for reduction of inequalities both within countries and between groups of countries. They both agree that inequality is a central component of both the world system and the stratification system of individual countries, with the result that reductions of inequality are difficult, though not impossible. Such reductions will inevitably be incremental, and the possibilities for achieving them are greater for some countries than others, as well as for some groups within a country than others. It would be true to say again that neo-Marxists are even less optimistic than structuralists of the possibilities of such reductions taking place in the immediate future, either within countries or between groups of countries.

CONCLUSION

We have reviewed rather briefly the five main theories of development—modernisation, dependency, classical Marxist, neo-Marxist and left structuralist. The modernisation and the classical Marxist approaches are both evolutionary theories stressing the importance of internal rather than external factors to development, as the table below shows. They are evolutionary theories in the sense that they envisage all countries going through the same series of stages leading from primitive existence to a state of generalised welfare. They differ, of course, on the nature of the stage of generalised welfare that societies ultimately arrive at. For the modernisation theory, it is the change in values and attitudes that is essential for high ratios of economic growth that gradually propel societies to the post-industrial stage whose features bear a striking resemblance to contemporary American society. For the classical Marxist approach, the struggle between the haves and the have-nots, between the bourgeoisie and the proletariat, inexorably drives all societies towards the communist stage where the distribution of resources is based on the principle of need. Both these theories suffer from two basic weaknesses— overgeneralisation and unwarranted optimism. They both tend to ignore the vast differences in the internal dynamics of countries, of how different countries fit into the world system and of the past history of countries, with the result that they grossly under-estimate the obstacles to development, and vice-versa they blandly overestimate the possibility as well as the pace of improvement in living standards. Thus, despite their very different ideological frameworks, both these theories are inadequate in helping us to understand the problems and prospects of development of third world countries.

Table 1.1: Typology of development theories

	Stress on internal factors	Stress on external factors	Interplay between external and internal factors
Evolutionary	Modernisation Classical-Marxist		Neo-Marxist
Non-evolutionary		Dependency	
			Left Structuralist

The dependency theory proved a much needed corrective to the modernisation theory, with its emphasis on internal factors, on the mutuality of interests between advanced industrial countries and third world countries, its westernised model of development and its overoptimism. The new emphasis on historical factors, conflict of interests, external factors and the dominance of the world capitalist system had a lot to commend it. It proved, however, an overgeneralised theory because of the overpowering influence it attributed to external factors. The world capitalist system has such a grip on third world countries that the prospects of development have been obliterated everywhere. Only a socialist revolution by the masses—the prospects of which are admitted to be negligible—can create the possibilities for development. Thus overgeneralisation and abject pessimism are the unacceptable features of the dependency theory as put forward by Frank, Amin and Wallerstein. In the hands of Cardoso and Faletto, internal political processes gain some importance but this puts these two writers as much in the neo-Marxist as in the dependency school.

As already mentioned, the neo-Marxist and the left structuralist perspectives are very similar in the method they use to analyse the process of development in third world countries. They both base their analysis on the interplay between three crucial variables: the influence of the world system, the nature of the state and the balance of political forces in individual third world countries. Neither approach is as optimistic as the modernisation and the classical Marxist approach, or as universally pessimistic as the dependency theory. They both insist that each third world country must be examined using a political economy approach that gives due weight to political and economic factors internally and externally.

Our preference is for the left structuralist approach because it does not make class the crucial variable of its analysis. It acknowledges that in Third World countries today ethnicity, tribalism and religion can be as important dimensions of political power as class. It recognises that only a small fraction of the population in third world countries is in full-time paid employment and an even smaller proportion belongs to trade unions or working class parties. In such situations it is inappropriate to make class the most important variable or to attempt to present ethnicity, tribalism and religion as mere manifestations of class. Evidence from so many third world countries shows that these variables are often independent of class both during times of political stability and during periods of civil strife.

What then are the policy implications of the structuralist approach? First, that the process of economic growth in third world countries will be both slow and uneven in the foreseeable future. Some third world countries will achieve rates of economic growth that are higher than those of advanced industrial societies, but for most of them their economies will grow either at similar or lower rates. In other words, economic inequalities between advanced industrial societies on one hand and third world countries on the other will narrow in the case of a few third world countries, but they will remain either constant or even widen for most of them.

Second, the dominance of the world capitalist system is so powerful that very few third world countries can counteract it even for short periods and none can do so indefinitely. Clearly, it is the very large countries such as China which can attempt to carve out their own independent brand of industrialisation and development, but as the post-Mao situation in China shows, even such countries can isolate themselves from the world capitalist economy for brief periods only. In view of this, and bearing in mind the overall adverse effects of this dominance on third world countries, the best strategy for third world countries is to increase the extent of economic co-operation between them. This will not be easy but, as the governor of the Central Bank of Kenya has argued in relation to Africa, third world countries 'have no alternative—for the present strategies of separate development efforts and reliance on aid and external markets will only perpetuate their economic and political weakness and increase their dependence on foreign countries, with all the implications of such dependence' (Ndegwa *et al.*, 1985, p. 26). A South-South rather than a North-South type of development is what third world countries need. Bearing in mind, however, the disunities among third world countries and the power of international capital, the prospects of a South-South type of development are at best modest.

Third, development in terms of reductions of inequalities within third world countries is far more difficult than in advanced industrial societies. On one hand, reductions of class and group inequalities are always more difficult in countries where conditions of scarcity prevail than in affluent countries, and on the other the political powers of workers and peasants *vis à vis* the dominant groups in third world countries is weaker than that of their counterparts in advanced industrial societies. Third world countries, therefore, with a capitalist pattern of economic development will continue to exhibit sharper inequalities within them than those found in advanced industrial societies. The only way out of this situation appears to be radical political changes leading to fundamental structural changes in the distribution of material resources, as the experience of China and Cuba suggests.

Fourth, the emphasis of the structuralist approach on outside, world factors does not imply that internal factors are unimportant to a country's rate and pattern of development. Thus improvements in education, reductions in high rates of population growth, political stability and other domestic factors are important to the prospects of economic development. But the extent to which such domestic factors promote economic growth depends on whether the external, international factors act in ways that are favourable to third world countries. It is true that there is an interplay between internal and external factors, but for most third world countries the external factors have the upper hand over domestic policies. Moreover, in many situations, domestic economic factors tend to exert a very significant influence on non-economic factors. Thus high rates of population growth and political instability in many third world countries are due in a significant degree to the low levels of economic standards for the majority of the population. It all suggests that the improvement in economic growth rates and the distribution of income must lie at the heart of the domestic policies of third world countries.

Finally, the way these policy implications have been expressed here indicates that, at present, the state of development theory is not of a standard that enables us to make generalised or predictive statements about third world countries often. It only provides us with a sketchy framework that we can use to analyse the development prospects of individual third world countries. Country case studies seem to be the best way forward at present for the refinement of a development/underdevelopment theory that can eventually be used for more generalised predictive statements. They provide firmer and more detailed evidence of the distribution of power within a country, of the relative position of the country within the world system and of how these influence the rate of growth of the national economy and the distribution of income within the country itself.

2 Economic Growth, Wealth and Income Inequalities

Inequality takes different forms—economic, political and social—and these interact with one another to produce composite forms of inequality and power. The relative importance of each form of inequality and power in the interaction process varies from one group of countries to another depending on the centrality and type of wealth ownership. In advanced industrial capitalist societies, where the means of production and distribution are owned privately and where class relationships are dominant, it is economic inequality and economic power that dominate the other two. In centrally planned societies of the East European model, where the means of production are largely owned by the state, it is political power that is the dominant force, while in third world countries of the capitalist mode, economic and political power vie with each other for the central role.

Inequalities are a central feature of all contemporary societies and they are usually supported by an ideology which legitimises them, i.e. makes them appear in varying degrees as right and proper, as inevitable and even as beneficial to all in society. This legitimation of inequality, however, is never total because competing notions—such as those of equality of opportunity, rights and citizenship—constantly challenge its supremacy. Conflicts over distributional issues, therefore, go on all the time, within and between countries, and they are normally conducted by politically acceptable methods. Only on rare occasions in advanced industrial societies and more often in third world countries do such conflicts take violent forms. As argued in the previous chapter, such conflicts range across class, race, gender and other lines and they are not merely internal domestic issues. They can incur the intervention of multinational companies, other countries and such international bodies as the IMF and the World Bank, if they are seen as a threat to the stability of the capitalist system. There have recently been numerous such instances, mostly in third world countries but several in advanced industrial countries, too. It is through such conflicts that reductions of inequality come about though, as the previous chapter again argued, such reductions are normally gradual and not necessarily cumulative. Neither privileged groups nor privileged nations give up or concede their privileges to other groups in society or other countries easily, let alone willingly.

The discussion in this chapter is confined to inequalities of income and wealth, partly because they are basic to other forms of inequality and partly because of data availability issues. The available data even on these two forms of economic inequality is inadequate in several respects and 'explained' trends or differences can, at times, be due as much to data inadequacies as to other factors. There are, however, many occasions where data is sufficiently adequate to warrant conclusions or observations on economic inequality.

ECONOMIC GROWTH AND INEQUALITY BETWEEN COUNTRIES

Whatever the inadequacies of data may be, there cannot be any doubt about the considerable expansion in the economies of all countries during the post-war period. The general picture is clear: the war-ravaged economies of Western Europe were the first to recover so that by the mid-1950s they were set on an expansionist course which appeared secure and indefinite at the time. The economies of third world countries as a group followed suit, and they witnessed unparalleled rates of growth down to the mid-1970s. The 1980s, however, have witnessed a slowing down of economic growth in all countries and even of negative rates in several countries, mostly in the Third World.

The result has been that the economic optimism of the 1960s and early 1970s has been followed by grave concern about the future of the world economy in general and of certain groups of third world countries in particular.

Table 2.1 provides the statistical evidence for these generalised conclusions. It shows that the economies of Third World countries grew at a faster rate than those of the advanced industrial countries during both the 1960s and 1970s but, of course, from a lower base. It also shows wide variations in the growth rates of the various groups of third world countries during this twenty-year period: the high-income oil exporting countries are leading the way, followed by the newly industrialised countries of Asia, and the African countries showing the lowest rates of growth in the world. There are also substantial variations between countries belonging to the same groups but not shown in Table 2.1. Using Africa as an example, Kenya's rate of growth in GDP during the period 1960–80 was higher than that of Tanzania, which was, in turn,

Table 2.1   Trends in average annual percentage change of GDP

Country Group	1960–73	1973–80	1980–85*
	%	%	%
I Developing Countries:	6.3	5.5	3.4
1. Low-income countries	5.6	4.9	7.0
(a) Asia	5.9	5.2	7.6
China	8.5	5.8	9.2
India	3.6	4.1	4.9
(b) Africa	3.5	2.7	1.1
2. Middle-income oil importers	6.3	5.6	2.1
(a) East Asia and Pacific	8.2	8.1	5.1
(b) Middle East and North Africa	5.2	7.1	3.5
(c) Sub-Saharan Africa†	5.6	3.6	1.4
(d) Southern Europe	6.7	4.8	2.0
(e) Latin America and Caribbean	5.6	5.4	0.7
3. Middle-income oil exporters	6.9	5.8	1.8
II High-income oil exporters	10.7	7.7	−2.1
III Industrial market countries	4.9	2.8	2.2

Sources: For 1960–73, *World Development Report, 1984*, table 2.1, p. 11.
      For 1973–80, *World Development Report, 1985*, table A.3, p. 149.
      For 1980–85, *World Development Report, 1986*, table A.3, p. 155.

  * Figure for 1984 is estimated; figure for 1985 is projected.
  † Excludes South Africa.

higher than that of Ghana, which, in turn, was higher than that of Uganda, and so on. Finally, Table 2.1 shows also the slowing down of economic growth in most countries during the 1980s, though it has affected some groups of countries more than others in a rather uneven way. A word of caution is necessary, however, for the figures in Table 2.1 refer to GDP rather than to GNP and, as Reynolds points out, this can exaggerate the extent of income available to residents of many third world countries since 'an appreciable percentage of what is produced may go to foreign suppliers of capital or labor' (Reynolds, 1986, p. 78). The distinction is not as important to advanced industrial societies.

What is significant, moreover, for individual people is not so much the national rates of economic growth but rather the size and rate of growth of their own individual incomes. These are issues which run throughout the rest of this book. Here we shall concentrate on the changes in per capita incomes in different countries which give some rough idea of the trends in income inequalities between countries. Trends in income per capita are obviously the result of the growth in national income and of the growth in the population of a country. Thus, within limits, it is quite feasible for a country to exhibit very high rates of growth in its national income but low rates of growth in the average income accruing to individuals. Vice versa, it is possible for a country to show rates of growth in per capita incomes that are higher than those in its national income, provided its rate of population growth is lower than that of the national income. It needs to be emphasised, however, that the relationship between population and economic growth is complex and will be discussed in a later chapter. Here we are simply concerned with the adverse statistical effects of high rates of population growth on incomes per capita rather than with the effects of population rises on economic growth which can be both positive and negative, depending on the overall situation prevailing in a country.

Table 2.2 shows that incomes per capita in low-income countries grew less than those of advanced industrial countries because of their higher rates of population growth. Similarly, other things being equal, incomes per capita in middle-income

Table 2.2 Average annual percentage change in population, GNP and GNP per capita

Country Group	Population		GNP		GNP Per Capita	
	1955–70	1970–80	1955–70	1970–80	1955–70	1970–80
I All developing countries	2.2	2.2	5.4	5.3	3.1	3.1
1. Low-income countries	2.1	2.1	3.7	4.5	1.6	2.4
(a) China	2.0	1.8	3.3	6.0	1.3	4.1
(b) India	2.2	2.1	4.0	3.4	1.8	1.3
(c) Other	2.4	2.7	4.4	2.7	2.0	0.0
2. Middle-income countries	2.4	2.4	6.0	5.6	3.5	3.1
II Industrial market countries	1.1	0.8	4.7	3.2	3.6	2.4
1. Europe	0.7	0.2	4.8	2.6	4.1	2.4
2. Japan	1.0	1.1	10.3	5.4	9.2	4.2
3. USA	1.4	1.0	3.4	3.1	2.0	2.1
III World*	1.9	1.9	5.1	3.8	3.1	1.9

Source. World Bank, *World Development Report, 1984*, table 5.1, p. 82.
Note: * Includes high-income oil exporters and industrial non-market countries.

countries would have been even higher had their population growth rates been lower. Moreover, the zero growth in per capita incomes in some third world countries shows in a striking way how high rates of population growth can depress living standards. More detailed figures, not shown in Table 2.2, indicate that some third world countries in Africa—Chad, Somalia, Niger, Madagascar, Uganda, Ghana and Senegal—experienced reductions in their per capita incomes, despite rises in their national incomes during this period (World Bank, 1981, table 1, p. 143 and table 2, p. 144). All these figures refer to the 1960s and 1970s, and there is no doubt that the situation deteriorated further during the 1980s in those third world countries where rises in national income have slowed down but population growth rates have not.

The overall net effect of the differential growth rates in population and national income has been to widen income inequalities between, on one hand, advanced industrial countries, and on the other most third world countries during the past forty years in both absolute and relative terms. The World Bank cites the example of India and the USA where the absolute gap in their per capita incomes widened from $6,860 in 1955 to $11,300 in 1983. Similarly, in relative terms, the American per capita income was forty-one times greater than that of India in 1955 but forty-four times greater in 1983. Similar and even wider gaps have occurred in the per capita incomes between advanced industrial societies and many other third world countries (World Bank, 1984, p. 6). All the evidence also suggests that, given the growth rates of even 1960–75, the gap in per capita incomes between these two groups of countries will remain a feature of the world economic landscape for centuries to come. Morawitz estimates that even Brazil will need 362 years before its income per capita catches up with that of OECD countries, while China will need 2,900 years. Given the severe economic difficulties experienced by Brazil in the 1980s, he has probably been overoptimistic (Morawitz, 1977, table 9, p. 29). For many other Third World countries there is no reason to believe that, on present evidence, they will ever catch up with today's affluent societies.

Thus, after forty years of economic growth, the majority of third world countries are no better off relative to the advanced industrial countries. Table 2.3 provides a snapshot of the distribution of incomes per capita in the world and, if figures ever speak for themselves, this is just one of those occasions: almost half of the world's population lives in countries where incomes per capita are well below the internationally acknowledged poverty line. This, of course, does not mean that all people in these countries are in poverty nor does it mean that no one is in poverty in other countries. These are issues to which we will return in the following two chapters. What these figures do show in the starkest of ways is that massive poverty exists in the midst of unprecedented economic affluence. Most of the world's wealth is consumed by a minority of the world's population—most of those living in the high income countries, and the very few who are affluent within third world countries.

Table 2.3   Income per capita and world population 1983

Income Group	Number of Countries	Total Population	Population as % of World Population
Below $300	28	2174.7 M	46.70
$301–$600	16	372.1 M	7.99
$601–$1000	12	303.4 M	6.51
$1001–$2000	21	342.1 M	7.35
$2001–$4000	18	400.5 M	8.60
$4001–$8000	12	420.4 M	9.03
$8001 and over	19	643.9 M	13.82
Total	126	4657.1 M	100.00

Source: Calculated from table 1, p. 174 of *World Development Report, 1985.*

Despite this overall gloomy picture, all the evidence also shows that a small number of third world countries have experienced significant improvements in their living standards during the post-war period, not simply in absolute terms but also relative to the standards prevailing in advanced industrial countries. These are, first, the rich oil exporting and, second, the Newly Industrialising Countries (NICs) of Asia—South Korea, Taiwan, Hong Kong and Singapore—and of South America—Brazil and Argentina. Development in the first group of countries is not of much theoretical interest for it is due to natural resources.

It is the latter group of countries that has been the centre of theoretical debates because the improvement in their living standards has been due to increased industrialisation and participation in the world trade of manufactured goods. Are the NICs the first wave of the industrialisation process that will slowly but surely envelope all third world countries, thus raising their standard of living and bridging or narrowing the income gap between North and South? Or is their industrialisation the result of such special and unique circumstances that it is unlikely to be reproduced by any, let alone by a large number of other third world countries?

The dependency theory sees industrialisation in the NICs as not only exogenous but also unlikely to spread to other third world countries. It is different from endogenous industrialisation because it is nothing more than 'assembly plant' operations of multinational companies. As such, it has limited implications for the local economy and it will last only as long as it serves the interests of foreign capital.

The orthodox Marxist and the modernisation theories on the other hand see industrialisation in the NICs as evidence of the inevitable march of industrialisation that will eventually engulf and benefit all third world countries. The distinction between endogenous and exogenous forms of industrialisation is of no relevance to these theories. Industrialisation may have been started largely by foreign capital, but this does not alter the fact that it sets in motion industrial, social and political processes that cannot be long held back or reversed.

Finally, the neo-Marxist and the radical structuralist positions see the NICs as part of the uneven and untidy process of industrialisation through which a few more third world countries will, with a great deal of difficulty, industrialise, but most will not in the foreseeable future.

Most of the empirical evidence from a variety of studies of varying theoretical viewpoints and sophistication shows that industrialisation in the NICs was the result of the convergence of both favourable outside factors and specific internal policies that cannot be easily replicated. It took place during a period when the world economy was expanding very rapidly and when international trade barriers were low. The internal policies consisted of strong government commitment to industrialisation, to the extent that it was prepared to offer multi-national companies fiscal and labour conditions that were most conducive to high profitability: low taxation rates and strict political control of trade union activity, as well as tax policies that benefited the top income groups and wages policies that were attractive to only a small section of the population.

Some of the NICs—Singapore and Hong Kong—also possessed unique historical and geographical conditions as entrepôts that made industrialisation easier. Reviewing the evidence of NICs, Bradford concludes that the advanced industrial countries have very little to fear from competition from the NICs in the foreseeable future because their numbers are not likely to grow much. In his words: 'The country composition of the tip of the proverbial iceberg will probably change somewhat in the coming decade, but the body of the iceberg will not become more visible' (Bradford, 1982, p. 24).

Writing from a neo-Marxist perspective, Sutcliffe arrives at a similar conclusion: he finds both the classical Marxist and the orthodox dependency positions wrong in view of recent empirical evidence. He concludes that industrialisation has been taking place in several third world countries, but it is the type of industrialisation that leads to internal polarisation where 'modern industry is growing at high and rising productivity levels and, at the same time, small-scale, more primitive industry survives at low, possibly declining productivity levels, but provides a meagre living for a growing share of the people' (Sutcliffe, 1984). In other words, technological industrialisation in NICs is confined to small enclaves and benefiting few people, while low productivity industrialisation continues unabated and even expands rather than being replaced by the former.

Finally, the evidence suggests that industrialisation has created severe political tensions in some NICs because of the polarisation of economic opportunities and incomes, with the result that its future is not as bright as it may appear. Nevertheless, it is not ephemeral and it cannot be wiped out at a stroke by multinationals if it ceases to serve their interests. Enough change has taken place to lay the foundations of industrialisation and to ensure its survival, even though its rate of expansion may not be as spectacular as it has been so far. In brief, the neo-Marxist and structuralist perspectives provide a better framework for understanding the uneven and the unsteady slow process of industrialisation taking place in third world countries, than the other approaches reviewed in the previous chapter. In terms of research, technological knowledge, capital availability, trade terms and political power, the cards are stacked far too much in favour of the advanced industrial countries to allow any more than a handful of third world countries to pose any real threat to their economic superiority.

To sum up this section: despite the enormous economic growth that has taken place since the end of the last war, only a small number of developing countries managed to narrow the gap with the advanced industrial societies. For most developing countries this gap has remained the same or even widened in both absolute and relative terms. This picture does not change substantially if a different definition of income is used for comparative purposes. It has been argued that the use of American dollars as the basis for comparing income inequalities between countries has the effect of exaggerating such inequalities because the same income has a higher purchasing power for basic commodities in the low-income than in the high-income countries (Kravis, *et al.*, 1982). This is a justifiable claim in relation to basic necessities produced within the country, but not for imported basic necessities. It does not apply, of course, to non-basic commodities nor does it take into account the fact that people's monetary incomes in advanced industrial societies are higher than those recorded if their social income is included, i.e. free or subsidised education, health, libraries, parks, street lighting, and so on. These services exist in developing countries, too, but at much lower standards. All these and other methodological difficulties in comparative studies of income do not change significantly the picture of gross inequalities that exist between the North and the South (Bigsten, 1983).

WEALTH INEQUALITIES WITHIN COUNTRIES

The discussion on inequalities in both wealth and income will be confined to income groups and will not cover such other important dimensions as race, religion, region or gender because of the lack of national and comparative data. The importance of these other forms of inequality, however, is recognised as significant in their own right which cannot always be subsumed under income groupings. This follows clearly from the structuralist perspective on development adopted in the first chapter.

Despite the absence of data on the distribution of wealth in most countries, it is important to include it for discussion because of the centrality of wealth to economic, political and social power. Wealth does not only generate income but can confer very significant amounts of power when held in large amounts. Clearly those whose wealth consists of simply their house or such-like items are in a very different position from those with large amounts of stocks and shares or land. It is clearly possession of exploitative wealth that confers economic, political and social power. The extent to which wealth is concentrated and inherited in a society is therefore 'of considerable relevance to the ways in which inequalities are structured and reproduced, and to the location of power in societies' (Cole and Miles, 1984, p. 15). As mentioned earlier, power is multifaceted and the possession of power in any one of its facets can generate power in the others and hence add to the total power possessed by a group or an individual. Very similar comments apply to power at the international level. Countries with superior economic power come to exercise also superior political and social power over others. Thus the widening or narrowing of the economic gap between advanced industrial societies and third world countries has implications also for their political and social relationships. In the same way that individual achievement for most people is thwarted in countries with excessive wealth concentration, so too at the international level economic progress of individual countries is held back when international wealth is overconcentrated in a few countries.

Table 2.4 shows that wealth is still heavily concentrated in advanced capitalist countries. The wealthiest 1 per cent of households own between one fifth and one third of the total wealth of their country; the top 5 per cent of wealthy households own between two fifths and two thirds of their national

Table 2.4   Distribution of wealth in advanced industrial societies

Country	% of Households/ Families/Adults	% of Wealth owned
	%	%
Australia 1967–68 (adults)	Richest 1	28.7
	5	56.6
	10	72.5
	25	92.1
Belgium 1969 (households)	Richest 1	27.8
	5	46.7
	10	57.4
	20	70.9
Canada 1970 (families)	Richest 1	19.6
	5	43.4
	10	58.0
	20	74.0
Denmark 1975 (households)	Richest 1	25.0
	5	47.0
	10	63.0
England and Wales 1972 (individuals)	Richest 1	31.7
	5	56.0
	10	70.4
	20	84.9
France 1975 (households)	Richest 1	12.5
	5	36.2
	10	51.7
	20	71.0
Ireland 1966 (individuals)	Richest 1	33.6
	5	63.0
	10	73.7
New Zealand 1966 (adults)	Richest 1	18.2
	5	44.5
	10	60.0
	25	84.7
Sweden 1975 (households)	Richest 1	17.0
	5	38.0
	10	54.0
	20	75.0

Country	% of Households/ Families/Adults		% of Wealth owned
West Germany 1973 (households)	Richest	1	18.7
		5	33.9
		10	45.3
		20	57.4
USA 1969 (individuals)	Richest	1	25.1
		5	43.7
		10	53.0

Sources: The main source was Alan Harrison, 1979.
For individual countries:
Canada, J. B. Davies, 1979
England and Wales, A. B. Atkinson and A. J. Harrison, 1978
France, A. Fouquet and D. Strauss-Kahn, 1984
Ireland, P. Lyons, 1974
Sweden, R. Spant, 1981.

wealth. The top 10 per cent own between two thirds and three quarters while the top 20 per cent of wealthy households own between three quarters and four fifths of their country's wealth. To put it in a different way, the vast majority of people in these countries, i.e. three fifths of households, own a small proportion, about one-fifth, of their country's wealth.

Moreover, table 2.4 underestimates the extent of wealth concentration, if wealth is defined narrowly in terms of the possession of land and such financial assets as shares, securities, bank deposits, and the like rather than widely, as the table does, to include people's housing and entitlement to retirement pension assets. It is wealth of the former type that confers economic power on its holders with all the implications outlined above. Evidence provided by a recent Royal Commission for England and Wales showed that most of the financial wealth is owned by a very small minority of individuals—350,000 individuals comprising 1.5 per cent of all wealth owners. Vice-versa, ownership of housing for personal use was widely spread among the general population. In the words of the Commission:

Persons with total net wealth between £5,000 and £20,000 held over 60%

of the value of all personally owned dwellings but less than 10% of the total for listed ordinary shares; conversely, individuals with net assets of £50,000 or more owned only 12% of the aggregate value of dwellings but 67% of the total for listed ordinary shares. (HMSO, 1977, p. 70)

Evidence from several advanced industrial countries shows that the recorded concentration of wealth, broadly defined, has declined over the years. Thus in Sweden the richest 1 per cent of households owned 50 per cent of the country's wealth in 1920 but only 21 per cent in 1975; and in England and Wales the richest 1 per cent of individuals owned 61 per cent of national wealth in 1923 but only 32 per cent in 1972. The same evidence, however, shows that this redistribution has been confined largely to the upper sections of wealth owners, 'between the very rich and the rich' (Atkinson, 1972, p. 22), rather than from the rich to the poor. Thus in England and Wales, the majority of wealth owners, 80 per cent, owned 6 per cent of marketable wealth in 1923 and 17 per cent in 1973; in Sweden the same group owned none of the taxable wealth in 1920 and 20 per cent in 1973. More detailed evidence shows that even this small redistribution of wealth towards the lower groups has been the result largely of the spread of home owner-ship rather than the spread of wealth narrowly defined.

As far as the redistribution of wealth from the very rich to the rich is concerned, the general picture that emerges from many countries is that some of it has been redistributed within families, in an effort to reduce tax liability, and only part of it has been the result of genuine spread of economic prosperity. There is also evidence that in some countries wealth concen-tration is largely hereditary rather than individually created. Harbury and McMahon examined the estates of deceased rich men—valued to £100,000 or more—in the UK in 1956 and 1965 and found that half of them had fathers who had left estates of £100,000 or more while 70 per cent had fathers who had left £25,000 or more in their estates. Moreover, these find-ings were not very different from those of Wedgwood that covered the years 1924–6, a fact which led them to conclude that 'the role of inheritance in the creation of the personal fortunes of top wealth owners ... has not changed very much since the mid-twenties' (Harbury and McMahon, 1973). In some other advanced industrial societies, the role of inheritance to wealth concentration appears not to be as prominent as it is in the UK. Davies argues that this is the case for both Canada and the USA, and he estimates that inherited wealth in the USA accounted for 'about 12 per cent of 1959 household wealth', a figure which is far lower than that pertaining to the UK (Davies, 1979). Though the role of inheritance to wealth concentration varies from one advanced industrial country to another, there is no doubt that it is, nevertheless, a major factor in both the stratification system of all countries at any one time and the transmission of economic power across the generations. The policy implications of all this is that the taxation systems on wealth that have so far operated in advanced industrial societies are not going to affect the degree of wealth concentration, particularly when they include a host of exemption clauses that either reduce or do away completely with a person's liability to wealth taxation. Claims by right-wing governments, as the Thatcher government in the UK, that privatising nationalised companies will lead to substantial reductions of wealth concentration are unfounded for all the evidence shows that the large shareholders eventually buy off most of the small shareholders.

Finally a word of caution concerning the comparability of national data on wealth distribution: bearing in mind the varying assumptions, bases of data estimation, reliability of data sources and such like methodological problems, it is not possible to draw reliable comparisons between countries. All that can be reliably said at present from existing data is that wealth concentration in these countries is high, that it is probably not as high as it was in pre-war days, that the degree of concentration varies slightly among countries and that wealth concentration is immune to reformist fiscal policies.

Wealth data are almost non-existent for third world countries but, bearing in mind their economic, political and social structures, one would expect wealth concentration to be even higher. Both the political pressures for wealth redistribution and the economic opportunities for wealth creation are weaker than those in advanced industrial societies, with the result that the tendencies for wealth concentration and wealth inheritance will be stronger. What little evidence there is relates to land ownership which is, of course, a very central form of wealth since the majority of the population live in rural areas and agricultural products are more important to the economies of third world countries than of advanced industrial countries. Table 2.5 shows the concentration of land in a large number of third world countries and, despite all the data problems, several observations can be made: the high concentration of land in all countries is the first and most obvious comment. In many third world countries a large proportion of the rural population is either landless or tries to earn a living from very small landholdings. Griffin provides evidence for several countries and shows, for example, that in the early 1960s in Morocco, almost 70 per cent of households were either landless or owned landholdings of less than two hectares, amounting to 16 per cent of cultivated land; in Equador in 1968 three quarters of all farms were less than five hectares making up 10 per cent of total farm area; and so on. Vice versa, most of the land was owned by a small minority of households and it was usually the best arable land (Griffin, 1976, tables 2.4, p. 85 and 5.7, p. 189). Second, land concentration in South American countries is the highest because of historical reasons relating to the colonisation policies of Spain and Portugal that resulted in the creation of large farms owned by Spanish and Portuguese at the expense of the indigenous populations. Third, evidence from several countries, particularly African, shows that in the modern commercial sector of agriculture, land concentration is higher than in the traditional section. It is generally accepted that the modern large-scale prosperous sector attracts more govern-ment subsidies than the traditional small-scale type of farming.

The result, therefore, is that public expenditure helps to increase income inequalities in rural areas (Ghai and Radwan, 1983, p. 20). Moreover, the commercialisation of agriculture in many third world countries has not only meant increased land concentration but the trend may well continue further in the future. The fourth observation relates to countries with low concentration ratios: they are countries where radical land reform measures were explicitly designed to spread land ownership. It is a reiteration of the point made earlier that wealth concentration of the exploitative type can only be reduced through direct radical measures and not through indirect mild reforms. Korea, Taiwan, Sri Lanka, Thailand, and the Philippines are all such countries and, interestingly enough, they are all Asian countries where political pressures and the fears of political revolutions are at their highest bearing in mind the examples of China and Vietnam. Land redistribution over the years in other third world countries has been of very modest proportions and unless radical land measures are introduced, the situation will remain the same in the future.

Table 2.5 Degree of land concentration in third world countries

Country	Year	Gini Coefficient
Bangladesh	1974	0.57
Colombia	1960	0.86
Costa Rica	1970	0.75
Dominican Republic	1970	0.79
Egypt	1960	0.63
Ghana	1970	0.64
India	1970	0.63
Indonesia	1974	0.57
Iran	1960	0.64
Iraq	1970	0.65
Jamaica	1970	0.80
Kenya	1960	0.54
Korea	1974	0.32
Lebanon	1960	0.70
Libya	1961	0.71
Malaysia	1971	0.54
Mozambique	1970	0.71
Pakistan	1970	0.52
Panama	1970	0.75
Peru	1970	0.92
Philippines	1971	0.51
Puerto Rico	1970	0.73
Sri Lanka	1970	0.41
Taiwan	1960	0.48
Thailand	1971	0.41
Tunisia	1960	0.67
Uruguay	1970	0.83
Venezuela	1970	0.92

Sources: Quan and Koo, 1985, table 3;
Griffin, 1976, table 8.4, 286;
Ghai and Radwan, 1983, table 3, p. 11.

Finally, data provided by Quan and Koo, on whose work Table 2.5 is largely based, show that land concentration in third world countries is far higher than income concentration and that 'it is the high concentration of land holdings that influences the unequal distribution of income' rather than the other way round (Quan and Koo, 1985). In fact, the situation is very similar to that of wealth and income in advanced industrial societies where the former is far more concentrated than the latter and, in its exploitative form, far more resistant to change.

The importance of wealth to economic inequality is far lower in societies where the means of production and distribution have been largely nationalised, as is the case in East European and several third world countries. Inevitably wealth concentration in these countries is low and it is restricted largely to non-exploitative forms of wealth, i.e. housing, very small plots of land, very small privately-run businesses and household valuables such as paintings, books, etc. There are, however, important variations even among these countries, particularly in relation to agriculture. In some countries, such as the Soviet Union, most land is nationalised or collectivised, whereas in some others, such as Poland, small independent peasant farms are still the major type of land ownership (Bergmann, 1975). Similarly, Hungary tolerates and sometimes encourages small businesses far more than other East European countries. Despite all these qualifications, the fact still remains that private wealth ownership is of far lesser significance in these countries than in capitalist countries.

INCOME INEQUALITIES WITHIN COUNTRIES

People's incomes are derived from three main sources: wealth, employment and state benefits. As expected, people with large amounts of wealth in the form of investment will derive a far greater proportion of their income from wealth than from employment earnings. Those with little or no wealth will clearly rely either totally or mainly on their earnings from employment or, if they are not in the labour market, from state benefits. In terms of the groups of countries we are considering, income from wealth is insignificant in the East European type of societies; income from state benefits is far more important in the advanced industrial societies than in third world countries irrespective of their political system; and income from employment is universally important though, in practical terms, of lesser importance in third world countries where rates of unemployment are very high.

This diversification of income sources inevitably means that income cannot be as highly concentrated as wealth and that its concentration has declined more over the years, largely because of increased employment opportunities and the introduction of social security benefits, particularly those that benefit most the low income groups. Despite the absence of privately owned wealth in East European societies, it does not necessarily follow that income inequalities will be lower than in capitalist countries. This is an empirical question to which we shall return later in this section. Thus wealth and income are related in several ways but they are also two different aspects of inequality that need separate documentation and discussion.

Debates about income inequalities face similar problems as those in the area of wealth but they are of far less severity. Data on income distribution are available for almost all countries and their reliability is far greater than in the case of wealth, with the result that more valid conclusions can be drawn both about the patterns of distribution within countries and comparisons between the distributional patterns of different groups of countries.

Before looking at the comparative evidence on income distribution, it is important to note that published income data do not take into account the value of occupational benefits which favour, in varying degrees, the highest income groups. Thus a recent study of 690 companies in the UK showed that occupational benefits for senior executives accounted for 'between 80 per cent and 100 per cent of basic salary' in 1987—a figure that is far higher than that of lower managers and, of course, of other socio-economic groups (Golzen, 1987).

Table 2.6 provides information on the income distribution patterns of a large number of countries, divided up into four groups according to their level of GNP per capita, but excluding East European type countries. The first general conclusion that emerges from the table is that income inequalities in the advanced industrial countries as a group are lower than those found in the other groups of countries. Using the proportion of national income accruing to the top 10 per cent of households, the highest figure found was 30.5 per cent in two countries, France and Australia, with all the remaining lying between 21 per cent and 30 per cent. In the upper middle income countries, the highest figure for the same income group was Brazil's, a staggering figure of 50.6 per cent, two other figures between 40 per cent and 50 per cent and all but two of the remaining between 30 per cent and 40 per cent. The two countries with figures lower than 30 per cent were South Korea and Israel, where special political and cultural factors apply.

The income distribution patterns found in the lower income countries as a group are very similar to those shown in the upper middle income group. The low income countries, however, exhibit a less unequal pattern of income distribution than the other two groups of countries but more unequal than that of the advanced industrial countries. A very similar picture emerges if one uses the bottom end of the income scale for comparison purposes, though the differences between the various groups of countries are not so wide. Using the Gini co-efficient as the yardstick of income inequality, the overall picture remains largely the same. Where data are available, the Gini co-efficient in advanced industrial countries is in the range of 0.30–0.39; in the low income countries it is 0.35–0.59; and in the other two groups of countries it ranges from 0.38 to 0.61 (Lecaillon *et al.* 1984, table 42, p. 207). In brief, then, income inequalities are at their lowest in advanced industrial societies, followed by the low income countries and with the middle income countries exhibiting the highest levels of income inequality.

The second general conclusion is that variations in income concentration within each of the four broad country groups are so wide that it is not possible to attribute them simply to levels of economic growth. Thus the Gini co-efficient for income distribution in France (0.39) is higher than that of Bangladesh (0.35), of South Korea (0.38), of Sri Lanka (0.35),

Table 2.6 Income distribution

Country	Year	Percentage share of household income, by percentile groups of households						
		Lowest 20%	Second Quintile	Third Quintile	Fourth Quintile	Fifth Quintile	Highest 10%
		%	%	%	%	%	%
1 Low Income Countries:							
Bangladesh	1976–7	6.2	10.9	15.0	21.0	46.9	32.0
Nepal	1976–7	4.6	8.0	11.7	16.5	59.2	46.5
Malawi	1967–8	10.4	11.1	13.1	14.8	50.6	40.1
India	1975–6	7.0	9.2	13.9	20.5	49.4	33.6
Sierra Leone	1967–9	5.6	9.5	12.8	19.6	52.5	37.8
Sri Lanka	1973	6.5	11.5	15.5	21.0	45.5	30.0
Kenya	1976	2.6	6.3	11.5	19.2	60.4	45.8
Sudan	1967–8	4.0	8.9	16.6	20.7	49.8	34.6
2 Lower Middle-Income Countries							
Senegal	1970	5.5	7.8	10.5	15.3	60.9	45.4
Indonesia	1976	6.6	7.8	12.6	23.6	49.4	34.0
Zambia	1976	3.4	7.4	11.2	16.9	61.1	46.3
Egypt	1974	5.8	10.7	14.7	20.8	48.0	33.2
El Salvador	1976–7	5.5	10.0	14.8	22.4	47.3	29.5
Zimbabwe	1969	3.0	4.8	7.2	17.0	68.0	55.5
Honduras	1967–8	3.2	4.1	7.7	17.5	67.5	50.6
Philippines	1985	5.2	8.9	13.2	20.2	52.5	37.0
Thailand	1975–6	5.6	9.6	13.9	21.1	49.8	34.1
Costa Rica	1971	3.3	8.7	13.3	19.9	54.8	39.5
Peru	1972	1.9	5.1	11.0	21.0	61.0	42.9
Turkey	1973	3.5	8.0	12.5	19.5	56.5	40.7
Colombia	1974	4.0	6.5	13.0	18.0	58.5	43.5

Table 2.6–continued

Country	Year	Percentage share of household income, by percentile groups of households					
		Lowest 20%	Second Quintile	Third Quintile	Fourth Quintile	Fifth Quintile	Highest 10%
		%	%	%	%	%	%
3 Upper Middle-income Countries							
Malaysia	1973	3.5	7.7	12.4	20.3	56.1	39.8
Chile	1968	4.4	9.0	13.8	21.4	51.4	34.8
Brazil	1972	2.0	5.0	9.4	17.0	66.6	50.6
Korea, Republic	1976	5.7	11.2	15.4	22.4	45.3	27.5
Argentina	1970	4.4	9.7	14.1	21.5	50.3	35.2
Panama	1976	2.0	5.2	11.0	20.0	61.8	44.2
Portugal	1973-4	5.2	10.0	14.4	21.3	49.1	33.4
Mexico	1977	2.9	7.0	12.0	20.4	57.7	40.6
Uruguay	1967	3.5	9.0	14.0	23.0	50.5	33.5
Venezuela	1970	3.0	7.3	12.9	22.8	54.0	35.7
Israel	1979–80	6.0	12.0	17.7	24.4	39.9	22.6
Hong Kong	1980	5.4	10.8	15.2	21.6	47.0	31.3
Trinidad and Tobago	1975–6	4.2	9.1	13.9	22.8	50.0	31.8
4 Industrial Market Economies							
Spain	1980–1	6.9	12.5	17.3	23.2	40.0	24.5
Ireland	1973	7.2	13.1	16.6	23.7	39.4	25.1

Italy	1977	6.2	11.3	15.9	22.7	43.9	28.1
New Zealand	1981–2	5.1	10.8	16.2	23.2	44.7	28.7
Belgium	1978–9	7.9	13.7	18.6	23.8	36.00	21.5
UK	1979	7.0	11.5	17.0	24.8	39.7	23.4
Netherlands	1981	8.3	14.1	18.2	23.2	36.2	21.5
Japan	1979	8.7	13.2	17.5	23.1	37.5	22.4
France	1975	5.3	11.3	16.0	21.8	45.8	30.5
Finland	1981	6.3	12.1	18.4	25.5	37.6	21.7
German Federal Republic	1978	7.9	12.5	17.0	23.1	39.5	24.0
Australia	1975–6	5.4	10.0	15.0	22.5	47.1	30.5
Denmark	1981	5.4	12.0	18.4	25.6	38.6	22.3
Canada	1981	5.3	11.8	18.0	24.9	40.0	23.8
Sweden	1981	7.4	13.1	16.8	21.0	41.7	28.1
Norway	1982	6.0	12.9	18.3	24.6	38.2	22.8
USA	1980	5.3	11.9	17.9	25.0	39.9	23.3
Switzerland	1978	6.6	13.5	18.5	23.4	38.0	23.7

Sources: World Development Report, 1985, Table 28, pp. 228–230
World Development Report, 1987, Table 26, pp. 252–253.

and of Yugoslavia (0.33). Looking at the issues in a different way, the highest proportion of income accruing to the lowest 20 per cent of households was 7.0 per cent in India for the low income group of countries; 6.6 per cent in Indonesia for the next group; 6.0 per cent in Israel for the next group, all of which compare favourably with the corresponding figures applying to several countries in the advanced industrial group. Thus variations within each group of countries and substantial overlaps between groups support the observation that historical and political factors are at least as important as economic growth for explaining the pattern of income distribution prevailing in any one country.

Lacaillon *et al.* arrive at a similar conclusion from their recent study of income distribution. While observing a general relationship between income levels and income distribution patterns, they note that other factors intervene to make this relationship far more complex. They show that, though income inequalities in South American countries vary a great deal, they include some of the highest in the world, reflecting past development policies that emphasised economic growth through import substitution industrial policies. African countries exhibit 'both the most equal and the least equal distributions', and, what is more, 'for the same GDP per head, the inequality in Asia is less than in African and Latin American countries', again a reflection of the importance of historical, political factors (Lecaillon *et al.*, 1984, pp. 36 and 40). Thus economic, cultural, historical and political factors interact to produce distinctive income inequality patterns.

Individual country studies also bring out the significance of political factors and of government policies in the reduction of income inequalities. Several studies have shown that the land reforms introduced by governments in Taiwan and South Korea have led to the reduction of rural inequalities simply because, on one hand they reduced the size of large estates, and on the other they 'established small owner-occupied farms as the dominant mode of production' (Reynolds, 1986, p. 71). Nyerere's agrarian policies are partly responsible for the low levels of income inequality in Tanzania, particularly when these are compared to those prevailing in neighbouring Kenya (Bigsten, 1983, chapter 7). In Britain income inequalities increased in the 1980s as a result of the fiscal policies pursued by the Thatcher government. The list of such examples is long, but they all endorse the importance of non-economic factors in shaping income inequality patterns. Economic growth by itself does not necessarily lead to the reduction of income inequalities, though it makes it easier for those political processes and government policies favouring reductions of such inequalities to have some effect. We shall return to this issue in this chapter.

The importance of political factors to the prevailing patterns of income inequalities is best shown in the case of East European types of societies. All the evidence shows that income inequalities in such societies are lower than those prevailing in capitalist societies, even after taking into account the importance of occupational benefits to people's monetary incomes. Thus the proportion of income accruing to the top 20 per cent of households in Yugoslavia, Hungary and Cuba in the late 1970s was 39 per cent, 36 per cent and 36 per cent respectively, which are lower than those prevailing in the vast majority of capitalist countries. The two main reasons for these lower figures are, first, the nationalisation of the means of production and distribution and, second, the lower ideological emphasis placed on the importance of inequality in terms of work incentives in society. The history of these countries also shows that income inequalities are at their lowest in the immediate aftermath of the revolutions or the other political processes that did away with the capitalist system and its established political order.

As the new political and economic elites, however, consolidate their power, they manage to win for themselves greater economic advantages *vis à vis* the rest of the population, which they are able to pass on to their children with the result that income inequalities increase over time and they also become entrenched, though not to the same extent as those of capitalist societies. There is a great deal of evidence that this is what happened in the case of several countries. In the Soviet Union, inequalities were reduced substantially in the early 1920s but they have increased since then, sometimes with the encouragement of the political leaders of the country (George and Manning, 1980).

China's policies towards both urban workers and farmers were, for many years, emphasising the reduction of inequalities though, in recent years, greater allowances have been made for work incentives that allow wider degrees of inequality. The case of Cuba illustrates the same trends in income distribution. Reviewing the data for these trends, Brundenius concluded that there was 'a radical redistribution of income in Cuba after the revolution with the major transfer of income to the bottom quantiles during the first years after 1959 and with more moderate transfers during the latter part of the 1960s and 1970s' (Brundenius, 1981, p. 154). Again, in recent years, the trend has been to consolidate entrenched patterns of inequality in Cuba. Hungary's example also fits in with this pattern— inequalities being reduced at first in a big way but gradually reasserting themselves over the years (Ferge, 1979). This and other evidence from other East European countries was reviewed by Lane, who reached a similar conclusion to the one outlined here.

> We may confidently generalise that it seems to be a general pattern in state-socialist societies that the period immediately following the national-isation of property and the seizure of political power is characterised by income equalisation. Later, with the consolidation of power by the new elites, greater differentials are introduced. (Lane, 1982, p. 61)

Though as a general statement this is correct, it needs to be qualified in at least one important respect. In such countries, political decisions can have far greater implications for income distribution than political decisions in capitalist societies, because of the state ownership of the means of production and distribution. It is, therefore, possible for political decisions favouring reductions of income inequalities to go contrary to the trend outlined above, as again the history of the Soviet Union shows. Income inequalities were reduced immediately after the revolution, they were increased under Stalin, they were discouraged under Kruschev and they were accepted under Brezhnev. Though political pronouncements do not always match up with reality, they can be influential.

The final comment about income inequalities is that they are not as wide as wealth inequalities in capitalist societies. In England and Wales the top 10 per cent of income earners received 23 per cent of gross incomes but 70 per cent of the country's wealth in the mid-1970s; in the USA the corresponding figures are 23 per cent, and 53 per cent respectively; and similar figures can be produced for other capitalist countries. Such comparisons are not possible for third world countries because of the absence of wealth data but one would expect a similar picture to emerge since both income and wealth are more unequally distributed than in advanced industrial societies. Only in centrally planned countries of the East European model are incomes more unequally distributed than wealth for the reasons already discussed.

ECONOMIC GROWTH AND INEQUALITY

The relationship between income inequality and economic growth has long been the focal point of debates in the social science literature. The two related facets of this debate are first, whether economic growth in itself reduces income inequalities and second, whether income inequalities encourage economic growth. We have already touched on the first but we need to develop it further before examining the second aspect of this relationship in some detail.

The issue concerning the effects of economic growth on the distribution of income in society has always been controversial, but it has gained added prominence since Kuznets's inverted U-curve hypothesis in 1955. Examining income data in three industrial societies—UK, USA and Germany—he found that income inequality was low during the pre-industrial period, it increased during the early period of industrialisation, it levelled off during the middle years and then it declined during the advanced stage of industrialisation. He was anxious to make clear that his conclusion was very tentative, since the data he used were inadequate in several respects, so much so that he felt his thesis 'is perhaps 5 per cent empirical information and 95 per cent speculation, some of it possibly tainted by wishful thinking' (Kuznets, 1955). Moreover, he was uncertain as to whether the same trends in income distribution would eventually take place in developing societies, since their political and historical heritage was different from that of developed countries in their pre-industrial phase. Thus it is 'far from safe to extrapolate economic or demographic aspects from the earlier records for the developed countries to current and prospective levels for the underdeveloped' (Kuznets, 1954, p. 151). In brief, Kuznets was recording what he found had been the experience of three industrial countries and he was calling for more research to test his hypothesis in other countries. The explanation he offered for the U-curve trends was that, in the pre-industrial societies, inequalities were low because the majority of people lived on the land; during the early stages of industrialisation and the mass rural exodus to the towns, the small sector of full-time industrial workers and the upper middle class gained most of the fruits of the increased economic growth; and it is only when all the sectors of the labour force were integrated in the industrial and political structure of the country that income became more equally distributed.

Ideas, however, are often interpreted to suit the dominant climate of opinion and Kuznets's hypothesis is no exception to this. The modernisation theory was beginning to gain general acceptance in the mid-1950s, with the result that Kuznets's findings, far from being a tentative hypothesis, were elevated to an iron law in the history of economic development. It was now claimed that it was both necessary and natural for inequality to increase during the early stages of economic development and that it would inevitably decline as the country became more affluent. Later rather than sooner economic growth would 'trickle down' from the higher to the lower socio-economic groups. The experience of advanced industrial societies was relevant to the development process of the developing societies, since the latter were merely going through the same stages that the former had gone through a couple of centuries earlier. History would repeat itself but much more quickly now, since developing countries would be assisted in their efforts by the rich world.

A great deal of research has since been done to test Kuznets's hypothesis but, interestingly enough, most of it is not along Kuznets's lines. It is not historical research examining the experience of countries over long periods of time but rather it is cross-sectional research looking at the distribution of income in a large number of countries at one point in time. Clearly there are serious problems in using cross-sectional data to test a hypothesis based on historical data. The whole exercise is implicitly based on a modernisation theory framework with all the problems that this theory encounters as Chapter 1 showed.

What cross-sectional studies therefore can show is simply whether the degree of inequality varies inversely with the level of economic growth prevailing in any one country. Kravis's work in 1960 was the first major cross-sectional study attempting to 'test' the U-curve thesis. Looking at income data from eleven countries, Kravis found that income inequalities were greater in low income than in high income countries, particularly because of the high concentration of income among the top income groups in developing countries (Kravis, 1960). His sample, however, was so small that only tentative conclusions could be reached, even in relation to the situation in 1960. Several other studies using the same methodology were conducted in the 1960s (Bigsten, 1983, Chapter 5) and arrived at similar results, i.e. economic growth and income inequality were inversely related and hence this 'confirmed' Kuznets's U-curve hypothesis.

The issue, therefore, appeared to be settled until Adelman and Morris's work in 1971 sparked off yet another round of cross-sectional studies. Using data from seventy-four developing countries during the period 1957–62, they found that economic growth led to an increase in both income inequality and poverty. The reason for this association, however, was structural, and hence economic growth could not be held responsible for the increased impoverishment of third world countries. In their words, 'economic structure, not level of income or rate of economic growth, is the basic determinant of patterns of income distribution' (Adelman and Morris, 1973, p. 186). In other words, it is not so much economic growth but a certain type of economic growth—that based on *laissez-faire* capitalist lines—which accentuates income inequalities in a country. It therefore followed that more economic growth of the same kind would not, as the Kuznets hypothesis claimed, bring about reductions in inequalities in third world countries. To quote them again: 'Piecemeal policies are unlikely to benefit the poor significantly unless accompanied by fundamental institutional reforms' (Adelman and Morris, 1973, p. 200).

It was not unexpected that Adelman and Morris were subjected to a great deal of criticism because their conclusion shattered the comfortable illusion of the establishment in the international economic development field that economic growth by itself would sooner or later solve the problem of extreme inequality and poverty—no radical changes in terms of land distribution or the terms on which aid was given or such like areas were necessary. Ahluwalia's study in 1974, on behalf of the World Bank, was the most important reply to the sobering conclusion of Adelman and Morris. Using data from sixty-six countries, he found no support for the Adelman and Morris thesis but instead 'corroborated' the U-curve hypothesis. Indeed, he found that improvements in education policies and reduction in population growth rates were sufficient to reduce income inequalities in third world countries (Ahluwalia, 1974). A more recent study, by an ILO team in 1984, has also given support, though qualified, to the Kuznets thesis. Examining income data from thirty-nine 'developing' and eight 'developed' countries, they concluded that their study 'has confirmed the Kuznets hypothesis on long-term changes in the distribution of incomes, but the sharp variation in the Gini co-efficient within each income group show the limitations of that hypothesis for interpretations of changes in individual countries' (Lecaillon *et al.*, 1984, p. 41).

To sum up: cross-sectional studies cannot prove or disprove Kuznets's claim of an historical trend towards reductions of income inequality as a country proceeds from an agrarian, pre-industrial economy to an advanced industrial stage of development. Only long-term historical studies can shed light on this hypothesis. Saith's verdict on cross-sectional studies, i.e. that they are 'arguably more of a hindrance than an aid to our comprehension of the relationship between economic growth and income distribution' (Saith, 1983), has much to commend it. They may, however, provide broad and tentative indications of the relationship between economic growth and income inequality at any one time within capitalist societies. Even so, there are such wide variations of income inequality within any one group that the relationship with levels of economic growth is only moderate, and it disappears altogether once East European countries are included in the tortured statistical exercises of cross-sectional studies (Papanek and Kyn, 1986). The levels of per capita income, at best, explain only a small part of the variations in income inequality between countries. Other factors, political, structural and historical, account for the rest.

Turning to historical studies of income distribution within third world countries, the picture is no less complex. There is no iron law linking patterns of income distribution to levels of economic growth; rather there is a complex web of economic, structural and political factors shaping the pattern of income distribution within countries. We can only refer to a few studies here to illustrate the complexity of the issue. Berry and Urrutia's study of Colombia showed that income distribution in urban areas worsened during the period 1930s–1950s and then improved slightly; for rural areas, income distribution worsened through the whole period; and the main beneficiaries of economic growth were the middle classes (Berry and Urrutia, 1976). Van Ginneken's study of Mexico confirmed that the main beneficiaries of economic growth were the middle classes and concluded that the trend in income inequality in Mexico 'does not follow the pattern which is predicted by the Kuznets hypothesis' (Van Ginneken, 1980, p. 146).

Brazil's income distribution trends have been widely studied and have been the centre of a great deal of controversy. Thus Morley's recent study claimed that economic growth increased inequality at first but Brazil reached the turning point on Kuznets's U-curve around 1970, with the result that the benefits of economic growth were at last 'trickling down' to the low income groups (Morley, 1983, p. 284). Cardoso's review of Morley's work, however, produces evidence from Brazil's 1980 census that was not available to Morley, to show that this was not the case. Thus the income share of the top decile was 40 per cent in 1960, 47 per cent in 1970 and 48 per cent in 1980; the corresponding figures for the share of the lowest 40 per cent of income earners was 12 per cent, 10 per cent and 10 per cent respectively (Cardoso, 1983).

The ILO study of rural areas in eight Asian countries

showed that, apart from China, income inequalities in rural areas worsened during the 1960s and early 1970s (ILO, 1977). Another ILO study of nine African countries during the 1960s and 1970s also found that the available data pointed 'to increasing inequalities in incomes and assets, as represented for example by the shares of the bottom 20 per cent to 40 per cent and the top 10 per cent to 20 per cent of rural households' (Ghai and Radwan, 1983, p. 4). Though the two ILO studies referred to rural areas, there is no reason to believe that the situation was any different in urban areas, bearing in mind the massive rural migration to the cities which is characteristic of all third world countries today.

Finally, Fields, reviewing the experience of thirteen third world countries, found no consistent pattern and concluded as follows: 'Growth itself does not determine a country's inequality course. Rather the decisive factor is the *type* of economic growth as determined by the environment in which growth occurs and the political decisions taken' (Fields, 1980, p. 94). In conclusion, neither cross-sectional studies nor historical studies support the view that all countries go through the same statges of economic inequality that Kuznets identified in his study of three European countries. Economic growth may be achieved through *laissez-faire* capitalism, through government controlled capitalism, or through East European type nationalisation, and each has different implications for the degree and pattern of income inequality prevalent in a country. It may well be that first world countries that adopted the *laissez-faire* path to industrialisation—as the three countries Kuznets study did—followed the U-curve route to income distribution but there is no logic or evidence to claim that countries which follow different paths to industrialisation will follow the U-curve route to income distribution. What determines the pattern and degree of income inequality in a country is not its level of economic growth but the type of industrial, agrarian and other relevant government policies that are being pursued.

The debate between the economistic U-curve and the structural-political explanation of income inequality has significant policy implications. The first implies that government redistributive measures are not necessary since economic growth will eventually take care of distributional issues. The second states clearly that explicit government policies are necessary for the reduction of inequalities. Moreover, the first implies that redistribution will impede economic growth while the second claims that it is possible to achieve growth with redistribution (Wright, 1978). Some writers in the second school go even further to claim that reduction of income inequalities is a necessary prerequisite to economic growth in third world countries. We now turn to examine the debates and the empirical evidence in this equally important area.

INEQUALITY AND ECONOMIC GROWTH

We now turn to the second part of the debate concerning the relationship between inequality and economic growth: is maximum inequality conducive to economic growth and do policies designed to reduce it undermine economic growth? Three main answers to these questions emerge from the various development theories discussed in Chapter 1. We shall discuss these first and then examine some relevant empirical evidence from the development of third world countries.

The first answer emerges from the modernisation theory in the form of the functionalist theory of inequality advanced by several sociologists, but particularly by Davis and Moore in the 1940s and Parsons in the 1950s (Davis and Moore, 1945; Parsons, 1951). Inequality is both necessary and beneficial to all in society, because it encourages economic growth. It does this by ensuring first, that the most able occupy the most important jobs in society and, second, that they continue to be motivated whilst in their jobs. Without the mechanism of unequal pay, incentives to work hard and to save would be undermined, economic growth would decline and everyone would suffer as a result. In the case of third world countries, the issue of savings is highly significant because without the savings of the rich, investment would decline and economic growth would inevitably suffer. Development 'must be inegalitarian' (Lewis, 1976, p. 26), or none at all; there can be no such thing as egalitarian economic development.

There is no good reason to discuss at length the weaknesses

of the functionalist theory for it has already been done several times (Tumin, 1953; Midgley, 1984; George, 1980). We shall instead comment briefly on those aspects that have particular relevance to third world countries. Whilst it may be true that the middle classes in the industrialising countries of the nineteenth century used their savings to advance the process of industrialisation, all the evidence shows that the elites of third world countries today are not behaving in the same way. Instead, as Todaro points out, they are inclined 'to squander much of their incomes on imported luxury goods, expensive houses, foreign travel, and investment in gold, jewellery and foreign banking accounts' (Todaro, 1977, p. 138). The reason, of course, is that they find themselves in a totally different economic, political and cultural situation, and not because they are psychologically different. It is yet another example of the inadequacy of the idea of the stages of economic growth that is so central to the modernisation theory.

The claim that unequal pay is necessary, inevitable and beneficial to all because it is the only known incentive for effort and work application is full of so many weaknesses that have been referred to by so many writers—talent is plentiful in society, family background rather than talent often decides who occupies the most important positions in society and non-economic incentives can be important to work effort and so on. Though it is one of those claims that is almost impossible to prove or disprove, it must be rejected on ethical grounds in the case of third world countries because its application has led to untold suffering and to the starvation and death of millions of people.

The second and third answers to the question emerge from the Marxist and structuralist approaches to economic development. Though the explanations are slightly different, they both see inequality as neither natural nor beneficial to all nor conducive to economic growth. Inequality is the result of unequal class power, according to the Marxist view, and of a dominant ideology which legitimises it. This explanation is adequate as far as it goes but it needs to be complemented by the structuralist explanation, for several types of economic inequality are the result of racial, religious, gender, professional, technical and educational forces which cannot be subsumed, as mentioned before, under the dimension of class. Both the structuralist and Marxist explanations see inequality as undesirable because, firstly, it benefits the few at the expense of the many and secondly, because it hinders economic growth, particularly in the case of third world countries. Greater equality would benefit economic growth in third world countries for at least three main reasons: it would improve the quality of labour through better education, health and nutrition; it would increase demand for locally produced basic needs since the low paid spend their incomes on such consumption, rather than on imported luxury goods as the rich do; and thirdly, greater income equality can have a positive psychological effect on the poor—it can encourage them to take an active part in the country's development process rather than being indifferent or even hostile (Todaro, 1977, pp. 156–7). Yet the structuralist nature of these explanations makes it abundantly clear that the road to reduced inequalities in third world countries is, by definition, slow and difficult, particularly in capitalist countries.

An examination of the development policies of third world capitalist countries suggests that government policies that reduce inequality are just as compatible with economic growth as unrestricted *laissez-faire* capitalism. Brazil, which has emphasised *laissez-faire* industrialisation and has made no attempts to redistribute land or property, has achieved respectable rates of economic growth but it has created a society where abject poverty on a large scale exists side by side with strikingly high levels of affluence. So it is possible to raise economic growth by adopting development policies that show no concern for income inequalities and for poverty. Korea, on the other hand, has adopted a development policy which involved land redistribution with a capitalist form of industrialisation and has also achieved respectable rates of economic growth but with reduced income inequalities. Several other capitalist countries can be cited as examples of economic growth being accompanied by unrestricted or restricted income inequalities.

What, however, of the contrast between capitalist and 'socialist' models of economic development? The comparison that most commentators use in this debate is that between the development policies of China and India (Byres and Nolan, 1976). They are both large countries, geographically and by population, they both began their development process in the early 1950s from very similar economic levels, but they have adopted different development policies. China has national-ised most land and it has given it to villagers to cultivate on a collective basis, while India has permitted the private owner-ship of land to continue with its characteristic feature of high levels of land concentration. China has nationalised most industries, and though it has accepted some outside aid mainly from the Soviet Union, it has emphasised the self-reliant path to industrialisation. India has left most industry in private hands and it has relied a great deal on outside aid and expertise for its industrialisation process. China has adopted very endogenous types of health and education provision stressing the satisfaction of the basic needs of the majority while India has used westernised forms of health and education provision. China has tried vigorously to control rural migration to the cities, while India has permitted a free flow of population and labour within its boundaries. Both China and India have attempted to reduce their rates of population growth but with China showing far greater success because of its more determined efforts and the greater integration of population policies with health, education and economic policies. In brief, China has adopted a structuralist egalitarian road to economic development, while India has followed an inegalitarian path, despite the rhetoric to the contrary that many of its five year plans use. The result has been that China has achieved higher rates of economic growth as well as higher rises in income per capita than India, together with a less unequal distribution of wealth, income, education and health, in terms of socio-economic groups, the urban-rural dimension, or between the sexes.

Critics of the Chinese model of development, however, point to the fact that, though all this may be correct, the fact is that it has been achieved through a great deal of authoritarian government planning and the repression of individual and political freedom. Without in any way wishing to belittle the importance of individual freedom as it is known in the West, one has also to acknowledge that there are different institutional methods of respecting individual freedom and the Chinese method is not necessarily inferior to the Indian method as far as the vast majority of the population is concerned. Freedom means more that the right to vote, of free speech and of free association. It also means the right to be consulted at the workplace, as well as freedom from starvation, disease and illiteracy. A truly free society fulfils, as far as it can, all these aspects of freedom, for they are truly indivisible and complementary.

The contrast between China and India suggests that, at the very least, reductions of structural inequalities are not incompatible with economic growth. In fact, they may well be a necessary prerequisite to long-term sustainable economic growth. The experience of China, however, also shows that, though the reduction of structural inequalities poses no problems and may be conducive to economic growth, excessive reductions of individual economic inequalities may well act as disincentives if they are not supported by public opinion. Cuba's experience has been very similar. Wealth inequalities can be substantially reduced but individuals need to be rewarded slightly unequally depending on their talents, effort and contribution to the nation's welfare if economic growth is not to suffer (Blecher, 1985). It is for this reason that both China and Cuba have, in recent years, sanctioned greater income inequalities to reward and to stimulate individual contribution (Trescott, 1985).

Clearly, there are immense problems of how individual contribution is defined and measured let alone the degree of inequality that is necessary to reward and encourage it. But a society which faces up to these problems and tries to find answers to them that command general support is a much fairer society than one which accepts both wealth and income inequality as natural and unalterable, and makes no attempt to control the excesses generated by the operation of the labour market. There is a great deal of difference between regulated and reduced inequality on one hand and unchecked, maximum inequality on the other.

CONCLUSION

Despite current economic difficulties, economic growth has been very substantial during the post-war period. Living standards have risen the world over, but economic inequalities between countries and within countries have not changed as much. Some third world countries have managed to narrow the gap between themselves and the affluent industrialised world, but for most third world countries the relative gap has remained unaltered. Similarly, wealth and income inequalities within countries have narrowed slightly, but this redistribution has been from the very rich and the very highly paid to the rich and highly paid. The bottom half of wealth owners and income earners have benefited very little from this redistribution. The most powerful, be they nations or classes and groups within nations, have been fairly successful in defending their relative living standards against the constant demands and pressures from the rest of the population. Power, buttressed by a favourable ideology, tends to produce a set of exploitative relationships that are not amenable to quick or substantial change. It is for this reason that the stratification system of the world and of individual countries will probably look very much the same for as long as one can see in the future, despite minor changes here and there.

The experience of the last forty years has dispelled several long-standing beliefs in the field of development. It has shown, first of all, that economic growth by itself does not reduce wealth or income inequalities. It has, secondly, shown that reductions in income and wealth inequalities are quite compatible with economic growth. There is no iron law linking economic growth with economic inequality. Thirdly, it has demonstrated that the real issue is not between equality and inequality in their global terms, but rather what types and degrees of inequality are desirable and possible at any one time in any one country, so that neither economic growth nor individual people suffer. In the same way that excessive equalisation of income can undermine economic growth, excessive inequalities can have the same effect and result in poverty and personal suffering in any country, but particularly in third world countries where living standards are so low that the end result can be tantamount to malnutrition and starvation. It is with these issues—poverty, malnutrition and starvation—that the next two chapters are concerned.

3 Poverty in Advanced Industrial Societies

Despite the substantial economic growth and the high standards of living that characterise affluent societies, poverty remains commonplace and, on present evidence, will remain so for the foreseeable future. Yet poverty in affluent societies is not a paradox but the inevitable result of the concentration of political and economic power and of the prevalent ideology that places private profit and economic growth above the satisfaction of basic needs for all. Clearly, it is not lack of resources that accounts for poverty in affluent societies but the pattern of distribution of these resources. In this chapter we examine the various definitions of poverty, the extent of poverty, the various population groups in poverty, the explanations of poverty, and the prospects for its reduction in the future.

DEFINITIONS OF POVERTY

Definitions of poverty are just as value-based as definitions of development, for they are both concerned with the satisfaction of human needs and the distribution of resources within and between countries. Being value-based means that no one definition of poverty commands universal support. Claims that definitions of poverty can be 'objective' or 'scientific' and hence universally acceptable do not stand up to any critical examination. However ingenious and complex the research design and however tortuous the statistical techniques may be, the questions asked to ascertain poverty, the indicators used to measure it and the decisions taken on the dividing line between poverty and non-poverty inevitably reflect the views and the values of some person or group, be they those of the researcher, the professional expert, the government, the media correspondent or the general public. Self-interest and personal social values largely account for such decisions. All this is generally agreed and an OECD report expressed this very well when it concluded that 'there cannot be any definition of "poverty" which is free from value judgements' (OECD, 1976, p. 62). What is not agreed, however, is whose interests and values are being served by the definitions adopted by governments for policy purposes. We shall return to this issue later on in the chapter.

The various definitions of poverty in advanced industrial societies have tended to be grouped under a subsistence or a relative heading. In one sense all definitions of poverty are relative because they represent, to a greater or lesser extent, the customs and living conditions prevailing at any one time in any one country. But this is not the real issue between subsistence and relative approaches to poverty. The crux of the matter is the degree of generosity that is built into the definition. Relative definitions are more generous than subsistence definitions, in terms both of the range of needs and the level at which these needs should be satisfied to ensure that people are not in poverty. Looked at in this way one might be tempted to say that all definitions of poverty are relative but some are more relative than others. This, however, would be an over-simplification of what are real differences between the two approaches.

Subsistence definitions are primarily concerned with ensuring that people have enough incomes to pay for those needs which are indispensable for their health and their physical survival. They tend to be the prevalent approach to the definition of poverty in countries whose economic standards of living are low. Thus definitions of poverty during the nineteenth and early twentieth centuries in today's advanced industrial societies as well as definitions in third world countries today are predominantly subsistence definitions. One of the clearest exponents of the subsistence approach was Rowntree, whose study of poverty in York at the turn of the century set the pattern for many a study for decades. He saw poverty in terms of a person's ability to pay for food, clothing, housing and a few household sundries, all at as low level as possible so long as the health of the individuals concerned did not suffer. His poverty line represented bare physical survival and it showed no concern for even the most customary of social needs, as the following quotation shows:

> A family living upon the scale allowed for in this estimate must never spend a penny on railway fares or omnibus. They must never go into the country unless they walk. They must never purchase a halfpenny newspaper or spend a penny to buy a ticket for a popular concert. They must write no letters to absent children, for they cannot afford to pay the postage. They must never contribute anything to their Church or Chapel, or give any help to a neighbour which costs them money.... The children must have no pocket money for dolls, marbles or sweets. The father must smoke no tobacco, and must drink no beer.... Should a child fall ill, it must be attended by the parish doctor; should it die, it must be buried by the parish. (Rowntree, 1901, pp. 133–4)

It can, of course, be argued with some justification that even this austere definition of poverty is relative since it reflected the living standards of the lower sections of the working class in Britain at the end of the last century. What cannot be argued, however, is that this poverty line is relative in relation to the living standards of either all sections of British society or even of the average standard of living prevalent at that time.

Though this early Rowntree approach has all but been abandoned in advanced industrial societies, it is very much the basis of most poverty studies in third world countries today. Indeed, many poverty studies in third world countries use a far more subsistence approach than Rowntree. Many of them define poverty, as we shall see in the next chapter, merely in terms of sufficient food to avoid starvation and death. As one member of the ILO team that examined poverty in Asia during the 1970s put it:

> In most exercises concerned with developing countries, the poverty lines are related to the absorption of a minimum diet based on nutritional requirements. The logic of such exercises is that since food is the most basic of the basic needs, the attainment of an adequate diet commands priority over other needs. (Naseem, 1977, p. 43)

Undoubtedly the prevailing national economic standards affect notions of what subsistence is, for poverty definitions tend to become more generous, though still of subsistence nature as the national economy grows. This is clearly shown by the fact that poverty definitions in third world countries vary in 'generosity', though they all hover around the point of subsistence. It is also shown by the fact that poverty definitions in advanced industrial societies became more generous, though again still of subsistence nature, as these countries began to be more affluent. Rowntree's second study of York in 1936 used a more generous subsistence definition of poverty in the sense that it included expenditure on some social needs such as newspapers, trade union subscriptions, travelling expenses to work, and the like. The result was that though this new definition of poverty was more generous than the first in terms of the rise in prices during the intervening period, it was not more generous in terms of the rise in wages (George, 1973, chapter 2).

It is true that both Karl Marx and Adam Smith referred to poverty in relative terms, i.e. that it should reflect the prevailing standards and norms of society. But it is equally true that neither spelled out what this meant in detail and, had they done so, they would have arrived at very different sums, bearing in mind their contrasting views on economic and social affairs. Indeed, it was not until the 1960s and 1970s that researchers began to define poverty in detailed ways that reflected social norms in terms of either the range of needs or the level at which these needs should be satisfied, or both. In more precise terms the poverty line that was now being adopted was higher than previous ones not only in terms of the rise in prices but also in terms of the rise in wages. The post-war rapid improvement in living standards in advanced industrial societies influenced the perception of poverty as researchers came to feel that their countries could afford to make better provisions for their poor than in the past. It seems most unlikely that these new perceptions of poverty would have come about without the very substantial rise in living standards during the post-war period. People's social horizons and researchers' conceptual frameworks are influenced by the material conditions within which they live.

Townsend is the best known advocate of the relative poverty approach and his poverty studies of the 1960s and 1970s constitute the real break from the Rowntree tradition. People are in poverty, he argues,

> when they lack the resources to obtain the types of diet, participate in the activities and have the living conditions and amenities which are customary, or are at least widely encouraged or approved, in the societies to which they belong. Their resources are so seriously below those commanded by the average individual or family that they are, in effect, excluded from ordinary living patterns, customs and activities. (Townsend, 1979, p. 31)

He operationalised this definition with a long list of sixty items, ranging from purely physiological—food, clothing, housing, work, environment—to purely social needs such as eating out in restaurants, having friends at home, going on holidays, and so on. He showed not only the very obvious statistical correlation between income and participation in or consumption of these needs but also that, at a certain point on the income distribution, participation in these activities or needs dropped very substantially. This point he defined as the deprivation threshold, i.e. the poverty line below which people are poor, not just unequal, in relation to the rest of the population.

Mack and Lansley used a very similar approach in their study of poverty in the UK in the early 1980s but with two significant improvements. They relied on public perceptions of what basic and relative needs are, rather than on their own judgements, and they distinguished between people who could not afford to have and those who simply did not want to have any out of the long list of basic and social needs.

The relative approach not only defines the poverty line at a higher level than the basic needs approach but it also sees poverty as part of the wider issue of income distribution in society rather than as a specific problem for a small group of people in society. For this reason, the relative definition of poverty has been criticised for confusing inequality with poverty. Theoretically, however, the two are different and it is quite possible to envisage a society in which relative poverty is abolished whilst inequality still exists. What is true, however, is that the relative approach questions fundamentally the prevailing pattern and ideology of income and wealth distribution, whilst the basic needs approach does not. Moreover, were a government willing and able to implement a pro- gramme that abolished or reduced substantially relative poverty, it would probably set in motion a chain of further demands that would threaten even more the prevailing pattern of inequality. It is for these reasons that the concept of relative poverty has been seen as the Trojan horse of equality and it has met with strong resistance from writers of right-wing ideology (Joseph and Sumption, 1979, p. 28). It is also obvious that the abolition of relative poverty is far more costly than the abolition of subsistence poverty and hence governments of all political orientations have so far shown little interest in it.

Government policies on poverty are influenced not so much by the findings of research studies and the arguments of academics but by wider political, ideological and economic considerations. As argued in the last chapter, the dominant ideology of capitalist societies sees inequality as both natural and necessary and this, together with the economic costs involved, has meant that, where poverty lines have been adopted by governments, they have been of the subsistence type. In fact, many countries in the industrialised world, let alone the Third World, do not have legally binding, statutory subsistence poverty lines. Clearly it is the values and the interests of the dominant groups in society that shape the government poverty line, which affects the daily lives of millions of poor people. A high poverty line inevitably means substantial vertical redistribution of income: a low line may involve very little, if any, such redistribution.

So far the two approaches to poverty have been presented as ideal types. In practice, however, research studies often use definitions that contain elements of both. The claim that the subsistence definition has lost all its usefulness and should be abandoned is misplaced, not only because it is the only approach that can be realistically used in third world countries but because it is a reminder that basic needs are absolute and not merely relative. The fact that the majority of people in some developing countries are undernourished or ill-housed has to be seen as such rather than as a relative condition. It is this absolute nature of basic needs that Sen has in mind when he argues that

> relative deprivation is essentially incomplete as an approach to poverty, and supplements (but cannot supplant) the earlier approach of absolute dispossession. The much maligned biological approach, which deserves substantial reformulation but not rejection, relates to this irreducible core of absolute deprivation, keeping issues of starvation and hunger at the centre of the concept of poverty. (Sen, 1981, p. 22)

The use of a simple poverty line—in relative or absolute terms—is inadequate in many ways as a measure of poverty in society. It does not take into account the depth of poverty, i.e. by how much people fall below the line, and it also gives the misleading impression that those just above the line are different from this on it or just below it. Suggestions for a band rather than a line of poverty do not really solve the border problems associated with the line of poverty. We simply need more detailed statistics about these issues. Another important issue that is often neglected is the duration and flow of poverty, i.e. how long people have been in poverty and what proportion of the poor at any one time have been in poverty before (Duncan, 1984). Data on poverty are very patchy and inadequate in several respects, as the discussion in the following section shows.

THE EXTENT OF POVERTY

Poverty studies have been few and far between and they have been concentrated mainly in the English-speaking countries. Moreover, the few attempts that have been made to standardise the level of poverty lines in different countries have met with little success, with the result that there is no generally accepted standard of measuring poverty in rich countries (Beckerman, 1979; George and Lawson (eds), 1980; Walker, Lawson and Townsend (eds), 1984).

The extent of measured poverty in any one country thus depends on the generosity of the poverty line used. The more austere the poverty line, the lower the proportion of the population found by research studies to be in poverty; and vice versa, the more generous the definition, the higher the proportion found to be in poverty, other things being equal. Another important methodological factor that seriously affects the extent of poverty uncovered by research studies is the income unit used. Household as a unit underestimates the extent of poverty compared to tax or family unit. Thus a British study showed that 'the proportion of tax units classified as below the poverty line is almost twice the proportion of households so classified' (Fiegehen *et al.*, 1977, pp. 44–5).

Post-war studies of poverty date back mostly to the early 1960s. The 1950s were a period of economic recovery and general reconstruction following the devastations of the last World War. Poverty was thus neglected and later 'rediscovered' by the studies of Harrington in the USA in 1962, of Abel-Smith and Townsend in Britain in 1965, of Paul-Marie de la Gorce in France in 1965, and of other researchers in other countries in the late 1960s and early 1970s. This period was thus a time of intense debate on poverty, of high-sounding political rhetoric, of government programmes declaring 'war' on poverty or 'positive discrimination' in favour of the poor. If research activity and political declarations were enough to

Table 3.1 Extent of poverty in various countries and national definitions of poverty

Country	Year	Percentage of Persons/Families Below Poverty Line	Definition of Poverty Line
		%	
USA	1960	20.2 of persons	
	1970	12.6 of persons	The food needs standard
	1980	13.0 of persons	of the United States
	1983	15.2 of persons	Department of Agriculture
UK	1960	2.3 of persons	
	1972	3.2 of persons	Supplementary Benefit
	1979	4.0 of persons	Level Line
	1983	5.2 of persons	
Australia	1972	10.2 of families	Government Commission of
	1981	11.8 of families	Enquiry into Poverty Line
Canada	1969	23.1 of persons	
	1980	15.1 of persons	Economic Council of
	1984	17.8 of persons	Canada Poverty Line

abolish poverty, the problem would have easily been solved. But government actions and policies lagged far behind and, in many instances, they were no more than of a token nature.

Table 3.1 shows the extent of poverty using national definitions. Though all the definitions adopted refer mainly to subsistence needs, they, nevertheless, vary in generosity because they are culturally defined, with the result that no firm country comparative conclusions can be drawn from the table.

No firm historical conclusions between countries can be drawn either, because some countries update their poverty line according to the more generous criterion of the rise in earnings. In a study of poverty trends in the USA, which adopts the prices indicator, over the period 1949–1979, it was found that poverty declined by 68 per cent using the prices indicator but it dropped by only 18 per cent when measured in relative terms that took account of the rise in earnings. Economic growth tends to reduce stagnantly defined poverty (Loeff, 1984). In the UK benefits were raised on an *ad hoc* basis up to the early 1970s, when they were linked to the wages or prices index, whichever was the higher; from the early 1980s they were linked simply to the prices index with the result that poverty figures for the 1980s are lower than they would otherwise have been. Similar comments apply to all other countries.

Despite these imperfections, Table 3.1 shows that in none of the rich countries has subsistence poverty been abolished, that

Table 3.2   Poverty in various European countries in mid-70s and standard definitions of poverty

Country	Percentage of households with incomes less than		
	40% of average equivalent disposable Income	50% of average equivalent disposable Income	60% of average equivalent disposable Income
France	8.5	14.8	28.2
Italy		21.8	
Netherlands	3.1	4.8	9.1
United Kingdom	0.9	6.3	14.4
West Germany	2.3	6.6	16.5

Sources: R. Walker, R. Lawson and P. Townsend, table 2.25, p. 71; for the 50% line, R. Lawson, 1985.

its extent has fluctuated but it has always remained substantial, and that it began to rise in the early 1980s, with the onset of the economic recession. Thus poverty is neither peripheral nor accidental to advanced industrial societies—it is endemic for reasons to be explored later in this chapter.

Table 3.2 is an attempt at some standardisation of poverty, though, as the authors point out, far from perfect. If one uses the 50 per cent level, then the extent of poverty in the mid-1970s varied from 4.8 per cent in the Netherlands to 21.8 per cent in Italy. The proportions are, of course, higher today, partly because of the economic recession and partly because of the cuts made in social security programmes in most countries.

All the figures in Table 3.1 and the first and second columns of Table 3.2 refer to people in poverty in austere terms. Thus the Report of the British Government's Advisory Body for Social Security acknowledged this in 1982 when it stated that the supplementary benefit rates 'are too near to subsistence level to provide an adequate standard of living for the poorest people in our society' (Second Report of the Social Security Advisory Committee, 1982/83, p. 94). The same observations apply to the Australian official poverty line, which was described by the government report adopted it as being so austere that 'It cannot seriously be argued that those below this austere line, whom we describe as "very poor", are not so' (Australian Government Commission of Enquiry, 1975, p. 12). Very similar comments apply to the American official poverty line because it is based on an economy food plan for 'temporary or emergency use when funds are low' (Orshansky, 1965). It is not designed for people in long-term poverty, it assumes the cheapest of meals and of other needs and, as Beeghley has shown, families in poverty are not just poor but desperate (Beeghley, 1984).

How many people then live below the official poverty lines of the rich countries? Clearly only rough estimates can be given, but the size of the group is substantial even by these austere definitions. The EEC estimated that in 1981, 10 per cent of the population of its members countries was in poverty and there is no reason to believe that this is any different in the other rich countries (Commission of the European Communities, 1981). In all probability the proportion is higher today and a figure of 12 per cent is the most likely. In other words, about 75 million are living in poverty using the 10 per cent figure or 90 million using the 12 per cent figure in the rich countries that the World Bank designates as industrial market countries. Moreover, the proportion and number of people living around the poverty line are far higher. In real life situations the living conditions of people on or just above the poverty line are not all that different from those living just below the line. Evidence from the UK shows that almost twice as many people live on the poverty line than below it, and the situation cannot be all that different in other countries. It also goes without saying that the proportion of people in poverty is even higher if one uses the figures of poverty studies which adopted more generous definitions of poverty. Townsend found that 22.9 per cent of the population in Britain in 1969 lived below his deprivation threshold, whilst Mack and Lansley found only 13.8 per cent were in severe poverty and another 8.4 per cent in poverty. In brief, the size of the population group living in poverty, however this is defined today, is quite substantial.

The vast majority of studies on poverty are cross-sectional studies taking snapshot pictures of poverty at one specific point in time. There are very few longitudinal studies showing the turnover among the poor population as well as the degree of persistence of poverty. One recent American longitudinal study provides much needed information on these issues. Using 5,000 families interviewed every year during the decade 1968–78, it found that 24.4 per cent of those in poverty in 1968 were also in poverty for one or more years during the subsequent decade; 5.4 per cent were poor for five years or more; 2.6 per cent were poor for eight or more years; and 0.7 per cent were poor for the entire period (Duncan, 1984, p. 41).

Though only a small proportion of the poor remained in poverty for most of the decade (eight years or more), the proportions were higher for certain groups of the poor— elderly women, and particularly the black, irrespective of whether they were men, women, elderly or non-elderly. Elderly black women, however, were the group most likely to be in persistent poverty. The corollary to all this is that there is a rapid turnover among the American poor with the result that one quarter of the American population experienced periods of poverty during the decade. Thus people drift in and out of poverty, though most hover around the poverty line to fall below it again. People who are in poverty in any one year are far more likely to be in poverty in the next year than the non-poor—at least fifteen times as likely (Duncan, 1984, p. 45). It appears that there is a pool of people consisting of the poor and the nearly poor who interchange positions frequently and who between them comprise the majority of the poor at any one time. The composition of this pool inevitably reflects the most vulnerable groups in society which are very similar in advanced industrial societies, as the following section illustrates.

All the data and discussion in this section related to advanced capitalist societies and not to East European countries. The evidence on poverty in these countries, unfortunately, is far too fragmentary and inadequate to permit any definitive statements. What evidence there is, however, suggests that poverty is at least as prevalent as in Western Europe. Using the Soviet Government's minimum wage as the poverty line, Mathews estimates that about 41 per cent of people at work received earnings that were below the poverty line in the late 1970s (Mathews, 1986, p. 27). McAuley, using Soviet Government data, estimated that in 1967 'some 61 per cent of the Kolkhozniki were below the [poverty] line' (M. McAuley, 1979, p. 10). Even if one argues that the minimum wage is too high as a poverty line, the proportion of people in poverty is still very high (George and Manning, 1980, p. 62). Very little is known about the situation in other East European countries but, bearing in mind the level of wages, the coverage of their social security systems and other such factors, there cannot be any doubt about the prevalence of poverty on at least as wide a scale as in Western Europe.

Before looking at the various groups in poverty, three points need to be made clear. First, these administrative categories of poverty are not the same as the causes of poverty. These categories reflect the workings of the social security system, whilst the causes of poverty are to be found, as we shall argue in the next section, mainly in the structure of society. Second, social class is an important dimension cutting across all these administrative categories of the poor: it is the low-paid worker of today who is most likely to be the unemployed person in poverty or the elderly person in poverty in the future, and so on. Other factors such as gender and race are also important but not as important as class on the whole. Often these three dimensions—class, gender and race—compound each other in poverty situations. Third, those with low incomes in poverty are also most likely to suffer from other forms of deprivation—ill-health, bad housing, low educational standards, and so on—all of which interact to create a structural network of social handicaps. The empirical evidence on this is substantial and it is generally accepted (Berthoud, 1976; Rutter and Made, 1976; Brown and Made, 1982). An official publication of the European Commission expressed the multiple deprivation syndrome very well:

> Social, economic and cultural handicaps tend to be cumulative. The poorest in society tend to have the worst health and the worst housing. If they do have a job . . . they usually have the worst working conditions and only work sporadically. One handicap generates another. Poverty is a cause of ill-health and ill-health is a cause of poverty. A child from a poor family tends to do less well at school. And if young people with education and skills do manage to find a job, it is usually an ill-paid job with no prospects. (Commission of the European Communities, 1983, p. 46)

Let us now examine the main population groups that are in poverty, beginning with the unemployed.

POPULATION GROUPS IN POVERTY

All the evidence shows that the numbers and proportions of the unemployed have increased considerably in all rich countries in the 1980s apart from a few exceptions such as Switzerland and Japan where the increase has been far more modest. In the ten EEC countries, there were 2,669,000 people officially unemployed in 1960 making 2.5 per cent of the working population; in 1970, the corresponding figures were very similar—2,169,000 and 2.0 per cent respectively; by 1980, however, they rose to 6,712,000 and 5.9 per cent respectively; and by 1983, they jumped to the staggering levels of 12,192,000 and 10.6 per cent respectively (Commission of the European Communities, 1983, p. 111). What is even more worrying is that the proportion of the long-term unemployed has increased even faster and it is this group of the unemployed who suffer most hardship—financial, social, emotional and medical.

Unemployment results in poverty in one obvious and one not so obvious way. First, unemployment means loss of wages and all the available evidence shows that, for the vast majority of the unemployed this means a drop of varying degrees in their incomes (Moylan *et al.*, 1984). Only a small proportion of the unemployed—those with large families—may find themselves not worse off financially, and this depends on their entitlement to social security benefit. To put this in a different way, full employment is the only sound basis for the eradication of poverty. Obviously it is not sufficient in itself, but it is a necessary prerequisite. Full employment accompanied by a wages system and a social security system that take account of the financial circumstances of the family is the key to an effective anti-poverty programme.

The second way in which unemployment results in poverty is that the social security benefits provided for it are intended to safeguard labour discipline and work incentives as much as to relieve financial hardship. The fact that the primary benefit is an insurance benefit inevitably means that the weak groups in the labour market do not quality; the fact that it is paid for a certain period of time only means that the long-term unemployed suffer. As one study of poverty in three communities in West Europe—UK, Germany and France—concluded

> the insurance-based schemes were suited to helping people who were generally in well-paid, regular work to survive short and infrequent spells of unemployment. But many of the unemployed were people who had never worked or had been badly paid and whose periods of unemployment were frequent and long; for them the schemes had little or nothing to offer. (Mittan *et al.*, 1983, p. 55)

It is for this reason that the existence of a means-tested benefit as a second line of defence is so crucial to the unemployed. Many countries do not have such a scheme and those which have such a scheme do not always provide adequate benefits. Moreover, at a time of an economic recession, social security benefits for the unemployed are not improved as logic and compassion would dictate but they become more punitive and less adequate in an effort to reduce expenditure and to force the unemployed to accept any type of job available.

It needs also to be stressed that the costs of unemployment are not just financial. There is considerable evidence that persistent and prolonged unemployment has adverse effects on people's health, on their family life and on community life in general (Sinfield, 1981; Fagin and Little, 1984; Burghes and Lister (eds), 1981). Moreover, the financial costs of unemployment are not merely short-term. They can be very long-term resulting in reduced life-earnings, lower pensions during retirement and reduced career opportunities of the children of the unemployed. All this lends support to the comment made

Table 3.3   Population groups in poverty, Britain, 1983

Population Group	Percentage of people in poverty with specified characteristics	Percentage of population with specified characteristics who are poor
1 Persons over pension age	38.8	12.0
(a) Married Couples	15.3	9.2
(b) Single Persons	23.5	15.4
2 Persons under pension age by Family Type	61.2	3.8
(a) Married Couples with Children	24.8	3.0
(b) Single Persons with Children	2.9	3.3
(c) Married Couples without Children	8.3	2.4
(d) Single persons without Children	25.2	7.4
3 Persons under pension age by Employment Status	61.2	3.8
(a) Full-time work or self-employed	24.5	2.0
(b) Sick or disabled for more than 3 months	2.5	4.5
(c) Unemployed for more than 3 months	19.1	12.9
(d) Other	15.1	7.9
4 All persons	5.2	5.2

Source: DHSS, 1986, table 2.

above that the abolition or substantial reduction of unemployment is a necessary, though not a sufficient, condition for the abolition of poverty.

The fact that the unemployed suffer from poverty is thus obvious and predictable. In Britain, the unemployed constituted 7.0 per cent of people in official poverty in both 1960 and 1972, but the proportion more than doubled as the size and duration of unemployment rose—it reached 19 per cent in 1983, as table 3.3. shows. The same table also shows that the risk of the unemployed being in poverty is second only to the single elderly and it is seven times greater than for those in employment. The duration of unemployment is a crucial factor to the incidence of poverty because of the way the social security system operates, and because savings gradually run out while personal and family needs inevitably increase. It is obviously true that the position of the long-term unemployed is worse in those countries where social security provisions are harsh—such as the USA—than in countries such as the UK, where they are less so (OECD, 1984, table 45, p. 89 and table 46, p. 90). It is equally obvious that the incidence of poverty increases if both spouses rather than one is unemployed—clear evidence of the importance of both spouses' wages to the family budget. Thus in Canada evidence shows that, where both spouses worked full-time all the year, the proportion in poverty was only 1.8 per cent; where only one spouse worked full-time, the proportion was 5.9 per cent where one spouse experienced unemployment the proportion rose to 12.5 per cent; and where both spouses experienced unemployment it rose even higher to 16.8 per cent (OECD, 1984, table 43, p. 89).

In conclusion, so long as benefits for the unemployed are based primarily on the insurance principle, so long as they are paid for limited periods of time, and so long as they are designed to serve labour discipline and work incentives, poverty among the unemployed will continue. The only real solution is the return to full employment, not only because wages provide a higher standard of living than benefits for most people but also because the much needed reforms of the social security system, so that it can benefit equally all socio-economic groups, are most unlikely to be undertaken during periods of economic recession.

The largest population group which relies on social security benefits is the elderly. Despite slight national variations, the proportion of the elderly has increased considerably in all advanced industrial societies, partly as a result of falling birth rates and partly due to greater longevity. Thus today the elderly, i.e. those aged 65 or over, constitute 12–15 per cent of the population of such countries and their proportion will increase in the near future. From the poverty angle, even more significant is the fact that the proportion of the 'very elderly', those aged seventy-five or over, has increased even faster and will continue to increase in the future.

These demographic trends have recently been accompanied by two labour market trends that increase the size of the elderly group relying on social security benefits. Due to the rise in unemployment, governments and employers have forced, pressurised and encouraged people to retire from work long before they have reached retirement age. Second, the proportion of the 'young elderly', i.e. those aged sixty to sixty-nine, in full-time or part-time employment has been declining for a couple of decades, but the pace has accelerated during the recession years. These trends, coupled with the rise in unemployment and the decline in rates of economic growth have raised anxieties about a country's ability to provide adequate pensions through the public sector. The recent 're-organisation' of retirement pensions in the UK, for example, is nothing more than a crude attempt to reduce the costs of retirement pensions to the government. The overall cost of pensions to society will not decline but some of the cost borne by the government will be shifted onto employers with all the exacerbation of inequalities that this involves.

The sources of income for elderly people are, in order of significance, government retirement pensions, occupational pensions, paid employment and savings. All the evidence shows that savings are a very minor source, that they are important mainly to people with high incomes during working life, and that they decline with advancing age. As mentioned earlier, paid employment has been declining over the years but it is still significant for those young elderly who are in good health. Occupational pensions have been increasing in importance over the years both in terms of the number of people covered and the amount of pensions they provide. Nevertheless, they are heavily class and sex biased: the higher socio-economic groups are more likely to be covered and to receive higher benefits than the lower socio-economic groups; men fare better than women, partly because of their superior position in the labour market and partly because of direct sex discrimination against women. Moreover, in many instances, occupational pensions are not increased annually to take account of even inflation, with the result that their value declines rapidly.

The state retirement pensions are the main source of income for the elderly and, though they differ in important details from one country to another, they are also similar in many important ways. Firstly, they are usually insurance-based, with the result that those population groups who did not work long enough would not quality or might qualify for reduced amounts of pension. Thus married women, disabled people, the long-term unemployed and some other groups run the risk of not receiving the whole or any amount of the state pension. Second, most retirement pension schemes provide earnings-related pensions with the result that those who were in low-paid jobs receive lower amounts than those in high paid jobs.

Bearing all these points in mind, it is not surprising that income inequalities in old age at least reflect and often surpass those prevailing during working life. Evidence from several countries—USA, UK, Switzerland—confirms this. Reviewing the position of American retirement pensioners, Crystal states that census data suggest that 'inequality within the elderly population is greater than inequality between elderly and non-elderly age groups, and greater than inequality within the non-elderly population' (Crystal, 1986). Reviewing the situation in Switzerland, Gilliand crisply sums it up: 'Retirement confirms previous inequalities; it frequently exacerbates the differences' (Gilliand, 1982).

Quin rightly warns us to 'beware of the mean' when discussing the financial circumstances of the elderly. There is such diversity in their circumstances that the 'average can be very deceptive'(Quin, 1987). This is all true and, after summarising the general position, we need to examine the position of the main sub-groupings among the elderly. The first general point to make is that for the vast majority of the elderly, retirement results in substantial loss of income. Retirement pensions are not only a portion of earnings but, often, they are not increased annually to keep up with the rise in wages and, sometimes, not even with the rise in prices. The second general point is that a proportion of the elderly have incomes that are below the poverty line—this proportion varies from one country to another but it is always a significant proportion. The third general point is that the financial conditions of the elderly have improved in all industrial countries over the years as a result partly of better state benefits and partly because of better private and occupational provisions. Governments find it difficult to ignore the value of retirement pensions for obvious political reasons (if for nothing else), with the result that retirement pensions are improved. In this way retirement pensions perform also an unanticipated function—they tend to protect other benefits against benefit-cutting governments. The fourth general point is that poverty among the elderly is higher than that of the general population in some countries but lower in other countries, as the various tables show.

Looking now at the various sub-groups among the elderly several important points emerge: firstly, the elderly living on their own are more likely to be in poverty than those living together as couples, because of a combination of age and gender considerations. Secondly, women are more likely to be in poverty than men, partly because their state and occupational pensions are inferior to those of men and partly because they live longer than men. Thus in Canada the poverty rate among women living on their own aged sixty-five and over was 52.6 per cent whilst for such men it was 43.6 per cent in 1984 (National Council of Welfare, table 16, p. 32); in the USA the corresponding figures for 1984 were 25.2 per cent and 20.8 per cent respectively (USA Department of Health, 1987, table 8, p. 74). Since the incidence of poverty increases with old age and since women live longer than men, it does mean that the vast majority of the very elderly poor are women. Atkins shows that in the USA in 1983, whilst 11.9 per cent of those aged sixty-five to seventy-four were in poverty, the corresponding figures for those aged seventy-five to eighty-four and eighty-five plus were 16.7 per cent and 21.3 per cent respectively (Atkins, 1985). Thirdly, poverty is more prevalent among certain ethnic groups in old age than it is for the elderly as a whole. The only reliable evidence on this comes from the USA but it is difficult to see why the situation would not be similar in other countries. Thus in 1982, 12.4 per cent of the white elderly in the USA had incomes below the poverty line, compared with the staggering figures of 35.6 per cent of black elderly Americans and 38.2 per cent of the elderly Americans of Hispanic origin (Estes, 1986). Finally, poverty is far more prevalent among the elderly with a working class background than those with a professional or managerial career. The working class elderly are less likely to have any significant savings, their occupational pensions are inferior and, sometimes, even their state pensions are lower than those of the elderly with a professional or managerial background. In brief, class, gender, race and age influence the incidence and

Table 3.4   Population groups in poverty, USA, 1984

Population of Group	Percentage of population with specified characteristics who are poor (poverty rate)
Above retirement age:	12.4
Unrelated Individuals	24.2
Family Members	6.7
Under retirement age:	14.0
Children under 18	21.0
18–54 years	12.3
55–64 years	10.3
Living arrangements of children:	
In two-parent or single male-headed families	12.5
In female-headed single-parent families	54.0
Employment status of working age population:	8.0
Worked during whole year full-time	3.0
Worked during part of year or part-time	21.0
Did not work at all during year	30.0
Race (figures refer to 1980)	
White	10.2
Black	32.5
All	14.4

Source: USA Department of Health and Human Resources, Social Security Adminis-tration, 1986.

Table 3.5   Population groups in poverty, Canada, 1983

Population Group	Percentage of population with specified characteristics who are poor (poverty rate)
Persons over pension age:	25.3
In Families	9.5
Unattached Individuals	57.5
Below retirement age:	
Two-parent Families	11.1
Female-Headed Single-Parent Families	49.1
Male-Headed Single-Parent Families	21.2
Age groups:	
Head of Family under 25	34.7
Head of Family 25–34	16.5
Head of Family 35–44	12.7
Head of Family 45–54	10.8
Head of Family 55–64	12.3
Head of Family 65+	11.1
Unattached Individuals under 25	49.3
Unattached Individuals 25–34	25.0
Unattached Individuals 35–44	23.0
Unattached Individuals 45–54	36.0
Unattached Individuals 55–64	40.8
Unattached Individuals 65+	57.5
Below retirement age:	
Neither Head of Family Unemployed	11.6
Head Unemployed	26.4
Major source of income of families:	
Wages and Salaries	6.3
Self-Employment	22.5
Government Transfers	47.2
Other	10.6
All	17.1

Source: Adapted from National Council of Welfare, Government of Canada, 1985.

depth of poverty in old age, sometimes separately but usually in interaction with one another.

Though some progress has been made in all industrial societies in improving the relative economic position of the elderly, a great deal more remains to be done, particularly in view of the higher aspirations of the elderly in the future. Today's elderly lived through the austere years of the 1940s and 1950s and their expectations are modest; tomorrow's elderly will be the children of the affluent 1960s and 1970s and they are not likely to be satisfied with the level of income that the elderly today receive. Their numbers will be large enough—despite their group divisions—to enable them to exercise far more influence on governments than they have done so far, not only in relation to incomes but also in terms of the wider aspects of the quality of life. Whether they do so or not, however, remains to be seen.

We now turn to examine the position of disabled people, which is by far the most difficult to assess for several reasons: the numbers of the disabled in the community are not known exactly; there are various degrees and definitions of disability; social security benefits for the disabled are the most complex; and so on. Despite all this, a number of general points can be made which apply to all industrial societies. First, the proportion of the disabled in the community is quite high. In Britain it is estimated that about 30 per cent of the population suffer for long-term illness or disability and of these, almost half are above retirement age, according to government statistics. Secondly, the type of benefit paid to disabled people depends not only on the degree of disability but the source of disability as well. This means that the occupationally disabled are likely to receive higher benefits and under easier qualifying conditions than other disabled persons. Thirdly, the proportion of disabled at work is far too low, bearing in mind their capacity for work. At times of high demand for labour, the disabled are offered employment while at times of economic recession they suffer more from unemployment than those who are not disabled. Fourthly, wages for the disabled are lower than those for other population groups because of the type of jobs that they do, which is at times the result of plain discrimination resulting from the belief that their work potentialities are limited.

Bearing all these points in mind, it is not surprising that the likelihood of being in poverty is higher among the disabled than the rest of the population below retirement age. Statistics are hard to come by in many countries, but in the UK, table 3.3 shows that 6.3 per cent of the disabled below retirement age were in official poverty in the 1980s. Townsend's study also showed that the elderly disabled and particularly those with

Table 3.6   Population groups in poverty, Australia, 1981–82

Population Group	Percentage of income units with specified characteristics who are poor (Poverty Rate)
Couple without dependents:	
head aged <65	4.7
head aged >65	5.4
Couple with dependents	11.6
Single parent	46.2
Single persons:	
aged 15–24	15.7
aged 25–64	14.1
aged >65	11.0
All	11.8

Source: Bradbury, Rossiter and Vipond, 1986, table 2.1, p. 16.

severe disabilities ran the highest risk among the disabled of being in poverty. Thus, higher rates of unemployment, low pay and inadequate social security benefits combine to create long-term poverty among the disabled. Moreover, the needs of the disabled in terms of housing, access to buildings, mobility, and so on, are at best partly recognised and partly catered for in some countries whilst in others they remain almost totally unrecognised and totally ignored.

We now turn to discuss one of the newest groups in poverty—one-parent families. Though comparative statistics on one-parent families are far from adequate they, nevertheless, enable us to draw several generalised conclusions about the demographic and socio-economic conditions of this population group. The first such conclusion is that the number of one-parent families has grown in all advanced industrial societies though at different rates. For example, in the UK, the proportion of one-parent families grew by 60 per cent between 1971 and 1982 whilst in Australia it rose by 70 per cent during 1974–82 (Cass and O'Loughlin, 1984). The main reason for this increase in the incidence of one-parenthood has been family break-up due to divorce or separation. There is no reason to believe that this trend will slow down in the future—if anything it will spread to all advanced industrial societies.

As a result of these demographic trends, the incidence of

one-parent families with children ranges from 5.6 per cent in Ireland to 27 per cent in Sweden. A glance at table 3.7 suggests that the incidence of one-parenthood may be loosely related to the level of economic standards in society and to the influence of religion. Thus Ireland with a relatively low standard of living and with a strong Catholic church has the lowest figure while Sweden with one of the highest standards of living has one of the highest figures.

The composition of the group of one-parent families in any one country seems to be related to its incidence. Thus in countries where the incidence is low, widows form a large part of one-parent families whilst the reverse is the case in countries where the incidence is high; in these countries it is the separated and the divorced that are the largest group. Similarly, whilst the vast majority of one parent families are headed by women—about four fifths—this proportion is even higher in countries where the incidence of one-parenthood is very low. One-parent families headed by men are a small minority and their financial circumstances are better than those headed by women with whom this section is primarily concerned (George and Wilding, 1972). Finally, it is important to bear in mind that the proportion of one-parent families at any one time is lower than the proportion of families which experienced one-parenthood status at some time or other. One British study, for example, found that though 8.4 per cent of sixteen-year-olds were living in one-parent families at the time of the survey, 12.2 per cent of them had experienced one-parenthood in their lives (Fogelman, 1983). This is the same observation that we made earlier in relation to poverty and unemployment.

The financial circumstances of one-parent families depend on several considerations: clearly where both parents, or at least the caring parent is very rich, the financial circumstances of one-parent families will be quite satisfactory. For the rest of one-parent families, however, their income position will depend on their incomes from work, on the social security benefits that they receive and on the number of children in the family. Other things being equal, one-parent families with only one child, particularly of school age, will be financially better off than those with a large number of children, particularly if

Table 3.7   Comparative data on one-parent families

Country	Year	Percentage of all families	Percentage of mothers in one-parent families in employment
Australia	1985	14.4	43.0
Belgium	1970	9.8	N/K
Canada	1979	12.3	63.0
Denmark	1980	12.0	89.0
France	1980	13.0	78.0
Germany, West	1977	9.1	63.0
Ireland	1975	5.6	N/K
Italy	1975	9.4	N/K
Luxembourg	1970	13.3	32.0
Netherlands	1977	10.7	25.0
Norway	1979	12.9	N/K
Sweden	1979	27.0	86.0
UK	1981	13.0	49.0
USA	1979	19.5	68.0

Source: Mainly from J. Millar, 1985.

they include under school age children, because mothers find it easier to obtain full-time employment. As table 3.7 shows, the labour market participation rate for one-parent families varies considerably between countries—from 25 per cent in the Netherlands to 86 per cent in Sweden. Several factors affect the employment of lone mothers: the labour market participation rate of married women, in general, the rate of unemployment, the type of social security benefit and the pre-school care facilities for children that are available. In countries where it is the norm for married women to go out to work and where care facilities for pre-school children are relatively easy to obtain, the proportion of lone mothers at work will be high provided the payment of social security benefits is not conditional to their being out of work.

Social security benefits for one-parent families vary considerably between countries. In the case of widows, all countries provide some kind of benefit though this varies in generosity and in the qualifying conditions. Nevertheless, it is recognised that family break-up through death merits state income support measures. This, however, does not apply to family break-up through divorce or separation because it is considered a voluntary risk. The result is that many countries make no special provision for one-parent families whatsoever. This is not so iniquitous if family allowances for all families are fairly satisfactory, as in France, for example. Thus a recent study reported that 'only a minority of French mothers (38 per cent) ... said their income had fallen, following their divorce, compared with 31 per cent who had said it had risen, and a third who reported no change'. This was due not to maintenance payments by fathers but to the scheme of family allowances and to child care facilities for all mothers (Baker, 1987). Some countries make special allowances for one-parent families and where this is coupled with high labour market participation rates, as in Sweden, the financial position of one-parent families is at its best (Kamarman and Khan, 1983). Their financial position is at its worst in those countries where no benefits are provided and they have to rely on their employment, their extended family or charity. Countries like Britain, which almost force one-parent families to choose between employment income and means tested state benefits, do not allow one-parent families to starve but they create a vicious poverty trap. If mothers work they tend to earn poverty wages and if they rely on means-tested benefit they receive poverty allowances. It was this state of affairs that the Government Committee on One-Parent Families in Britain had in mind when it concluded that:

> in terms of families with children ... there can be no other group of this size who are as poor as fatherless families of whom so many lack any state benefits other than supplementary benefit or family allowance, whose financial position is so uncertain and whose hope of improvement in their situation is relatively so remote. (The Finer Report, 1974, p. 269)

Despite these variations in benefits and employment rates, evidence shows that one-parent families headed by women are more likely to be in poverty than other families in all advanced industrial countries: they are twice as likely in Britain and Germany, four times as likely in the USA, Canada and Australia, three times as likely in the Netherlands, and so on. These comparative statistics may not be totally accurate but they do reflect the seriousness of the economic disadvantages suffered by this population group. It needs to be added, however, that though one-parent families are more likely to be in poverty than most other groups in some countries (USA, Canada and Australia) it is not the case in other countries (Britain, France).

Despite a great deal of discussion in recent years on the inadequacies of the social security system for one-parent families, it is most unlikely that any specific social security benefit will be provided for this population group in all countries in the foreseeable future. Apart from reasons of direct financial costs, there are the fears that such a benefit will undermine the stability of the family and will thus create even more one-parent families (Brown (ed.), 1984, pp. 18–20). It would not be too cynical to say that had one-parent families been headed mainly by men, a better set of social security benefits would have been devised by now in most advanced industrial countries. Bearing in mind these difficulties and the fact that the interchange between one-parent and two-parent family status is on the increase, the best way out of the present stalemate may be the provision of better economic and child care policies for all families with children, irrespective of their parenting statuses. This approach, however, raises questions about the vexed relationship between incomes from work and family responsibility, which we examine in the following section. Before doing that, however, it is useful to examine briefly the 'feminisation of poverty' thesis that is closely related to the poverty of one-parent families.

The 'feminisation of poverty thesis' has acquired several meanings since it was first put forward by D. Pearce (Pearce, 1978). As coined by Pearce, the thesis claimed that, despite the substantial increase in women's participation in the labour market, the growth of social security expenditure, the new anti-discrimination legislation, poverty among women had increased in contrast to the situation of men, where poverty had decreased. The explanation of this trend was that the causes of women's poverty were different from those of men's poverty. In policy terms, this meant that women of all classes and races should unite around a common economic strategy that would abolish women's poverty.

In this section we are concerned with the descriptive aspects of the thesis, i.e. that poverty affects women more than men and we will return to its explanatory and policy aspects in the final section. In its descriptive aspect, the thesis refers to at least three related claims: the incidence of poverty is higher among women than among men; the number of women in poverty is greater than that of men; and the incidence as well as the extent of poverty among children is greater in households headed by women than other households. All the evidence used so far in this section supports these claims. It has already been shown that the female elderly are more likely to be in poverty than the male elderly; that women below retirement age heading families are more likely to be in poverty than men heading families; and it will be shown in the following section that women are more likely to be earning low wages than men. If the incidence of poverty is greater among women than men, then it follows that the number of women in poverty is higher than that of men, particularly since women live longer than men in the age group where the incidence of poverty is high. As for the third claim, it is certainly true that the incidence of poverty among children in female-headed households is higher than that for children in male-headed households, be they two-parent or one-parent. What is not correct is the claim that most children in poverty are in female-headed households, bearing in mind that the vast majority of children live in households officially headed by men. In Britain, for example, 80 per cent of all children in 1980 lived in two-parent families and the remaining 20 per cent in one-parent families—male and female-headed—so that, despite the greater incidence of poverty among children in female headed households, the majority of children lived in two-parent male headed households. Finally, the claim that poverty among men has declined whilst poverty among women increased over the years may be true of the USA, but not necessarily of other countries. In Canada, for example, the incidence of poverty among single-parent families headed by non-aged women was the same in 1984 as in 1980—46.4 per cent—whilst that of such families headed by men rose from 8.1 per cent to 11.4 per cent during the same period (National Council of Welfare, 1985, p. 31). In Australia the position was again different: during the decade 1971–81, the incidence of poverty for single-parent families headed by women rose from 38 per cent to 50 per cent, whilst the corresponding figures for male-headed single-parent families were 16 per cent and 19 per cent respectively. Economic, demographic and social security factors combine to produce different trends in different countries—the only common element is the upward trend in poverty for all types of families since the mid-1970s when the economic recession hit all advanced industrial societies (Cass, 1986, p. 22). In summary then, the feminisation of poverty thesis is essentially correct though some of its detailed claims are not substantiated by comparative evidence.

All the groups discussed so far are either totally or partially outside the labour market—they have either retired or are out of work. We now turn our attention to those who are in full-time employment but who are still in poverty. A distinction must be made at the outset between low pay and poverty at work. They are two different concepts and, though they overlap at times, they need separate discussion. Not all the low paid are in poverty because many of them are single people whose low pay is adequate to lift them above the poverty line or they are married women who are mostly second earners in the household. Vice versa, not all the people at work in poverty are low paid—most of them are but a small proportion may be earning good eages though inadequate for their family needs due to the size of their families.

Low pay is as difficult to define as poverty and it is also just as universal. Traditionally it has been seen as the lowest decile of the earnings distribution. A more recent definition advanced, under the auspices of, among others, the European Social Charter, is the equivalent of 68 per cent of the national average wage, a figure which is similar to the lowest decile. Interestingly enough, the Charter urged governments to ensure that workers were paid at least this wage so that their families could enjoy 'a decent standard of living' (Winyard, 1982).

Field has estimated that in Britain 25 per cent of adult male and female workers were receiving wages that were below the level set by the European Social Charter. Indeed, the proportion was far higher for women—they constituted almost three quarters of the 25 per cent. Moreover, the proportion of the low paid had remained fairly constant for several years

reflecting the rigidity of the earnings structure that is characteristic of industrial societies. Thus, the bottom decile of the
earnings distribution of male manual workers in Britain has
remained pretty constant for a century now: in 1886 it
amounted to 68.6 per cent of the median wage, while in 1982 it
was 68.3 per cent with the highest variation being only 2 per
cent during the whole period. Women's wages have shown an
equal degree of rigidity but with slightly wider variations: in
1938, the corresponding figure was 64.3 per cent of the median
wage while in 1982 it was 69.2 per cent with a variation of 8 per
cent (Field, tables 1.1, p. 8 and 1.3, p. 11). Similar figures and
trends apply to other advanced industrial societies. There has
also been a fairly constant relationship between the average
earnings of men and women over the years but with a slight
improvement in the position of women in recent years. In
Canada, for example, the average earnings of women
amounted to 47 per cent of men's in 1971 and 55 per cent in
1982 (National Council of Welfare, table 45, p. 59). The
statutory provision of a minimum wage ought in theory to
improve the position of the low paid but in practice it achieves
far less than it promises for minimum wages are always set at
low levels and they are usually inadequately enforced.

As mentioned several times in this chapter, people at work
are less likely to be in poverty than those not at work. Nevertheless, the incidence of poverty among this group is still quite
high: In the USA, 3 per cent of all people of working age who
were in full-time employment all the year round in 1984 were
in poverty; the proportion rose to 24 per cent for those who
worked for part of the year or part-time (USA Department of
Health and Human Resources, 1987, table 1.3, p. 77). In
Canada, 4.7 per cent of heads of families and 9.0 per cent of
unattached individuals who worked full-time during the whole
year of 1983 were in poverty; the corresponding proportions of
those working part-time were 23.7 per cent and 49.1 per cent
respectively (National Council of Welfare, 1985, tables 25,
p. 41 and 26, p. 42). Similar figures could be produced for
other countries but it would not alter the basic conclusion that
the incidence of poverty is lower among people at work than
out of work. This is particularly true where both parents are at
work. A recent study in Britain showed that the number of

families in poverty would have trebled had it not been for the incomes of working wives (Layard *et al.*, 1978, p. 25). Canadian data confirm this: the poverty rate for families with two earners was three times lower than for families with one earner in 1983.

Despite the fact that the incidence of poverty among those at work is low, the proportion of poor people who are in full-time work or whose parents are in full-time work is higher because of the large size of the population group at work. Thus in Britain, in 1981, 24 per cent of those in poverty were people where the individual or the head of the family was at work; in Canada, in 1983, 57.8 per cent of families in poverty were headed by persons who worked or were actively searching for a job; and so on. The general conclusion therefore is that, despite the fact that the incidence of poverty among people at work is relatively low, they make up a very large part of the poor population. Low wages in relation to family needs are therefore responsible for the poverty of a large section of the population.

Two types of benefits are provided to families with children in different countries irrespective of whether the head of the family is at work: family allowances or tax allowances. The first are cash transfers while the second are income tax rebates or deductions. The value of these two benefits, individually and together, varies considerably among advanced industrial countries. One study showed that the combined value of these benefits to single income married couple families with two children as a percentage of an OECD benchmark wage varied from 2.5 per cent in USA, to 5.7 per cent in Australia, 9.0 per cent in Canada, 9.7 per cent in France, 10.7 per cent in Sweden, 13.1 per cent in Britain and the Netherlands, 15.6 per cent in Norway and New Zealand, 17.9 per cent in Austria and reached the highest figure of 26.6 per cent in Belgium in 1984 (Oxley, 1986). Thus countries vary a great deal in the degree of financial support that they provide to families with children.

In some countries, such as Britain, a special means-tested benefit is provided to families with children where the head of the family is at work, but his or her wages are inadequate for family needs as officially prescribed. It is a form of direct wage supplementation based on a family means-test. Despite its many weaknesses, this scheme has proved of benefit to many low wage earners with children. Before the scheme was introduced in the early 1970s, people in poverty due to low wages accounted for 48 per cent of all people in poverty whereas in 1983, as mentioned above, the figure was halved to 24.5 per cent.

There is no doubt that the arrival of children reduces family income for all families irrespective of their socio-economic group. Thus, in addition to the question of poverty among families where the parents are at work, there is the additional issue of whether governments should bear the cost of maintaining children and, if so, what proportion, or whether the whole cost should fall on the parents. The response of governments so far has been incoherent but it has one common strand: governments should not bear the whole cost of maintaining children even at the basic level when their parents are at work. Fears that such a measure would undermine work incentives and parental responsibility are one set of reasons. The other set of reasons for not providing family allowances of even subsistence level is the financial cost of such a measure and its implications for both horizontal and vertical redistribution of income in society. It will ultimately mean that the labour market will become less important in determining the living standards of families than it is today.

Finally, a look at the very obvious relationship between social class and poverty: as expected, poverty is primarily a problem for working class groups. Canadian data, for example, show that the incidence of poverty among families where the head was in a managerial position was only 2.6 per cent compared with 20.7 per cent for heads in service occupations and 22.9 per cent for farming and fishing (National Council of Welfare, table 29, p. 43). Moreover, it is more than likely that poverty among managerial and professional groups is of the transitory short-term type rather than of long-term duration that often spans the person's whole lifetime, and sometimes continues to the next generation, as is the case with poverty among the lower socio-economic groups. This inverse relationship between class and poverty applies not only to families where the head is in full-time employment but it extends to families or individuals suffering from unemployment and disability, or who are retired or who live in one-parent families. Class, gender and race are the basic forces that combine to create structural situations that inevitably create poverty amidst unprecedented affluence. It is to these issues that we now turn and their implication for policies for the alleviation of poverty.

WHY SO MUCH POVERTY?

The main theories of wealth and poverty at the international level were discussed in Chapter 1, where it was also indicated that very similar theories apply to the situation prevailing within countries. The various theories of poverty in advanced industrial societies have also been discussed extensively elsewhere and there is no need to repeat the discussion here (Holman, 1978; Townsend, 1983); instead we will comment briefly on the individualistic explanations and then develop in more detail the structuralist approach to poverty, before we examine the relationship between poverty and the social security system.

Individualistic explanations see poverty as the result of the values, attitudes and skills of individual people and they therefore advocate policies that would change these characteristics and thus reduce or abolish poverty. We already discussed the culture of poverty, or the cycle of deprivation thesis in Chapter 1 and there is no point in going over the issues again. As far as the lack of skills approach is concerned, it is obviously true that there are people whose skills are low and they tend to occupy low paid jobs. But their low skills are often—though not always—the result of family and economic background rather than their own personal inadequacies or their explicit decisions. Above all, what the culture of poverty explanation implies is that, if the values and the skills were changed, no one would be earning low wages and thus no one need be in poverty. Clearly this is not a convincing argument because so long as there are low-paid jobs some people have to do them. One needs to examine the reasons why these are low paid jobs rather than simply concentrate on those who do these jobs.

For this reason the culture of poverty has to be seen in

conjunction with the functionalist theory of inequality that was discussed and rejected in Chapter 2. What these two theories together maintain is that the most able and the most motivated occupy the best paid jobs while the least able and the least motivated occupy the worst paid jobs to the benefit of the whole society—of both the winners and the losers. The two theories, individually and together, try hard, but very unconvincingly, to justify the grossly unequal distribution of income and wealth and hence poverty in society.

Individualistic explanations are just as untenable in the case of women and ethnic groups who tend to occupy low-paid jobs. Clearly this is not due to the fact that women or such groups are either less intelligent or less motivated or even less skilled than others; rather it is the result of the operations of the market with all its prejudicial practices that result in the majority of these jobs being performed by women and ethnic groups. It is, of course, true that there are some individuals who prefer not to work hard or long hours and they find themselves and their dependents in poverty. But it is totally misleading to use the exceptions as the basis for explaining the condition of the whole group. For all these reasons individualistic explanations are unconvincing and one needs to turn to some form of structuralist explanation for the incidence of poverty.

Structuralist explanations argue that the vast majority of the poor are in poverty because of the ways that the economy and the political system of their country operates. In the same way that structuralist explanations of development on a world scale attribute the poverty of third world countries to mainly international forces that are beyond their control, so structuralist explanations of poverty within a country see the causes of poverty in mainly national forces that are beyond the control of individual poor people. Again there are the same two main subdivisions in the structuralist approach—the Marxist and the non-Marxist, which is adopted here. Production for private profit inevitably means a continual attempt by the owners and managers of businesses to pay as little in wages as it is necessary in order to maximise profit. The result is that those areas in the labour market where labour is weak either because of lack of organisation, or lack of bargaining power, or because of surplus of labour or because of the gender or ethnic composition of the particular occupation or such like reasons, wages will be lower than in other areas where labour is strong. All this has to be seen in the context of inherited wealth, family background and educational achievement, for all these structural forces reinforce one another.

There is a wide range of inter-related ways in which these forces operate to create and maintain both wealth and poverty in society. The inheritance of private property means that some people have a better start in life than others; the child's family background affects its educational achievement; the region in which a person lives affects his/her occupational and employment opportunities; the decision of a multinational company to close down operations in a country results in loss of jobs for many people; a person's type of employment may be hazardous and hence he or she may be more likely to suffer from industrial diseases or occupational accidents; the absence of adequate minimum wage legislation means that some jobs will pay poverty wages; the ways in which governments raise their revenues affects the net incomes of different groups in society differently; the demand for labour in a particular area or business; the type of social services provided affects people's educational, employment, health and other statuses differently; the degree of prejudice and discrimination against certain ethnic groups affects the type of jobs they do, the wages they earn, and whether they are in poverty; social attitudes towards women and their role in society influence their educational, employment, health and other statuses differently; and so on, for the list is endless.

Thus class, gender and ethnicity are the main determinants of a person's life chances and whether he or she will be wealthy, comfortably well off or impoverished in societies where grossly unequal earnings from private property and from work are the norm. There are situations where one or other of these three factors is more important than the others but it is not possible to explain the poverty of women or of ethnic groups always through the discriminatory practices against them. Class often combines with either gender or race or with both to create poverty situations. It is when the three reinforce each other that the worst cases of poverty are created. Thus the group most vulnerable to prolonged and extreme poverty in the USA is elderly black women of working class background (Sarvasy and Allen, 1984).

The structuralist explanation of poverty does not deny the individuality of people; it does not create social cages in which all people are trapped and from which they can never escape. It does recognise that some individuals move up and some move down the social scale, but such movements are normally of limited range. Upward and downward mobility is mostly between adjacent rungs on the social scale and very rarely from one end of the scale to the other. Most people live their lives at or around the same position on the ladder as their forefathers. When this is seen in the context of a reward system from work that accepts gross inequalities, it is inevitable that some people will find themselves in poverty. These people are not just any people—they are primarily from family backgrounds at the lower end of the social scale. Some see them as failures, others as victims—perhaps it is best to see them in neutral terms as those who did not make it because the cards were heavily stacked against them from the day they were born.

Poverty is therefore endemic in capitalist societies—it is part and parcel of the working of the system. Capitalism has an inherent tendency to create poverty as part of the process of generating wealth. It is partly for this reason that all advanced industrial societies have developed elaborate social security systems over the years. There were, of course, other reasons for the development of social security schemes—the maintenance of political stability, the encouragement of consumer consumption in order to boost employment, the enforcement of labour discipline, and so on. Though we are primarily concerned with the aim of social security to achieve a basic minimum for all in society, the importance of the other aims will also be discussed, for they often modify and, at times, override it. The values and power structure of the capitalist system inevitably cast their shadow on the social security system. It is extremely difficult, and perhaps not possible, to create a social security system that does not bend to the pressures from the private market and the dominant groups in society, with the result that it serves their interests at least as much as those of working class people for whom it was ostensibly created.

Expenditure on social security has grown considerably during the post-war years as table 3.8 shows. Alber's work also shows that not only expenditure grew but also that 'the pace of this increase accelerated over time'—at least up to the mid-1970s after which the pace slowed down, but it still remained faster than it was in the 1950s and 1960s (Alber, 1983, p. 160). This growth in social security expenditure has been the result of two main factors: the growth in the numbers of people dependent on social security benefits; and a real improvement in the level of social security benefits.

The growth in the numbers of beneficiaries has been the result of demographic, social, labour market and social policy changes. The demographic changes refer to the increase in the elderly, and particularly the very elderly, discussed earlier in this chapter. The social changes refer to the increase in the number of one-parent families and, to a lesser extent, the increased tendency of young single people to live away from their parental households. The labour market trends cover the rise in unemployment and early retirement. Social policy changes include the creation of new benefit schemes over the years or the expansion of existing schemes which took place during the three decades 1950–80. During the 1980s, however, the trend has been halted and to some extent reversed with governments in several countries chipping away at existing schemes.

As far as the second main reason for the growth of expenditure on social security, the value of benefits has risen not simply in relation to the rise in prices but also in relation to the rise in net wages and, to a lesser extent, in relation to gross wages. During the 1980s, however, governments in several countries have attempted to restrict the rise in benefits, particularly for certain groups—the unemployed, the young, strikers, and the like.

Thus the rise in social security expenditure has been the result of factors, many of which are not directly concerned with the reduction of poverty. In particular, three reasons account for this failure of rising social security expenditure to abolish poverty. Before we look at these reasons, however, it is

Table 3.8 Social security expenditure as percentage of gross domestic product or percentage of net material product, West and East European countries

Country	1950	1960	1965	1970	1975	1980
			Gross domestic product			
Australia	—	7.7	8.3	8.0	10.7	12.1
Austria	12.4	15.4	17.7	18.6	20.2	22.4
Belgium	12.5	15.3	16.1	18.1	23.6	25.9
Canada	—	9.2	9.4	11.8	14.7	15.1
Denmark	8.4	11.1	12.2	16.4	22.4	26.9
Finland	6.7	8.8	10.6	12.8	16.1	18.6
France	12.6*	13.2	15.6	15.3	24.1	26.8
Germany, West	14.8	15.4	16.6	17.0	23.5	23.8
Greece	—	—	9.2	10.8	10.8	12.2
Ireland	8.9†	9.3	10.3	11.6	19.7	21.7
Italy	8.5	11.7	14.8	16.3	23.1	18.2
Japan	—	4.9	5.1	5.4	7.6	10.9
Netherlands	7.1	11.1	15.5	20.0	26.8	28.6
Norway	5.7	9.4	10.9	15.5	18.5	20.3
New Zealand	—	13.1	11.5	11.5	12.5	14.4
Portugal	—	5.3	5.3	5.7	11.0	10.1
Spain	—	—	—	—	11.7	16.1
Sweden	8.3	10.9	13.6	18.8	26.2	32.0
Switzerland	6.0‡	7.5	8.5	10.1	15.1	13.8
UK	10.0	10.8	11.7	13.8	16.2	17.7
USA	—	6.8	7.1	9.6	13.2	12.7
			Net material product			
Bulgaria	—	10.7	10.0	13.7	16.0	15.1
Czechoslovakia	—	15.4	18.2	18.0	17.2	18.9
Germany, East	—	—	12.8	13.1	15.3	17.0
Hungary	—	8.8	10.7	11.0	14.8	18.2
Poland	—	8.9	9.3	10.7	11.0	15.7
USSR	—	10.2	11.6	11.9	13.8	14.1

Sources: 1950 Column, Alber, 1983
Other Columns, ILO, 1985
Notes: * refers to 1952 † refers to 1953 ‡ refers to 1951

important to record the fact that poverty levels would have been far higher had it not been for the payment of social security benefits. Beckerman examined the impact of social security expenditure on poverty in four countries in the mid-1970s—Australia, Belgium, Britain and Norway—and concluded that 'The benefits have reduced the incidence of poverty in the countries taken as a whole from about one quarter of the population to about one tenth, although there are considerable variations between countries' (Beckerman, 1979, p. 26). The country variations are obviously the result of the structure of the social security systems of particular countries and the direct concern of this with poverty alleviation rather than with other objectives.

The first reason why social security systems, despite their increased expenditures, have failed to abolish poverty relatively defined, is that they are all dominated by labour market considerations. This means that those with a strong position in the labour market do well out of the social security system and, vice versa, those whose position is weak do badly. This relationship between labour market position and social security protection is manifested in several ways. In the first place, those who have not paid the necessary number of insurance contributions or, as in the case of East European countries, who have not been in full-time employment for the required number of years, do not receive any benefit or, at best, receive reduced amounts of benefits. Clearly, it is the low-paid and the irregularly employed who suffer from this situation, i.e. the very groups of people who are most in need of social security protection.

In some countries, married women who took time off work to bring up their families also suffer from the insurance or work principle. In the second place, many countries provide benefits whose amounts are related to the recipient's previous earnings from work. Despite the many variations to this formula, the end result is again the same—those in greatest need receive the least degree of protection from the social security system. The more unequal the distribution of wages, the more unequal social security benefits are likely to be, with the result that the social security system gives most to those who have most. The final main link between the labour market and the social security system is manifested in the treatment of the unemployed. Benefits for the unemployed tend to be lower than other benefits; they are paid for shorter periods of time; and they are subjected to greater scrutiny than other benefits. Moreover, such benefits are not paid when the person concerned is deemed to be voluntarily unemployed, to have been involved in industrial misconduct or to be partaking in a strike. In most East European countries, unemployment is not even recognised. In all these and other ways labour market considerations result in giving least or no protection to those most in need and, therefore, poverty is allowed to exist despite massive social security expenditure.

The second reason for the failure of social security systems to abolish poverty is that their national assistance schemes range from the totally inadequate to the less than adequate. If insurance schemes have been seen in the social security literature as the first line of defence against loss of income from work, assistance schemes have been considered as the safety nets to catch those who fail the insurance test and thus to ensure that no one lives in poverty. This has been the rhetoric but the reality has always been very different. Some countries do not have a national scheme of assistance at all: the most that they provide for those who do not qualify for insurance benefits is occasional lump sums from voluntary or statutory bodies to avoid extreme starvation. Other countries provide assistance benefits that vary in generosity from one part of the country to the other but they are always less generous than insurance benefits, not only in amount but in the qualifying conditions, too. Finally, there are the few countries which have an assistance scheme for the whole country whose benefit is almost the same in amount as insurance benefits and to which all citizens are entitled.

The Beveridge Report that became the foundation for the post-war social security system in Britain envisaged that the two schemes—insurance and assistance—should ensure that no one had an income below the poverty line when out of work. In practice this has not proved completely successful, partly because labour market considerations at times override the principle that no one should be in poverty, and partly because many people do not apply for assistance benefits out of ignorance, pride, or the fear of stigma. Nevertheless, countries with national assistance schemes provide a better system of defence against poverty than countries with patchy or no assistance schemes at all. There is also a tendency for universal assistance schemes to apply less harsh means-tests than patchy assistance systems in terms of both the resources that are disregarded before the payment of benefit as well as the range of related people that are considered legally responsible for maintaining one another. It is mainly for this reason that, for example, the British system of social security is more successful in reducing poverty than the American system—85 per cent success as against 37 per cent (Atkinson, 1985, p. 83).

The third main reason for the failure of social security systems to abolish poverty is that most national schemes are not directly concerned with the incomes of those in full-time employment. As we saw earlier in this chapter, all countries assume that parents are responsible for the maintenance of their children but some qualify this to a greater extent than others. At one extreme there are those countries which provide no direct cash benefits to parents for their children even though they may permit parents to pay less in income tax on account of their having children. Then there are those which provide such cash benefits but they vary a great deal in generosity and qualifying conditions (Borowczyk, 1986). In no country, however, is the cash benefit sufficient for the total maintenance of a child. In other words, governments share in varying degrees with parents the cost of children, but they never bear it entirely. Finally, there are those few countries which have means-tested benefits for families where the head is in full-time employment. Such countries should, in theory, be able to abolish poverty among the families of wage earners; in practice, they do not because the payment of the benefit is influenced in a variety of ways by fears that it may undermine work incentives. Having initially proclaimed their intent to protect living standards among wage earning families, they come to undermine it in practice. Nevertheless, such schemes provide one of the best, if not the best way, of protecting the families of wage-earners against poverty.

The failure of social security systems to abolish poverty, despite their rising costs in all countries, has revived interest in schemes which integrate the taxation and the social security system and which ensure that poverty is abolished. The Negative Income Tax (NIT) and the Basic Income Scheme (BIS) are the two main proposals that have received wide discussion in recent years (Ashby, 1984; Dilnot *et al.*, 1984). Both schemes envisage the abolition of social security schemes as they are today—the abolition of insurance contributions, of retirement pensions, unemployment benefits, all the other insurance benefits, as well as national assistance schemes and family allowances. In their place every individual or family, according to NIT, whose income falls below a certain line, will receive from the Income Tax department a supplement which will bring its income either up to the line or just below it. The BIS envisages the payment of a weekly amount to everyone irrespective of any other income that person may have from employment or from elsewhere. These are interesting ideas but clearly they are not practical politics.

If poverty is to be reduced, it will be through reforms of the existing social security systems. Three such reforms are the minimum necessary, as the previous discussion has indicated. First, the relaxation or preferably the abolition of the insurance or work principle so that the groups that are weak in the labour market are not excluded, as they tend to be at present, from receiving a benefit as of right. Second, the establishment of national assistance schemes for those who fall through the insurance net or for whom there is no insurance benefit—as is the case for one-parent families. It would be even better if such groups had their own specific insurance benefit, provided the emphasis on the insurance principle was more nominal than real. Third, the establishment of a social security system for those in employment whose wages are insufficient for the needs of their families. Another way, but a more expensive one, of achieving this is the payment of family allowances, that are sufficient for the whole cost of maintaining children, to all families.

The extra costs involved in implementing this type of anti-poverty social security system are not great and there is no doubt that advanced industrial societies can afford them. What is lacking is not the economic resources but the political will and it is difficult to see any evidence that this is likely to change in the near future. The current economic recession has not prevented governments from increasing expenditure on defence or on law and order, but it has been used as a reason for reducing benefits, particularly those for the unemployed who are the victims of the recession.

It has been argued that poverty cannot be abolished until unemployment rates decline and rates of economic growth rise. This will, on one hand, reduce the cost of social security and, on the other, improve the country's economic ability to protect the poor. Certainly a full-employment situation provides a more favourable economic environment but it does not necessarily lead to the abolition of poverty. After all, poverty was still rampant during the full employment years of the 1960s and early 1970s. Nevertheless, it is true that the reforms necessary for the reduction of poverty are less likely to be introduced during periods of economic recession than during periods of full employment and high rates of economic growth. It is simply politically more difficult to undertake such reforms even if in resource terms they are quite viable. Poverty is both a political and an economic issue and its abolition presupposes a climate that is favourable from both the economic and the political point of view. The upshot of all this is that governments in advanced industrial societies are most unlikely to implement policies in the near future that abolish or reduce poverty substantially.

Poverty is thus endemic to capitalist systems on two inter-related levels. It is, in the first place, created by a private-profit-oriented market system and it is, in the second place, continued on a reduced scale through social security systems that are themselves dominated in varying degrees by the practices, the values and the interests of the private market. In the final analysis, the operations of the private market benefit most the higher socio-economic groups in society and in this way the abolition of poverty becomes an issue of vertical income redistribution in society. The situation is not substantially different in the centrally planned societies of Eastern Europe where work incentives and income inequalities dominate government policies. Privileged groups in any society rarely, if ever, give up their wealth and privileges willingly to others and it is difficult to see why they would behave differently today in the case of poverty and particularly relative poverty. It follows, therefore, that only strong political pressure by either the poor or by a major political party can bring about the required changes in the wages and social security systems. On present evidence neither is in sight: the poor are divided and powerless despite their large numbers, whilst the major political parties are concerned primarily with economic growth and only secondarily with redistribution and the abolition of poverty. Thus poverty is likely to remain part of the economic and social structures of advanced industrial societies for as long as one can see in the future.

4 Famine, Starvation and Poverty in the Third World

Millions of people die every year from poverty, starvation and famine in third world countries. There are numerous estimates of the magnitude of this gruesome tragedy such as that of UNICEF, that in 1978 more than 12 million children under the age of five died of hunger; (quoted in the Brandt Report, 1980, p. 16) or that of the second Brandt Report that every two seconds of 1983 'a child will die of hunger and disease' (Second Brandt Report, 1983, pp. 9–10); and so on. Without exception all these estimates show how colossal this waste of human life is in third world countries today. This, of course, has always been the case and it also happened to European countries earlier in their history, though not to the same horrific extent. The crucial difference between then and now is not only the scale of the human catastrophe, but the fact that today it is generally recognised that this massive loss of life is happening at a time when food stocks in rich countries are so plentiful that they are being destroyed or being piled up at great cost to individual governments. It is objectively an unnecessary waste of human life because the world produces far more than enough to feed everyone. In the words of the FAO: 'On the one hand, overall agricultural supplies have remained ample, and unmarketable production is burdening the budgets of several industrial countries. On the other hand, food shortages and emergency situations have proliferated in the developing world' (FAO, 1984, p. 1).

This, however, is only part of the story—that part which is generally recognised. The other part, which is not generally recognised, is that starvation and famine in third world countries is often—though not always—happening when food exports from the very same countries are taking place in order either to pay off international debt or to satisfy the demand for certain products in the rich countries. As the report of the international committee chaired by Michael Manley—former prime minister of Jamaica—and Willy Brandt—former chancellor of West Germany—pointed out: 'Sudan, shortly before the famine of 1985, had increased its food exports threefold in an effort to gain foreign exchange and relieve its debt burden' (Manley and Brandt, 1985, p. 15). Malnutrition is also common in many third world countries where the best land is used to grow fruit or flowers for export to the rich world, rather than a staple diet for the people.

The definitions of poverty used in advanced industrial societies are not sensitive enough to cope with the breadth and depth of deprivation in third world countries. A much wider continuum of deprivation is necessary for this—one that begins with famine, moves on to starvation or malnutrition and, for most third world countries, ends with subsistence poverty while for a few it extends to relative poverty or rather affluence poverty. Despite the many problems resulting from the data that are available or not available, certain important general statements can be made about the prevalence of these problems and their incidence in the foreseeable future. As the reader would expect by now, it is a pretty depressing picture and a gloomy future that will emerge from this analysis.

FAMINES

Poverty, starvation and famine overlap and they are inter-related but conceptually they can be seen as three different processes. Starvation is the constant undernutrition and mal-nutrition that often goes unnoticed by governments, experts, the mass media and others in positions of authority. Famine is the abrupt and usually publicised collapse of food supplies so that people die in noticeable numbers. Clearly there cannot be famine without starvation, but it is quite possible—indeed it is more often than not the case—for starvation to exist without a famine taking place. Similarly, starvation implies poverty but the opposite is not the case for poverty is a less stringent form of deprivation than starvation. In brief, famine is the glaring tip of the massive deprivation iceberg that terminates the lives of millions of people or turns them into miserable forms of existence. Definitional debates concerning the dividing line between poverty, starvation and famine are as long-standing and unresolved as they are largely unimportant. As William and Paul Paddock commented on this issue: 'Perhaps when a man keels over and collapses from lack of food, then that can be accepted as the dividing line between malnutrition and starvation. Perhaps when whole families and communities keel over, then it can be called a famine. All this, unfortunately, is bad scientific terminology' (Paddock and Paddock, 1967, p. 50).

Famines in third world countries have recently received a great deal of publicity and they have aroused immense popular sympathy and concern in rich countries. Spontaneous popular movements, such as Band Aid, Live Aid, Sports Aid, and so on gave expression to these feelings and also raised large sums of money for famine victims. But the roots of famine are far too deep for such events to have anything more than a passing and slight beneficial effect. Unfortunately, there is also the danger that such well-intentioned events can have a detrimental effect on efforts to reduce famine by concealing the structural causes of famines, by concentrating on the pitiful plight of the victims, by praising the generosity of their general publics and by not condemning the policies of their governments.

Two main explanations of famines have been put forward over the years: the Food Availability Decline (FAD) theory, and the Food Maldistribution theory. The essence of the FAD theory is that a series of serious national disasters, such as droughts, floods, earthquakes, result in such sharp declines in the volume of food produced that inevitably large groups of people and perhaps the whole region cannot find enough to eat. Everyone in the famine area is more or less affected— famines are no respecters of rank, status, race, age or sex. Sometimes the FAD theory is linked to the Malthusian claim that famines are one of nature's ways of dealing with excessive population growth rates. Thus, either because of natural disasters, or excessive procreation, or both, the amount of food available is not enough to feed everyone and famines become inevitable. In other words, at best no one is to blame and at worst the famine victims themselves are responsible for their plight.

But how natural are these 'natural disasters'? Drought is natural in the sense that it cannot be prevented, but it is not natural in the sense that more often than not its effects can be prevented through better irrigation systems. Hurricanes cannot be prevented, but their destructive effects can be substantially reduced through better building construction; tidal waves may not be preventable but their consequences can be largely prevented through better construction works; and so on. Thus, these disasters are not natural because so much can be done to prevent their ill-effects. What is needed is sufficient capital and the political will to apply modern methods of prevention to age-old problems—something which has been done to a large extent in rich countries.

If the causes of famines are 'natural disasters', according to the FAD theory, the effects of famines are indiscriminate. Yet all the evidence from the potato famines of Ireland to the rice famines of India and China, to the maize famines of Africa, to the wheat famines of Europe, and so on, shows that it is the poor who are the victims of famine (Dando, 1980). Without doubt, the rich and the powerful never starve—even during famines. The idea that whole communities, villages, towns or societies are wiped out by famines is fanciful, and it is not corroborated by empirical evidence. Examining the incidence of several famines, Sen has shown not only that they affect the poor, but also that they can occur even at times when food production per capita in both the country and the affected region is rising and when food is being exported. Thus it is not general food shortages that cause famines but the maldistribution of the available food supplies (Sen, 1981).

Indeed, it is often the case that while some groups starve or die during famines, other groups prosper as a result. It is not uncommon for wealthy groups to benefit at the expense of the starving during famines. There is a great deal of evidence to support this from Sen's work and elsewhere. A recent report by an international group of experts sums this up as follows:

Some of the richest families in the Indian state of Bengal made their fortunes during the famine in 1943. Similar fortunes are currently being made in Africa and there is no doubt that the lasting impact on the African political economy of each cycle of famine is an increase in the gap between the rich and the poor. After the Sahel famine in the 1970s, there was a marked shift of livestock ownership from the small herdsmen to absentee merchants. (Independent Commission on International Humanitarian Issues, 1985, p. 64)

A recent World Bank report was even more specific about the predicament that faced small herdsmen and farmers during the famine in Ethiopia: having been weakened by the drought, they were annihilated by the rich merchants and farmers.

In Sidamo province in the south of Ethiopia three rainless years have made it difficult for cattleherders to sell their drought-starved animals. In the past, a bull would sell for about $200. During the drought, a lean bull sold for $20 to $40 at most. To make things worse, grain prices increased while cattle prices dropped. (Reutlinger and Pellekaan, 1986, p. 26)

All this is not to deny the fact that droughts or floods can cause substantial reduction and disruption in food supplies. What is being denied is that these phenomena are natural in the sense that their ill-effects cannot be prevented; that all famines are accompanied by sharp reductions in food production; and that everyone is equally affected in famine stricken areas. Vulnerability to famine may be increased by these 'natural disasters' but neither do they always cause famine nor does famine take place only during such disturbances. It is for these reasons that the FAD theory cannot explain famines and one has to look to food distributional theories for a satisfactory explanation.

All distributional theories link famine to poverty in one way or another. In its simplest form, this approach claims that famines strike those population groups who cannot afford to pay for their food, i.e. the impoverished groups. The report of the independent commission referred to above expresses this approach quite well: 'Famine, a short-term phenomenon, is inescapably linked to persistent long-term poverty. Rich people don't starve. . . . Even in famines there is always some food. Who has ever seen a starving military officer or merchant, let alone aid worker? It is a question of who has access to that food' (Independent Commission on International Humanitarian Issues, 1985, p. 63). The quotation refers to recent famines in Africa but similar situations applied to famines in European countries. Thus, during the Irish famine of 1846, when people were dying in large numbers, a local relief inspector noted: 'On Saturday, notwithstanding all this distress, there was a market plentifully supplied with meat, bread, fish, in short, everything' (Quoted in Woodham-Smith, 1962, p. 159).

Sen's work provides a more sophisticated explanation—the legal entitlement to food thesis. People suffer from famine because they cannot establish their entitlement to food in legally enforceable ways. A person's legal entitlement to food 'depends on what he owns, what exchange possibilities are offered to him, what is given to him free, and what is taken away from him' (Sen, 1981, pp. 154–5). In other words, whether a person suffers from famine depends on whether he or she produces enough food that he or she can keep for her/his own use; on whether he or she can afford to purchase food either through her/his own resources, or through grants from the government, or whether there are others who can sustain him/her through the famine period. Thus people's legal entitlement depends on their economic power which, in turn, involves political considerations. In general, therefore, Sen claims, famines and food problems are political issues. As he puts it in another publication: 'There is no such thing as an apolitical food problem' (Sen, 1983). The strength of Sen's approach is its precision and its acknowledgement that economic and political power combine to decide who are affected by famines. The main weakness of Sen's approach is that it concentrates exclusively on the power of individuals and it tends, therefore, not to take adequately into account the national and international forces that shape the patterns of both the production and distribution of food between as well as within countries.

Structuralist accounts, of both the Marxist and non-Marxist variants, place famines within the national and international political economy. Griffin, writing from a non-Marxist structuralist perspective, sees famine as the result of both internal and external factors that are interlinked. At the national level, one has to look for an explanation of famines 'to the distribution of income and wealth; to organisational mechanisms which supplement income in determining entitlements to food, e.g. rationing systems; and to institutional arrangements concerned with property rights which govern access to productive assets, the most important of which are land water rights' (Griffin, 1985, p. 188). These internal factors are reinforced by the international relationships between countries in the sense that governments of rich countries 'are biased towards landlords and their allies rather than towards the peasantry and other ordinary working people' (Griffin, 1985, p. 193). A very similar position is taken by Susan George, writing from a Marxist dependency perspective. She sees famines and starvation in third world countries as the inevitable outcome of the world capitalist system that creates the exploitative chain which begins in the world's metropoles and multinational agro-businesses and runs down to the governments and elites of third world countries, and then further down to the local landlords and through them to the small farmers or landless labourers at the end of the ladder (George, 1985, p. 12). Thus, if Sen's approach concentrates on the power or lack of it at the individual level, structuralist theories concentrate on classes, the state, international companies and other structural factors for an explanation of famines.

Despite their differences, all the structural explanations see famines as part of poverty and of the wider issue of income and wealth distribution in society. The solutions that they propose, therefore, go beyond the immediate amelioration of famines to include the redistribution of economic resources and power along the lines discussed in Chapter 1. There is no point in going over these proposals again; instead we shall concentrate on the debates concerning the measures that are necessary to deal with the immediate problems of feeding and helping the famine victims. A great deal of recent discussion on this topic has understandably centred on the real practical problems of how to get food and other forms of aid to the victims, on ensuring that aid does not fall into the wrong hand and so on. Recent experience on food aid in Africa is far from reassuring on all these issues. Here, however, we shall concentrate on some of the more fundamental objections to famine relief and to food aid programmes.

Though there is general agreement that food aid is necessary to relieve the immediate hardship caused by famine, there are fears that, if continued beyond the crisis situation, it can have serious undesirable consequences for the recipient countries. The three most important objections to prolonged food aid programmes are, first, that they can undermine local agricultural production; second, that they can encourage idleness; and, third, that they can create or simply increase dependence on unnecessary foreign products (Second Report of the Foreign Affairs Committee, 1985, appendix 16). Clearly, if food is given free for long periods of time in an area where food is grown, then food prices may fall and local food production may decline. These effects, however, should not be exaggerated because food is often grown for personal consumption rather than for sale and thus demand for local food may not decline unless food aid saturates the local market. As far as the decline in national food production is concerned, this is the result of several interlocking structural factors and it is therefore no surprise that attempts to establish a connection between the volume of food aid programmes and food production have come to nothing. Dawson's study of food aid programmes and food production in a number of Asian and African countries for the period 1960–74 concluded as follows: 'Statistics of food output in countries which receive large amounts of food aid do not indicate a relationship between the aid and poor food production performance'. In the case of Africa, where food production had declined, he noted that 'the decline in African food output per head during the 1970s predated and led to the recent considerable expansion of food aid' (Dawson, 1985).

The claim that prolonged food aid programmes undermine work incentives and encourage idleness is as old as poor relief itself. It has been widely used over the centuries in different forms and guises, ranging from the dominant belief in pre-industrial societies that the poor should be paid low wages for otherwise they would not work hard, to the 'less eligibility' principle of poor relief in eighteenth- and nineteenth-century Britain, demanding that the amount of relief should be lower than the lowest wages in the labour market if work incentives were to be preserved. As shown in the previous chapter, traces of such fears are still found in the social security programmes of all advanced industrial societies. It is also an argument that has been used by right-wing writers against aid programmes in general, as we shall see in the next chapter. This is not the place to review the literature on the effects of benefits on incentives, and all that can be said is that it is a thesis that is difficult to substantiate by empirical evidence. Mere references, such as those in a recent Oxfam publication, to instances where food aid was thought to have encouraged idleness are not sufficient. Thus one Oxfam fieldworker in South India reported: 'Even in Divi, where relief was needed, continued distribution of free food and supplies became counter-productive. Villagers came to find it more attractive to sit by the roadside waiting for distribution than to go back to work' (Jackson and Eade, 1982, p. 16). This tells us nothing about the kind of work that was being offered or the type of wages that were to be paid. Nevertheless, this fear has been taken very seriously by international relief bodies, with the result that food aid is often made available on condition that its recipients participate in community work programmes. The usefulness of such work programmes, however, is variable if the test applied assesses their contribution to the local economy and to people's living standards, rather than simply keeping people employed.

The last criticism of food aid programmes—that they can create or simply increase dependence on foreign types of food—is real, and it is part and parcel of the wider problem of the penetration of the economy and culture of third world countries by the ideology and the products of the rich countries, sometimes with catastrophic effects. Thus food aid in the form of tinned milk or milk powder discourages breast feeding, increases dependency on imported products and it can also lead to increased infant mortality when used in unhygienic conditions, particularly polluted water. Though there is some substance in this argument, it should not be confined merely to the practices of the poor, because the living styles of the rich in third world countries do even more to increase dependency on foreign products.

Food aid programmes are necessary to relieve the immediate situation of famine and hunger. Clearly they are no substitute for the reforms that are necessary to reduce poverty and inequality. It has always to be borne in mind that usually there is no shortage of food in third world countries affected by famines. The cause of most famines is not general lack of food but the unequal distribution of food or of the money to buy it, or of both. On this, most people are now in agreement even though they disagree sharply on the kind of policies that are necessary to rectify the situation. In the final analysis, famine is a political issue just as development, poverty and starvation are. Political issues need political solutions, but until these are found (if ever) food aid will be necessary to reduce mass deaths in famine-stricken areas in the Third World.

STARVATION AND UNDERNUTRITION

The dividing line between famine and starvation is often fuzzy at the edges, and what one person considers famine another may view differently. The brief definitions offered at the beginning of this chapter are a starting point but they lose their precision when one delves into them in more detail. A group of people may, for example, be starving for years, largely unnoticed, but when their plight comes to light and when the numbers dying come to be seen as excessive, that situation may be redefined from one of starvation to one of famine. At what point in this worsening of the situation lies the critical dividing line is a matter of judgement. Some situations clearly constitute famine and others starvation but many others are a messy mixture of the two—the degree of slippage between famine and starvation varies from one situation to another and from one observer to another. George Bernard Shaw brings this out very well in one of his plays as follows:

Malone: 'Me father died of starvation in the black 47. Maybe you've
        heard of it?'
Violet: 'The Famine?'
Malone: 'No, the starvation. When a country is full of food and export-
        ing it, there can be no famine. Me father was starved dead; and
        I was starved out to America in me mother's arms.'
                                   (G. Bernard Shaw, 1930, pp. 147–8)

Official figures provided by such international bodies as the FAO, the World Bank, the IMF and so on do not use the word starvation but refer mainly to undernutrition and occasionally to malnutrition. In this section, we shall be using these figures as indicators of different degrees of starvation. Undernutrition and malnutrition are sometimes used interchangeably and, though there is a relationship between the two, undernutrition refers to the quantity of diet while malnutrition refers to the quality of people's diets. In the more precise language of FAO, undernutrition means 'inadequacy in the quantity of diet, that is, in the calorie intake which, continued over long periods, results in either loss of normal body weight or reduction in physical activity or both'. Malnutrition, on the other hand, refers to the 'inadequacy of the nutritional quality of the diet which, if made good, enables a person to lead a healthy active life' (FAO, 1963, p. 36). A person may thus be malnourished even if he may not be undernourished. Since the statistics used below refer to undernutrition only, the size of the starvation groups would have been higher had they covered malnutrition as well as undernutrition.

As the reader will be aware by now, there is no agreement on what constitutes undernutrition, let alone malnutrition, on a world scale. There are the very obvious complicating factors of age, sex, height, occupation, climate, and so on, which render any scientific estimate of the number of people undernourished in third world countries impossible (Pacey and Payne, 1985). Indeed, it has recently been argued that under conditions of prolonged deprivation, the human body learns to adapt to substantially less food without any ill-effects. The implication of this is that the number of people who suffer from the ill-effects of undernutrition is far lower than that estimated by international bodies and dieticians (Sukhatme, 1982).

Even if there was agreement on what constitutes adequate nutrition, there would still be immense problems in quantifying the size of the nutritional problem on a world scale. Ideally, one would need national surveys and these do not exist in the rich let alone the poor countries. International bodies like the FAO, WHO and the World Bank, therefore, estimate the extent of undernutrition in third world countries by taking into account income distribution patterns and energy contents of diets in different countries and relating these to the various FAO/WHO undernutrition lines. It is clearly a complex and difficult exercise, and inevitably the statistical results can be nothing more than rough estimates. Nevertheless, the various estimates of undernutrition in third world countries agree on one point: the vast scale of the problem.

The various statistical estimates of the extent of under-nutrition are, from the methodological point of view, of two types: those which use calorie consumption as their measuring device and those which adopt income levels as proxies of food consumption. Both will be used in this section and, as will be seen, the size of the problem is huge by both standards. Beginning with calorie consumption, the most recent and most rigorous estimate of undernutrition in third world countries comes from a World Bank Report by Reutlinger and Pellekaan. Using as its nutrition standard the benchmark developed by a WHO/FAO expert committee (Report of a Joint FAO/WHO expert committee, 1973), it estimated that 34 per cent of the populations of eighty-seven developing countries, i.e. 730 million people, had diets which did not provide enough calories for an active working life; and 16 per cent or 340 millions did not have enough calories to prevent stunted growth and serious health risks. The report commented that, of the two standards, the first 'is the better guide to the harm that inadequate diets impose on development' (Reutlinger and Pellekaan, 1986, p. 17). The second standard is clearly much harsher and refers to those who suffer *serious* health risks as a result of their inadequate diets.

Table 4.1 provides detailed information for different groups of developing countries and shows that, as expected, under-nutrition is most acute in low-income countries. It should also be added that the study does not include China and, though it probably overestimates slightly the proportion of people who are undernourished, it certainly underestimates substantially the actual numbers of people undernourished. It is also worth pointing out that, though the incidence of undernutrition may be at its highest in Sub-Saharan countries, most of the undernourished people live in the populous countries of Asia. Understandably, the mass media of the industrialised countries

Table 4.1 *Undernutrition in developing countries, 1980*

Country Group or Region	Number of countries	Below 90% of FAO/WHO standard†		Below 80% of FAO/WHO standard‡	
		% of population	Population in millions	% of population	Population in millions
All Developing Countries	87	34	730	16	340
Low-income Countries*	30	51	590	23	270
Middle-income Countries	57	14	140	7	70
Sub-Saharan Africa	37	44	150	25	90
East Asia and Pacific	8	14	40	7	20
Middle East and North Africa	11	10	20	4	10
Latin America and Caribbean	24	13	50	6	20

Source: S. Reutlinger and J. van Holst Pellekaan, *Poverty and Hunger*, World Bank, 1986, table 2-3, p. 17.

* Below $400 per capita income in 1983 for low income countries; above $400 for middle-income countries.
† Calorie intake not enough for an active working life.
‡ Calorie intake not enough to prevent stunted growth and serious health risks.

concentrate on the pitiful plight of the famine-stricken, dying victims of Africa, and they neglect totally the desperate conditions of the much larger numbers of people in the villages and the cities who are not dying of famines but whose health suffers and whose lifespan is shortened as a result.

Other estimates of undernutrition in third world countries have reached similar conclusions. The FAO estimated that, in the mid-1970s, 19.3 per cent of the population of ninety developing countries or 436 million were undernourished, i.e. had less than 1,500 calories per day. Interestingly enough, it also showed that Asia and the Far East not only contained the largest number of the undernourished—303 million—but it also exhibited the highest incidence of undernourishment— 23.1 per cent of their population had less than 1,500 calories per day (FAO, 1982, table 2-1, p. 75). Moreover, the report referred to a problem that is common to all these global estimates of Third World starvation—they tend to underestimate the size of the problem because they 'disguise any deficiencies in food consumption at the local and area level while even where a household as a whole is above the poverty line, food distribution patterns within the family may result in inadequate nourishment of women and children' (FAO, 1982, p. 75).

The most recent estimates of the extent of undernutrition/ malnutrition by the FAO are shown in table 4.2. The measure of undernourishment used is less generous than the 'active working life' measure used by Reutlinger and Pellekaan but more generous than their 'maintaining of physical health' standard. It refers to the calories that are necessary for preventing ill-health and for maintaining 'the activity associated with eating, washing, dressing, etc., as well as minimum movement and other activity needed for communication' (FAO, 1987, p. 19). The table shows that the extent of undernutrition is higher in Africa than the other regions. A classification of countries by economic grouping shows, as expected, that the least developed countries had the highest rate of undernutrition—36 per cent—in 1979-81. It needs to be stressed again that the criterion used for undernutrition 'is likely to underestimate the actual incidence of undernutrition, because of the very low level of activity implied' (FAO, 1987, p. 19).

Estimates of undernutrition based on income levels arrive at very similar conclusions. The work of the World Bank staff is again one of the main sources of information. Thus Ahluwalia and his associates at the World Bank estimated that in 1969, 30.9 per cent of the population of forty-five Third World countries or 370.4 million people had incomes less than $50 per year; and 48.2 per cent or 578.2 million had incomes below $75. Moreover, the majority as well as the highest incidence of low incomes were again found in Asian countries. (Ahluwalia, *et al.*, 1974). Relating these incomes per capita to calorie consumption was not possible without further information, but they were accepted as evidence of the extent of absolute poverty in the Third World, i.e. of undernutrition or starvation. In a later study, Ahluwalia and Carter used as their benchmark the income per capita that was necessary for the purchase of basic food sufficient for 2,150 calories per person per day, and found that 38.4 per cent of the population of thirty-five countries, or 643 million were below this nutritional level, with Asia again faring worse than other parts of the Third World. The general conclusion of the study was: 'Almost 40 per cent of the population of the developing countries live in absolute poverty defined by income levels that are insufficient to provide adequate nutrition by South-Asian standards' (Ahluwalia and Carter, 1979, p. 463). It is, perhaps, necessary to point out again that these estimates do not include China and several other third world countries, with the obvious result that the number of people, though not the proportion, shown as undernourished is an underestimate of the actual figure. The general conclusion, therefore is as bleak when one uses income levels as proxies of undernutrition as when one adopts calorie-intake levels—starvation on a massive scale in the midst of global super-abundance of food.

Having surveyed the present extent of undernutrition, or starvation or absolute poverty in third world countries as a whole, we now move to the equally important but more difficult issue of the trends in the incidence of these conditions during the last twenty years or so. All the evidence shows that food production in absolute and in per capita terms has increased over the years not only on a global scale but also in the group designated as developing countries. However, rises

Table 4.2 Extent of undernutrition in ninety-eight market developing countries

Region	Number (millions)		Per cent	
	1969–71	1979–81	1969–71	1979–81
Africa	81	99	29	26
Far East	303	313	31	25
Latin America	53	56	19	16
Near East	34	25	22	12
Total	472	494	28	23

Source: FAO, 1987, table 3.1, p. 22.

in food production in absolute or per capita terms are no guarantee that the extent of starvation will decline in corresponding degrees—at the end of the day it is a country's and the individual's ability to obtain food that is the crucial factor. Nevertheless, food increases do make distributional issues easier, and this is reflected in figures of undernourishment: the proportion of the population in third world countries that is undernourished has declined slightly over the years, though the absolute numbers of the undernourished have increased. Reutlinger and Pellekaan show that the proportion of people in the eighty-seven developing countries covered by their study whose calorie intake was below 90 per cent of the FAO/WHO requirement declined by 0.06 during the period 1970–80, while the corresponding figure for calorie intakes below 80 per cent of FAO/WHO requirement was even smaller—only 0.02. Bearing in mind current rates of population growth, it was not unexpected that the numbers of people with calorie deficient diets increased during the same period: for the 90 per cent standard, numbers increased by 10 per cent, i.e. from 665 million to 730 million, and by 14 per cent for the 80 per cent standard, i.e. from 300 million to 340 million. Moreover, if one looks at the thirty low income countries within the overall group of eighty-seven countries, the situation deteriorated both in relative and in absolute terms: the proportions of undernourished people for the two calorie-intake standards increased by 0.04 and 0.03 respectively, while the absolute numbers increased by 41 per cent and 54 per cent respectively. In other words, the slight relative improvement that has taken place during the decade is confined to the fifty-seven middle-income countries in the eighty-seven strong group of developing countries (Reutlinger and Pellekaan, 1986, table 2-4, p. 18). It must also be borne in mind that these changes are based on what Reutlinger and Pellekaan acknowledged to be 'the rather optimistic assumption that income distribution did not change during the decade; this probably overstates the improvement' (Reutlinger and Pellekaan, p. 18). The most recent FAO study shows very similar trends—an increase in the absolute numbers of the undernourished but a decrease in the proportion with the exception of the least developed group of countries where the proportion rose from 34 per cent in 1969–71 to 36 per cent in 1979–81. Finally, it must also be pointed out that the overall improvement or worsening of the situation refers to the country or group country level and inevitably masks differences at lower geographical levels. These variations within countries will become evident in the discussion below.

Similar conclusions are arrived at if one uses income levels as proxies of undernutrition. Thus Ahluwalia and Carter estimated that the proportion of the population undernourished declined in all sub-groups of developing countries during the period 1960–75. In terms of absolute numbers, however, there was an overall increase of 7.8 per cent from 597 million to 644 million, and an even sharper rise of 16.4 per cent for the low income countries (Ahluwalia and Carter, table 11-3, pp. 478–9). It must be remembered, however, that this study covered the most favourable years in terms of economic growth in third world countries, and it is not unexpected that its conclusions are less pessimistic than they would have been had it extended to the mid-1980s.

What of the immediate future? Most of the projections were made in the 1970s, and they were based on the optimistic assumption that the high rates of post-war economic growth would continue to the year 2000, with the result that the incidence of undernutrition would decline substantially in both the low and middle income countries. Thus Ahluwalia and Carter estimated that the percentage of population in starvation poverty would decline from 38 per cent in 1975 to 20 per cent in developing countries as a group by the year 2000. Similarly

Table 4.3 *Trends in undernutrition rates by income levels**

Group of countries	Number in millions			Percentages		
	1960	1975	% change 1960–75	1960	1975	% change 1960–75
Low-income Developing Countries	(10) 438	510	+16.4	61.7	50.7	–19.8
Middle-income Developing Countries	(10) 86	81	–5.8	49.2	31.0	–37.0
High-income Developing Countries	(16) 72	54	–25.0	24.9	12.6	–49.4
All Developing Countries	(36) 597	644	+7.8	50.9	38.0	–25.3

Source: Adapted from M. S. Ahluwalia and N. G. Carter, 1979 table 11-3, pp. 478–9. Numbers in brackets indicate the number of countries in the group.

Note. * Income sufficient for 2,150 calories per person per day.

the World Bank estimated that, if past economic growth rates continued, then the percentage of population in poverty by the year 2000 would be halved in relation to the figure of 1975, with an even sharper decline for the middle and high income groups of developing countries (World bank, 1978, table 34, p. 33). These projections cannot be taken seriously now, in view of the recession that engulfed the world in the 1980s and which, as it is generally agreed, has affected the poorest sections and the poorest countries more severely than other groups and other countries. The only tentative projection possible is that the incidence of undernutrition in low-income countries will, at best, remain constant and, at worst, may increase in the years between now and the end of the century.

Having reviewed the evidence on undernutrition or starvation at the global level, we now turn to look at the evidence from research studies in individual countries. Most of these studies have been conducted under the auspices of various international bodies, particularly the ILO and the World Bank, and they are often comparable in broad terms. For the sake of clarity, the discussion will look at undernutrition country by country, beginning with Asian countries, then Latin American and finally African countries.

Naseem's study of absolute poverty in rural Pakistan during 1962–73 is worth discussion in detail, because it is a good example of the issues and the dilemmas facing poverty researchers in developing countries. He defined as poor 'those with an income less than the amount associated with the purchase of an adequate diet' (Naseem, 1977, p. 43). In other words, poverty was seen exclusively in terms of food and no account was taken of any other necessities, basic or otherwise. Having done this, he had to decide what kind of diet was necessary that would provide a person with a daily intake of 2,100 calories which was considered necessary in Pakistan. The FAO recommended diet was rejected because, being a balanced diet, it gave due attention to such items as meat and fruit, with the result that it was expensive and hence 'beyond the reach of all except the very high income groups in a country such as Pakistan' (ibid., p. 43). Ordinary people in Pakistan rely on getting most of their nutrition through cereals, despite the fact that such a diet is seriously lacking in other nutrients. He therefore adopted the diet recommended by a Pakistan government department that reflected local conditions and was, therefore, cheaper. The diet was costed but even then it proved too 'high' since it meant that 85 per cent of rural households would have been in poverty. In other words, it would have been unrealistic to use as a poverty line a diet that was officially considered necessary and which was inadequate by international standards but which would, nevertheless, classify most people in Pakistan as poor. Thus three lower poverty lines were adopted, illustrating the point made in the previous chapter, that the fact that a poverty line is relative to the standard of living prevailing in a country does not make it relative in the sense of being generous.

The research method also illustrates the constraints imposed on researchers involved in policy-making studies, since they are anxious to use poverty lines that would be acceptable to governments. It is worth recording that the government diet which Naseem reluctantly reduced to make it more realistic, would be totally unacceptable as a poverty diet in affluent countries and it was made up as follows in kilograms per person per day: wheat 0.343; rice 0.068; pulses 0.025; sugar 0.078; milk 0.171; meat 0.018; fruits and vegetables 0.093; oils and fats 0.016. Naseem's approach is clearly reminiscent of Rowntree's in York in 1899, though it did not include any other basic items apart from food.

Table 4.4 shows that the extent of starvation poverty in Pakistan was massive whichever of the three 'poverty lines' was used: it ranged from 43 per cent to 55 per cent to 74 per cent of the rural population—the figures shown in the table. It also shows that the extent of poverty remained constant during the ten year period covered by the study, despite the fact that during this period agricultural production increased substantially as a result of the Green Revolution. The explanation for this 'paradox' lies in the type of growth strategy adopted by Pakistan—a strategy which, as Naseem pointed out, 'included no place for a serious land reform and concentrated on promoting a technology which led to reduced demand for labour, greater land concentration and increased landlessness' (ibid., p. 60).

Other figures show that the extent of starvation poverty in

Table 4.4   The incidence of undernutrition poverty, Bangladesh, India and Pakistan

Country	Author	Year	Per cent of population in poverty		
			Rural	Urban	Total
Pakistan	M. Naseem	1963–4	72	—	—
	,,	1971–2	74	—	—
	W. V. Genneken	1971	65	55	—
India	Dandicar and Rath	1960–1	40	50	—
	P. Bardhan	1968–9	54	41	—
	M. S. Ahluwalia	1956–7	54.1	—	—
		1960–1	38.9	—	—
		1966–7	56.6	—	—
		1973–4	46.1	—	—
	NSS	1973–4	—	—	46
Bangladesh	A. Khan	1963–4	40.2		
		1973–4	78.5		
	United Nations	1980	80.0		

Pakistan is higher in rural than in urban areas, and that the poverty gap is also deeper. Genneken's figures showed that 55 per cent of the urban and 65 per cent of the rural population were in poverty in 1971 (Van Genneken, 1976, table 18, p. 37).

Poverty studies have featured prominently in India both during the colonial period and since independence. The Indian poor have been studied in more repetitive detail than the poor of any other developing country, even though their number and situation may not have changed very much in recent years. As Sen put it: 'The Indian poor may not be accustomed to receiving much help, but he is beginning to get used to being counted. The poor in this country have lately been lined up in all kinds of different ways and have been subjected to several sophistical head counts' (Sen, 1974, p. 67).

Several of the studies of poverty in India defined it not only in terms of food requirements, but included such other basic needs as housing, clothing, fuel, etc. These studies will be considered in the next section, while here we will briefly summarise the findings of studies on starvation poverty, i.e. on undernourishment. The extent of undernutrition discovered by these studies varies according to which part of India they refer to, according to the number of calories considered necessary, according to the frugality of the diet adopted, and other methodological reasons. Dandekar and Rath used as their poverty line the amount of money that was necessary to purchase a low cost diet that provided 2,250 calories per day. They found that 40 per cent of the rural and 50 per cent of the urban population lived below this poverty line in 1960–1 (Dandekar and Rath, 1971). They also found wide regional variations in the extent of poverty, reflecting the varying economic conditions prevailing in different parts of India. Bardan, using an income poverty line for the rural areas that was the same as that of Dandekar and Rath but a slightly higher one for urban areas, found that in 1968–9, about 54 per cent of the rural population and 41 per cent of the urban population were in poverty, thus reversing the rural/urban position in relation to this type of poverty (Bardhan, 1974, p. 120). Findings from several other studies continued to be divided in the issue of urban/rural poverty. The United Nations Economic Commission for Asia and the Far East found the incidence of poverty to be higher in urban areas, while the Planning Commission for India figures for poverty for 1977–8 suggested the opposite: '48 per cent of the rural population and 41 per cent of the urban population' (Quoted in Sinha, *et al.*, 1979, p. 27). One of the few studies referring to the whole country is the National Sample Survey of India, quoted by Sinha *et al.*, which suggests that about 46 per cent of the total population was in poverty in 1973–4. These studies have used a calorie intake of about 2,200 per person and it is, therefore, not unexpected that the FAO more stringent definition of undernourishment of 1,800 calories for 'reference man' and 1,500 calories for 'reference woman' has inevitably led to lower estimates of people suffering from undernutrition. The Fourth World Food Survey showed that, according to these nutrition standards, only 17.4 per cent of Indians—20.8 per cent in urban and 16.6 per cent in rural areas—were undernourished in the early 1970s (FAO, 1977, table 11 2.6, p. 58).

One of the central questions that poverty studies have tried to answer is whether absolute poverty in India and particularly in the rural areas has increased or decreased over the years. It is a crucial question, for it reflects on the growth strategies

Table 4.5 Incidence of subsistence and starvation poverty in Latin American countries, 1970

Country	Percentage of households below the subsistence poverty line*			Percentage of households below the destitution line†		
	Urban	Rural	National	Urban	Rural	National
Argentina	5.0	19.0	8.0	1.0	1.0	1.0
Brazil	35.0	73.0	49.0	15.0	42.0	25.0
Colombia	38.0	54.0	45.0	14.0	23.0	18.0
Costa Rica	15.0	30.0	24.0	5.0	7.0	6.0
Chile	12.0	25.0	17.0	3.0	11.0	6.0
Honduras	40.0	75.0	65.0	15.0	57.0	45.0
Mexico	20.0	49.0	34.0	6.0	18.0	12.0
Peru	28.0	68.0	50.0	8.0	39.0	25.0
Panama	—	—	39.0	—	—	25.0
Uruguay	10.0	—	—	4.0	—	—
Venezuela	20.0	36.0	25.0	6.0	19.0	10.0
Latin America	26.0	62.0	40.0	10.0	34.0	19.0

Source: O. Altimir, Poverty in Latin America: a review of concepts and data, *CEPAL Review*, No. 13, April, 1981, table 2.

Notes: * This line represents the destitution line plus an amount for other basic needs; housing, clothing and sundries.
† Households below this line 'very probably suffer from severe nutrient deficits' (Altimir).

supported by international bodies and adopted by governments in India which emphasise agricultural growth through improvements in technology. The ILO studies of poverty in various states of India concluded that starvation poverty either increased or remained constant, despite yearly fluctuations during the decade 1961–71, as table 4.4 shows. Taking a longer period, 1956–74, Ahluwalia reached very similar conclusions, even though he presents them in a less pessimistic style. Using as his poverty line the amount of income necessary to purchase a low-cost diet providing 2,250 calories per person per day, he found no consistent upward or downward trend in the extent of poverty in rural India. 'The percentage in poverty declines initially from over 50 per cent in the mid-fifties to around 40 per cent in 1960–1, rises sharply through the mid-sixties, reaching a peak in 1967–8, and then declines again' (Ahluwalia, 1978). This finding was confirmed by Rao, who concentrated on starvation poverty in rural India for the same period. He found that the incidence of this type of poverty was 52.3 per cent in 1965–6 and with minor fluctuations over the years it was 51.0 per cent in 1973–4 (Bhanoji Rao, 1981). Leaving aside matters of detail, the general conclusion of the various poverty studies is, as Cutler notes, 'that over the 1960s and early 1970s there was little or no change in the proportion of the Indian population living in absolute poverty' (Cutler, 1984). Since this was a period of steady industrial and agricultural growth in India, the inescapable conclusion must be that the main beneficiaries have been the better-off groups in Indian society, evidence again of the wider argument that unregulated capitalist economic growth in developing societies does not benefit the poor as much as it does other socio-economic groups, at least in its early stages.

Bangladesh is one of the poorest countries in the world, with a per capita income of $130 in 1983 and one would therefore expect a very high proportion of the population to be in starvation poverty. Rahman Khan's study, however, illustrates how the extent of poverty can be made to appear lower than it is by adopting very low poverty lines—a process similar to that adopted in Pakistan by Naseem. He rejected the FAO recommended diet as a useful poverty line because, though it provided a balanced diet—i.e. it provided not only for adequate calories but also for vitamins and protein—such a diet was too expensive and 'few Bengalis can hope for the "luxury" of such a diet' (Khan, ibid., p. 139). Had he used this diet as a poverty line, about 88 per cent of the rural population would have been in poverty. He therefore adopted a cheaper diet that would simply provide 2,150 calories per person per day. But even by this standard, the extent of poverty would have been too high and he finally settled for the two lower poverty lines—the first providing 90 per cent of the required 2,150 calories and the second providing even less, 80 per cent only. His findings were that in 1963–4, 40.2 per cent of the rural population of Bangladesh were in starvation poverty of the first type and 5.2 per cent of the second type. Thus the extent of poverty was halved through the redifinition of the FAO poverty line.

As far as trends of poverty were concerned, he found that there was a consistent and sharp increase over the years, particularly of the second type. Thus, while 40 per cent of the rural population was in starvation poverty in 1963–4, 78.5 per cent were in the same condition in 1973–4; the rise in the more extreme type of poverty, i.e. less than 80 per cent of calorie intake, was even sharper: it rose from 5.2 per cent in 1963–4 to 42.1 per cent in 1973–4 (Khan, ibid., table 48, p. 147). The main reasons for this rise in undernutrition were, as Khan points out, the decline in real wages in rural Bangladesh and the increase in landlessness during this period—both the result of the unregulated capitalist type of economic development pursued in the country. A more recent study showed that in the early 1980s, nearly 80 per cent of 4,000 rural households had inadequate food. As expected, the extent of under-nutrition varied by occupational grouping: 'Over 95 per cent of wage labour households suffered from inadequate food intake, wheras the percentage was 61 in households in business' (United Nations, 1987, p. 120).

We have discussed the extent of poverty in India, Pakistan and Bangladesh in some detail in order to illustrate some of the issues and controversies involved in defining and measuring absolute poverty. We now move on to discuss the situation in Latin American countries. During the mid-1970s, the United Nations Economic Commission for Latin America (ECLA) embarked on an ambitious project to measure the incidence and gap of poverty in Latin America as part of the new international orientation on development that emphasised the satisfaction of basic needs. It was felt that more precise knowl-edge of the dimensions of poverty would perform the twin functions of making planning administratively easier and of persuading international bodies and governments to exert greater efforts in solving the problems of poverty. Two poverty lines were constructed by the researchers: the first was the amount of money necessary to purchase the quantity and quality of food for an adequate diet as laid down in the FAO/WHO guidelines of 1973. This diet was certainly better in both quantity and quality than any of the diets used to measure starvation poverty in Asia discussed in the previous section, and the figures in table 4.5 are not therefore comparable with those of previous tables on Asian countries.

A number of general points merge from table 4.5. First, the

extent of starvation poverty varied quite substantially in Latin America from 1 per cent in Argentina to 45 per cent in Honduras; second, the extent of poverty is higher in rural than in urban areas in all countries; and third, about one fifth of all households in Latin America had incomes that were insufficient to pay for an adequate diet. An empirical study of nutrition in ten Latin American cities in 1966–9 confirmed the high levels of starvation poverty recorded in Table 4.5. It showed that the proportion of families in the sample in this type of poverty ranged from 18 per cent in Caracas to 29 per cent in Bogata and to 56 per cent in Quito. It also showed that poverty was associated with large families and particularly with low education and low wages (Musgrove, 1985).

Malnutrition to this extent in these cities is an indication of the maldistribution of income and wealth, rather than the absence of adequate national resources to provide an income to all families for basic nutritional needs. It is difficult to be certain about the incidence of undernutrition in more recent years, but it has probably increased in many Latin American countries. On one hand, economic growth continued to rise, but in many Latin American countries inflation rose much faster than wages, thus making the position of low income groups even more difficult. Allen, for example, points out that between 1977 and 1980, the minimum wage in Brazil rose by 20 per cent while the cost of food rose by the staggering figure of 428 per cent. She provides more specific data which show that between November 1982 and September 1983 'a Brazilian family paid 250 per cent more for the five basic food commodities of rice, beans, milk, sugar and cooking oil, while wages increased by only 90 per cent' (Allen, 1985, p. 5).

It is generally acknowledged that Sub-Saharan countries suffer more from widespread malnutrition than any other regions in the world, irrespective of whether malnutrition is measured in terms of income per capita or in terms of calorie-intake. Davies showed that, apart from the Ivory Coast, all the Sub-Saharan countries exhibited malnutrition rates in double figures reaching the highest point of 54 per cent of the population in Chad in 1974. Moreover, during the period 1969–74, the incidence of malnutrition increased in more Sub-Saharan countries—thirteen—than it decreased—seven—and the rate of increase was sharper than the rate of reduction (Davies, 1980, table 2.3, p. 69).

The situation was only slightly better in North African countries: malnutrition ranged from 17 per cent in Algeria and Tunisia, to 26 per cent in Egypt and 38 per cent in Morocco in 1977 (Kavalsky, 1980, table 1, p. 145). During the late 1970s, however, economic growth in North Africa was far higher than in Sub-Saharan countries with the result that the incidence of undernutrition declined in the former but not in the latter countries. The work of Reutlinger and Pellekaan showed that in Sub-Saharan countries during the period 1970–80, 'the share of the population with deficient diets increased slightly, and the absolute numbers increased markedly' (Reutlinger and Pellekaan, 1986, p. 3). Moreover, on present evidence, malnutrition rates are likely to remain pretty much the same in the foreseeable future. It is this general food insecurity which will almost inevitably erupt again in famines somewhere in Africa at some time in the near future. Many of the Sub-Saharan countries will need to increase food imports if they are to avoid starvation, for their agricultural output is not growing fast enough and the patterns of income distribution are not changing. Their economies, however, are not in a position to finance food imports without relying on increased foreign borrowing with all the problems that indebtedness causes, as we shall see in the next chapter. As Kirkpatrick and Diakosavvas point out, only '"concessionary finance" from the international bodies can enable them to purchase enough food to alleviate the situation without plunging them further into debt' (Kirkpatrick and Diakosavvas, 1985). This, as we shall see later, is in short supply.

The ill-effects of malnutrition on health are severe for all age groups but particularly so for very young children. Countries with high rates of malnutrition exhibit also high rates of infant mortality, high rates of stunted physical growth in terms of both weight and height and high incidence of disabilities. This is so because undernutrition usually goes hand in hand with insanitary housing conditions, polluted water, lack of adequate medical services, and so on. It is for these reasons that the high rates of child malnutrition shown in Table 4.6 are particularly worrying. The efforts of international bodies to

Table 4.6   Percentage of children suffering from malnutrition, 1975–81

Country	Mild malnutrition§	Severe malnutrition†
Africa		
Sierra Leone	24	3
Burkina Faso	N/K	40
Burundi	30	3
Ethiopia	60	10
Niger	17	9
Somalia	16	N/K
Congo	30	1
Ivory Coast	23	28
Nigeria	24	16
Sudan	50	5
Egypt	47	1
Liberia	17	2
Morocco	40	5
Tanzania	43	7
Tunisia	60	4
Uganda	15	4
Botswana	27	N/K
Equador	40	N/K
Kenya	30	2
Asia		
Yemen	54	4
Nepal	50	7
Bangladesh	63	21
India	33	5
Pakistan	62	10
Turkey	44	24
Burma	50	1
Indonesia	27	3
Philippines	40	3
Thailand	51	2
Korea	16	N/K
South America		
Bolivia	41	1
Haiti	70	3
Peru	42	2
Nicaragua	65	3
Honduras	29	2
El Salvador	52	6
Guatemala	69	4
Costa Rica	46	1

Source: UNICEF, 1985, table 2, p. 114–15.
Notes: * Mild malnutrition: between 60 per cent and 80 per cent of the desirable weight for age.
   † Severe malnutrition: less than 60 per cent of the desirable weight for age.

improve rates of vaccination and immunisation are meeting with some success but as UNICEF recognises 'protection against all of the illnesses and dangers of growing up in poverty will only happen when poverty itself is overcome' (UNICEF, 1985, p. 43).

SUBSISTENCE POVERTY

As with undernutrition, we begin our assessment of subsistence poverty with Asia, then move to Latin American countries, and finally we examine the situation in Africa.

Subsistence poverty has been defined to include expenditure not only on basic food requirements, but also some expenditure on minimum requirements for such other basic necessities as clothing, housing and a few sundries. Most of the studies have attempted to do this by simply adding on to the cost of minimum food requirements a sum that is a small proportion of food expenditure, since it is well-known that the poor spend a very high proportion of their income on food. Several studies in many countries, as well as general expenditure data in advanced industrial and third world countries, show this. Subsistence poverty studies have taken this into account in varying ways and varying degrees, as will be shown below. It goes without saying, of course, that the extent of subsistence poverty is far greater than that of undernutrition or starvation poverty, even though it is not always possible to quantify this difference.

Several of the ILO studies in Asia defined poverty in subsistence terms, as well as in starvation terms. Rajaraman's subsistence poverty line for rural Punjab consisted of 80 per cent expenditure on food and 20 per cent on non-food items— clothing, fuel, services and miscellaneous (Rajaraman, 1977, p. 67). Nayyar's poverty line for Uttar Pradesh was made up of 73 per cent expenditure on food and 27 per cent on non-food items (Nayyar, 1977, p. 97). Similarly, Kurian's poverty line for Tamil Nadu consisted of 70 per cent expenditure on food and 30 per cent on non-food basic necessities (Kurian, 1977, p. 118). All three writers found that subsistence poverty in the rural areas increased during the decade 1961–71). In the relatively prosperous Punjab it rose from 18.4 per cent to 23.3 per cent; in Uttar Pradesh it increased from 57 per cent to 80 per cent; and in Tamil Nadu, it rose from 69.8 per cent to 74 per cent. Nayyar's study in Tamil Nadu also shows how much more widespread subsistence than starvation poverty is. For the same two years, starvation poverty was 47.9 per cent and 48.6 per cent respectively—about two thirds of subsistence poverty. Using a less generous definition of subsistence poverty, UNICEF estimates that during 1977–81, 51 per cent of the rural and 40 per cent of the urban population were in poverty.

Subsistence poverty is equally widespread in other Asian countries, as Table 4.7 again shows. Based on World Bank data, the table shows that subsistence poverty is higher in rural than in urban areas and it is in double figures everywhere. The indicator of poverty used by Bussink was the amount of money needed to purchase a cheap diet that would provide 2,150 calories per day, plus a very small addition for other basic necessities. The author of the report, however, argued that even this poverty was too generous, because it denoted 'an extraordinary high incidence of poverty' and suggested a lower poverty line that would 'probably give a reasonable indication of the income needed to avoid significant malnutrition' (Bussink, 1980, pp. 11–12). Again, the anxiety of the researcher is not that the poverty line is by any 'scientific standards' too high but that it results in classifying a large proportion of the population as poor. The even more stringent definition adopted by UNICEF again results in lower figures of poverty for all these countries. The only country that had really relatively low levels of subsistence poverty was Korea, whose living standards are higher than those of other countries and whose economic policies emphasised issues of redistribution. A study of poverty in Thailand by Krongkaew showed that the World Bank figures were not too far out and that the extent of subsistence poverty had declined over the years as a result of the type of agricultural development pursued in the country. In his words, Thailand 'started with about 16 million poor persons (that is 57 per cent of the total population of about 28 million) in 1962–3 and ended up with about 11 million poor persons (24 per cent of 46 million) in 1981. The development policies in Thailand have thus been successful in this regard' (Krongkaew, 1985). Yet the reduction of subsistence poverty was not accompanied by a reduction of income inequalities. In other words, had a more generous poverty line been used, the conclusion concerning the reduction of poverty over the years might have been different. It is quite possible for a country to reduce starvation and subsistence poverty without necessarily reducing the extent of income inequalities, as shown by the customary gini coefficients.

We have already referred to the Latin American studies by ECLA on undernutrition or destitution as it was called by Altimir, one of the authors of these studies. Here we shall develop the definition of subsistence poverty used in the studies and describe the incidence of this type of poverty over the years in Latin America. Altimir's definition of these two poverty lines—subsistence and destitution—were based on the consumption patterns of urban and rural households—not of all households but of low-income households, an important distinction with clear implications for the levels of both destitution and subsistence poverty lines. His analysis of consumption expenditure among low-income urban households showed that these income groups 'devoted between 40 per cent and 50 per cent of their total consumption expenditure on food. On this basis, poverty lines were drawn for the urban areas in all the countries considered, at twice the amount of the minimum food budget' (Altimir, 1981). A similar procedure was adopted for rural areas, where it was found that households spent a lower proportion of their income on non-food items than was the case in urban areas. All this means that subsistence poverty lines in urban areas were twice as high as destitution lines, while for rural areas, they were 75 per cent higher. Thus national subsistence poverty and destitution lines were constructed that reflected rural and urban consumption patterns on food and basic non-food items of low-income groups. These lines, however, were more generous than those used in poverty studies in Asia and Africa, even though the methodology was similar—another illustration of the basic argument that the calculation of basic needs satisfaction inevitably reflects the living standards of a country.

Table 4.7   Incidence of subsistence poverty in Asia

Country	Author	Year	Per Cent of Population in Poverty	
			Rural	Urban
Afghanistan	UNICEF	1977–81	36	18
Bangladesh	UNICEF	1977–81	86	86
Burma	UNICEF	1977–81	40	40
India	UNICEF	1977–81	51	40
Indonesia	UNICEF	1977–81	51	28
Indonesia-Java	Bussink	1977	80	66
Korea	Bussink	1971	14	20
Korea	UNICEF	1977–81	11	18
Malaysia	UNICEF	1977–81	38	13
Malaysia	Bussink	1977	55	25
Nepal	UNICEF	1977–81	65	55
Pakistan	UNICEF	1977–81	29	32
Philippines	Bussink	1977	59	60
Philippines	UNICEF	1977–81	41	32
Thailand	Bussink	1977	43	17
Thailand	UNICEF	1977–81	34	15

Sources: Bussink, 1980;
    UNICEF 1985, table 6, pp. 122–3.
Note: UNICEF definition of subsistence poverty level 'that income level below which
    a minimum nutritionally adequate diet plus essential non-food requirements is
    not affordable (UNICEF, 1985, p. 128).

As expected, Table 4.5 showed that the extent of subsistence poverty was higher than the extent of destitution in all countries at the national, urban and rural levels. While a grand total of 19 per cent of all Latin American households was below the destitution line, the corresponding figure for subsistence poverty was 40 per cent. It is also clear from the table that the incidence of both subsistence poverty and destitution is considerably higher in the rural than in the urban areas.

Economic growth rates were fairly high in Latin American countries during the 1970s and it is therefore useful to see whether these have been reflected in a corresponding reduction of subsistence poverty rates. Table 4.8 uses the same methodology as table 4.5 and shows quite clearly that both the incidence and the depth of subsistence poverty declined very slightly indeed in all ten countries during the period 1970–81— from 39 per cent to 35 per cent and from 5.3 per cent and 3.6

per cent. As with undernutrition, so too with subsistence poverty, the recession of the 1980s may well have halted and even reversed this trend. Inflation rates that far exceed the rise in earnings inevitably hit the lower income groups hardest. Evidence on both the incidence and gap of poverty is very useful indeed, for it provides as clear an indication as is possible on whether subsistence poverty could be abolished easily in economic terms. Honduras, with 64 per cent of the population in subsistence poverty and with a poverty gap of 21.8 per cent will find it almost impossible to raise the financial resources to lift everyone of its citizens above the poverty line. Argentina, however, with an 8 per cent poverty incidence and 0.5 per cent poverty gap should have no difficulty, in economic terms, in doing away with this type of poverty. Clearly, however, it is not simply economic factors but political factors as well that determine the incidence and depth of poverty in any society. There is now abundant evidence to support Molina's conclusion that in several Latin American countries 'the problem of poverty is increasingly linked with the lack of equity in the distribution of national resources rather than limitations of such resources' (Molina, 1983).

Table 4.8   Incidence of subsistence poverty in Latin American countries

Country	Population below the subsistence poverty line			
	1970		1981	
	Per Cent	Poverty Gap	Per Cent	Poverty Gap
Argentina	8.0	0.5	8.0	0.5
Brazil	49.0	8.2	43.0	4.2
Chile	17.0	1.9	16.0	1.6
Colombia	45.0	7.7	43.0	5.3
Costa Rica	24.0	3.6	22.0	2.7
Honduras	65.0	23.1	64.0	21.8
Mexico	34.0	3.9	29.0	2.6
Panama	39.0	6.8	37.0	5.7
Peru	50.0	13.4	49.0	12.8
Venezuela	25.0	2.8	24.0	2.6
All ten countries	39.0	5.3	35.0	3.6

Source: Sergio S. Molina, Poverty: description and analysis of policies for overcoming it, *CEPAL Review*, No. 18, December, 1982, table 1.

The situation is slightly different in Sub-Saharan countries where the limitation and the distribution of resources may be equally responsible for the massive incidence of poverty. Poverty studies do not reflect adequately the comparative extent of subsistence poverty in African countries, because they use definitions which understandably reflect the living conditions of these countries. Bequele and Hoeven explain that the subsistence poverty line used in African studies consists of 'first, estimating the cost of a healthy, low cost local diet for the average family or families of different sizes, and then adding on the cost of basic non-food items such as clothing, housing and education' (Bequele and Hoeven, 1980). Despite the similarity of definition to those in Asian and Latin American studies, there can be no doubt that the poverty lines used in Africa are lower than those used elsewhere, with the result that the figures in table 4.9 are not really comparable with those in tables 4.7 and 4.8. Nevertheless, they show that subsistence poverty is very high and that it is higher in rural than in urban areas. Moreover, the incidence of poverty increased during the 1970s and this increase 'does not seem to be confined to countries with stagnant growth. Indeed even in countries where average incomes are thought to have increased, such as Ethiopia, Kenya and Zambia, it appears that the real incomes of the poor have declined' (Bequele and Hoeven, 1980). Again, the conclusion is similar to that of Asia and Latin America: economic growth, though important for the reduction of poverty, is not sufficient—it needs to be complemented with government policies which ensure that the fruits of economic growth trickle down to the lowest socio-economic groups in society. Moreover, there are situations where economic growth resulting from excessively inegalitarian development policies leads to higher, not lower, rates of poverty.

We have now reviewed the extent of undernutrition and subsistence poverty in several countries in Asia, Latin America and Africa. No doubt the findings are inadequate and inaccurate in several ways, but this does not change very much several general conclusions that emerge from this review: the incidence of both undernutrition and subsistence poverty is unacceptably high; it is usually higher in rural than in urban

Table 4.9   Incidence of subsistence poverty in Africa

Country	Author	Year	Per cent of population in poverty Rural	Urban
Algeria	UNICEF	1977–81	N/K	20
Benin	UNICEF	1977–81	65	N/K
Botswana	UNICEF	1977–81	55	40
Botswana	Watanabe	1975	55	N/K
Barundi	UNICEF	1977–81	85	55
Chad	UNICEF	1977–81	56	30
Cameroon	UNICEF	1977–81	40	15
Egypt	UNICEF	1977–81	25	21
Egypt	Radwan	1974	28	N/K
Ethiopia	UNICEF	1977–81	65	60
Ghana	Bequele	1970	50	N/K
Ivory Coast	UNICEF	1977–81	26	30
Kenya	UNICEF	1977–81	55	10
Kenya	Ghai	1974	40	4
Lesotho	UNICEF	1977–81	55	50
Liberia	UNICEF	1977–81	N/K	23
Madagascar	UNICEF	1977–81	50	50
Malawi	UNICEF	1977–81	85	25
Mali	UNICEF	1977–81	48	27
Morocco	UNICEF	1977–81	45	28
Rwanda	UNICEF	1977–81	90	30
Sierra Leone	Bequele	1977	66	65
Sierra Leone	UNICEF	1977–81	65	N/K
Somalia	UNICEF	1976	70	42
Somalia	UNICEF	1977–81	70	40
Sudan	UNICEF	1977–81	85	N/K
Tanzania	UNICEF	1977–81	60	10
Tunisia	UNICEF	1977	15	20
Tunisia	Ginneken	1970	60	40
Zaire	UNICEF	1977–81	80	N/K
Zambia	UNICEF	1977–81	N/K	25
Zambia	Bequele	1974	52	24

Sources: UNICEF, 1985, table 6, pp. 122–3;
A. Bequele and R. van der Hoeven, 1980;
B. Watanabe and E. Muellor, 1984;
W. van Ginneken, 1976;
D. Ghai *et al.*, 1979;
S. Radwan, 1977.

areas; in many countries it has not declined over the years and in some it has, in fact, increased; the prospects for the immediate future are not encouraging for many countries;

economic growth by itself does not abolish poverty; the quality and quantity of diet used to measure poverty in many third world countries would be considered unhealthy in all advanced industrial societies; and the roots of poverty are to be found in both the economic and political structure of the country, as well as in the location of the country within the world system. We shall take up this final point in some detail in the next chapter and examine it in the context of the theoretical framework arrived at in the first chapter. In the following section, however, we shall review the role of social security in combating poverty in an attempt to draw some parallels with the corresponding situation in advanced industrial societies that was examined in the previous chapter.

SOCIAL SECURITY AND SUBSISTENCE POVERTY

We noted in the previous chapter that, despite the fact that the social security systems of advanced industrial countries have grown substantially in terms of people covered, risks catered for and volume of expenditure, they have failed to abolish poverty, even though they have contributed a great deal to its reduction. We attributed this failure to the dominance of the interests and the values of dominant groups in society, as they manifest themselves in both the private market and the rules and regulations of the social security system itself. Nevertheless, social security benefits have prevented a large proportion of those in financial need—though not all—from living in poverty.

Social security systems in third world countries are dominated even more by the economic interests and the values of the dominant groups and hence the protection that they provide to those in greatest need is negligible. Let us develop this theme step by step, because it illustrates how the state in third world countries serves the interests of dominant groups—almost at the total neglect of the interests of the needy. Despite the many variations in the social security systems of third world countries, it is possible to make a number of general points which apply to them all in varying degrees.

In the first place, social security provision is predominantly in the form of insurance benefits, along lines similar to those prevailing in advanced industrial societies. Indeed, it would be most surprising if the situation were different, because the social security systems of several third world countries were started during the colonial period and they were replicas of the systems prevailing in the imperial countries. Even countries which started their social security systems after independence used the systems prevailing in advanced industrial societies as their model, often under the general guidance of such international bodies as the ILO and the International Social Security Association (Mouton, 1973, Chapter 1). It is, however, a simplification of a complex situation to attribute the insurance nature of social security systems in third world countries solely to the influence of colonial powers. The fact is that the insurance principle serves the interests of dominant groups quite well, and it is no surprise that the elites of third world countries have espoused it. If it had not been in existence, they would most probably have invented it or something like it!

Secondly, the coverage of insurance benefits is, by its very nature, limited to those in regular and full-time paid employment. In other words, social security schemes in third world countries cover the minority of the population—government employees, workers in large multinational firms, and other well-paid employees. The majority of the population is excluded—the rural population, the self-employed in the cities, the urban workers who are in and out of work, and so on. Thus social security systems in third world countries are inevitably far more tied to the interests of the well-paid section of the population than the systems of advanced industrial societies. As a result, the vast majority of the elderly, the sick, the unemployed and so on are offered no protection from their country's social security system. It is often claimed that the family systems of third world countries are cohesive enough to take care of their needy members. It is an argument identical to that used in the past in advanced industrial societies and it is as void of meaning today as it was then. How can impoverished children help impoverished parents? Or destitute relatives help one another? The concept of filial responsibility is used by governments first as a convenient excuse to neglect the interests of the majority of their people, and second as an alibi to turn 'a public issue into a private trouble' (Neysmith and Edward, 1984). Third, insurance benefits are financed by contributions from employees, employers and the central government, with the result that they involve a regressive form of income redistribution—from the poor to the well-paid. It is generally accepted that employers pass on the cost of their contributions to consumers in varying degrees in the form of higher prices; it is also well-documented that indirect taxes form the greater part of government revenues in third world countries, apart from the fact that direct taxes are not very progressive (Todaro, 1977). The net result is that the lower income groups as consumers and as tax payers subsidise the insurance benefits received by the middle and higher income groups.

The main social security benefit for the poor is means-tested public assistance. The qualifying conditions and the amount and type of benefits paid under this scheme, however, are such that it has a minimal effect on the relief of poverty. The qualifying conditions are such that they exclude most of the rural poor, the able-bodied urban poor, those with relatives who are deemed financially liable to provide assistance and many other groups. The result is that very few qualify and those who do may receive either occasional lump sums or regular payments of very low amounts. Midgley's work provides the most convincing evidence that the overall effect of insurance and assistance benefits, i.e. of the total social security system 'not only reinforces existing inequalities but aggravates them and makes the position worse than it is' (Midgley, 1984, p. 183).

Bearing in mind the power structures and the nature of the State in developing countries, it is both understandable that social security schemes would reflect and even reinforce existing income inequalities and that government measures to change this would have to await changes in the prevailing power structures. It is not possible at present to extend the coverage of insurance schemes to all or to most of those now excluded for financial and political reasons. Reformist governments in third world countries, however, may find it possible to improve the coverage, conditions of entitlement and level of benefit of public assistance schemes. The major argument against this has been that the costs would be too high. This may be true for some countries but not for others, depending on the nature of the improvements. As Midgley points out again, the fact that 'some poor countries, such as India and Sri Lanka, have old-age assistance schemes while other far wealthier developing countries do not, suggests that resource constraints are not the only obstacle to the creation of such schemes' (Midgley, 1984).

Moreover, figures of public expenditure provided in table 4.10 show that expenditure on social security is far lower than on other services, particularly defence. It is, of course, true that expenditure on education and health and other such services is just as necessary as expenditure on social security, but it is difficult to argue as convincingly for expenditure on defence. In the political realities of the third world, however, the likelihood of governments diverting resources from defence to public assistance are as remote as they are of reducing the scope of insurance schemes to the advantage of assistance benefits. Social security benefits, as well as other public services, are shaped primarily by the interests of the dominant groups in any society but particularly so in third world countries, where the poor have so little political power. The reduction of poverty is as much a political issue in third world countries as it is in rich countries, but it is politically an even more difficult task because the poor have even less political power and because the limitation of economic resources is far more real than it is in rich countries.

The impoverishment of women merits some separate discussion because it cannot be explained completely in socio-economic terms. A great deal of it is attributable to cultural values which consider women as inferior to men and thus render them less able to compete in the allocation of scarce resources. This is not the place to discuss the position of women in third world countries but several points that are relevant to our theme can be made briefly.

Firstly, women's work is of vital importance to both the economy of third world countries and to family budgets. In many third world countries, women either do most of the agricultural work or their share equals that of men. Clearly,

Table 4.10 Central government expenditure, 1982

Group of countries	Percentage of Total expenditure						Total expenditure as expenditure of GNP
	Defence	Education	Health	Housing welfare and social security	Economic services	Other*	
I Low-income countries†	18.5	5.5	3.0	5.0	25.2	42.8	16.3
1. India	20.2	1.9	2.2	4.3	24.3	47.1	15.1
2. Other low-income	16.2	10.6	4.0	6.0	26.6	36.6	7.3
3. Sub-Saharan Africa	9.5	15.6	5.3	4.2	24.5	40.9	18.0
II Middle-income countries	12.1	11.6	4.7	17.7	21.4	32.5	25.8
1. Oil exporters	9.0	12.6	3.6	10.5	23.5	40.8	30.4
2. Oil importers	15.0	10.4	6.2	24.1	19.1	25.2	23.5
3. Sub-Saharan countries	12.4	16.2	5.8	4.9	20.7	40.0	33.1
III High-income oil exporters	24.8	8.2	5.5	9.1	20.9	31.5	31.1
IV Industrial market countries	13.9	4.8	11.7	40.4	9.7	19.5	30.1

Source: World Bank, World Development Report, 1985, Oxford University Press, 1985, table 26, p. 224.
Notes: * It covers mainly expenditure for the general administration of government.
 † Does not include China.

this varies from country to country reflecting the socio-economic conditions and cultural traditions of the country. Government statistics usually underestimate the extent of female agricultural work, but a recent United Nations Report gave due recognition to women's work by pointing out 'that women provide 60 to 80 per cent of the agricultural labour in Asia and Africa; in Latin America, ... the percentage is 40 per cent (United Nations Report of the Secretary General, 1978, p. 5). Even in societies which enforce rigid segregation of the sexes, women's work contribution remains substantial: they are simply forced to work either at home or in sex-segregated groups (Beneria (ed.), 1982, Chapters 1, 3 and 4).

Secondly, the mechanisation and commercialisation of agriculture in many third world countries has had an adverse effect on both men and women but particularly so on women. Discussing the effects of the Green Revolution in parts of India, Gita Sen concludes that, as far as women were concerned, its main result was 'to narrow the range of tasks done by them and to place them at the lower end of a hierarchy of permanent and casual labor' (Beneria, p. 47). Thus women not only contribute substantially to economic growth but they tend to be more exploited than men, particularly in the more recent types of commercialised agriculture.

Thirdly, women's work in household tasks such as fetching water and fuel, preparing food and child minding are simply enormous in impoverished societies. When this amount of work is added onto paid employment or work in their own fields, the enormity of the burden becomes crystal clear. Yet, despite this very heavy burden, women's work tends to be undervalued in their own societies, by international development agencies, and, sometimes even by themselves.

Fourthly, women's earnings are therefore crucial to the household budget. In fact, in female-headed households they are the main source of income, for there are no social security benefits for the vast majority of such families in the third world countries.

Fifthly, there is substantial evidence which shows that non-pooling of family incomes is the normal thing in many third world countries—to a far greater extent than in affluent societies. Moreover, it is often socially accepted that the husband has a right to a certain proportion of the family income for his own personal, leisure pastimes.

Sixthly, it follows from all this that women are likely to consume less food than men, even in poor households, often to the detriment of their health. It is generally known that in some countries tradition demands that men are served first at meal times and that they have first choice of the best food (Gulati, 1981; Schofield, 1974). The same practice even extends to young children, with the result that several studies have found that the proportion of malnourished girls is greater than that of boys (Sen and Senqupta, 1983, pp. 855–64). Dyson and Moore show that in many parts of India child mortality rates are sex biased to the disadvantage of girls, and that these rates are the result of 'old-age practices of discrimination against females in respect of food and medical care' (Dyson and Moore, 1983). Thus the reduction of under-nutrition and poverty among women is a more difficult and complex task because it involves a complex range of class and gender factors solidified through age-old practices and beliefs.

CONCLUSION

The three measures of poverty used in this chapter—famine, starvation and subsistence poverty—represent stark realities in the daily existence of hundreds of millions of people in third world countries. Despite the harshness of the poverty definitions, the general conclusion is that poverty is of gigantic dimensions and it will continue unabated in many countries to the year 2000 and beyond on present evidence (Griffin, 1987, Chapter 2). The famines in African countries of 1985 that were projected on the television screens around the world gave rise to numerous types of spontaneous as well as organised, voluntary as well as government, aid activity that brought some welcome temporary respite to the terrifying scenes of suffering, but it has not obviously changed the underlying complex web of internal and external factors that make famine and starvation so widespread and so difficult to reduce. It is these factors that the next chapter attempts to explore.

5 Why so much Poverty and Starvation in the Third World?

Poverty and undernutrition afflict the majority of the population of third world countries and they cannot, therefore, be explained as simply the result of the maldistribution of income and other resources within individual countries, as is the case with poverty in affluent societies. They are also the result of the limitation of resources of individual countries, for even if their national income was distributed equally, it might not always be sufficient to eradicate poverty. It can in fact be argued that in the low-income countries of the Third World, poverty is primarily the result of the inadequacy of national resources and only secondarily the result of the maldistribution of these resources, despite their very unequal distribution. In the upper middle income group of third world countries, the position is the exact opposite, whilst in the middle income group both factors are probably of equal importance, though only a country by country assessment can reveal the exact situation. We have already discussed the reasons for the maldistribution of resources within countries that result in poverty in the case of affluent societies and, there is no point in repeating the arguments here. Instead, we shall concentrate on the specific factors that account for the overall limitation of resources in third world countries.

It is clear from the discussion in Chapter 1 that these reasons are both internal and external, and that different theories tend to emphasise one of these two groups of factors more than the other. The approach adopted in this book is that, whilst both groups of factors are relevant, it is the external group that has the upper hand, for it usually sets the agenda within which the internal factors operate. The internal factors that will be discussed briefly here are geographical conditions, social values, population and government policies. Most of the chapter will be given to three major external economic factors—trade, aid and international debt—for it is these that condition the economy of third world countries.

INTERNAL FACTORS REPONSIBLE FOR POVERTY

Adverse climatic and physical conditions have long been cited by some as either the primary or one of the main reasons for the poverty of third world countries. Too much rain in the tropics means the multiplication of pests and locusts, the constant erosion of soil, the proliferation of weeds, and the spread of ill-health and diseases through flies, snails and numerous other pests. Vice versa, too little rain and excessive heat result in the deterioration of soil, the withering away of grass and bush, and thus the gradual destruction of the environment and of agriculture. Kamarck's work represents the most coherent exposition of this view. Indeed, the most important question that needs to be answered for him is how third world countries have managed to achieve so much during the postwar years, rather than why they have achieved so little. Agricultural production as well as industrial manufacturing are inevitably made more difficult by the harsh climatic and physical environment, in the obvious ways just mentioned but also because they make human toil and exertion far more onerous than it is in the more temperate zones of the world (Kamarck, 1976). In these circumstances one has to marvel at the achievements of third world countries rather than be despondent about their slow pace of economic growth.

It is, of course, easy to point to parts of Africa, Asia, Latin America and elsewhere in the Third World where there is either too much or too little rain and where the soil is unsuitable for cultivation. But it is equally easy to point to other parts, very often within the same country, where climatic and soil conditions are most favourable for agriculture. Moreover, it is just as easy to point to very affluent societies where climatic conditions are very harsh—Canada and Iceland for example—or where the soil is poor and the land is mountainous and rocky—Japan and Switzerland—or where there are no rich mineral deposits Denmark, Holland and Belgium, to name but a few. Climatic and physical conditions may be encouraging or discouraging for economic development but they do not influence to any substantial degree, let alone determine, its course and pace. The relationship between these physical factors and national standards of living is, as Galbraith puts it, 'so erratic as to be flatly worthless' (Galbraith, 1980, p. 16). Moreover, some of these physical factors are not always wholly natural, but they are at times largely man made. Deforestation, soil erosion and desertification are sometimes the result of certain types of economic policy that abuse the environment in an effort to maximise produce and profit as quickly as possible. Fortunately, too, there is plenty of evidence which shows that these processes can be reversed, given the right kind of policies. Israel, Holland, China and other countries offer examples of such successful land reclamation projects (Griffin, 1986). In our technological age, the environment is far more at our mercy than it ever was, for better or worse.

As we saw in Chapter 1, the question of values and attitudes is at the heart of the modernisation theory of development. The issue was discussed at some length and here it is only necessary to remind the reader of the main conclusions of that debate. Values are very difficult to define and to measure, and inevitably research findings can be both ambiguous and contradictory. Nevertheless, most of the evidence shows that values and attitudes in third world countries are not anti-development and that, given the right economic opportunities, poor people in both rural and urban areas show plenty of initiative and are prepared to work hard. In his recent work on development in Africa, Harrison comments that the traditional view that 'the African farmer was a hopelessly inefficient stick-in-the mud, unwilling to give up traditional methods' is totally wrong. Instead, African farmers 'are among the most inventive and adaptable in the world' (Harrison, 1987, p. 73), and he cites several examples of farmers being quite receptive to new ideas, provided they were given the required assistance and guidance by governments. There may well be some situations where the attitudes of poor people appear too accommodating to their impoverished conditions, but these attitudes can be changed, not through preaching and lecturing but mainly through changes in the material conditions that gave rise to and propagated those attitudes over the years. Structure rather than culture lies behind the condition of poverty at the individual, neighbourhood and national level, and hence the solution to poverty is through structural rather than cultural change.

The relevance of values and attitudes to economic development has taken many forms over the years. Initially, the argument was that third world countries lacked the entrepreneurial spirit that is fundamental to industrialisation. Recently values and attitudes have been linked to the question of population growth which, in turn, is seen as an obstacle to development. Official concern that the poor at the national and international level multiply too fast for their own good and for that of others has been a recurring theme in the history of nations. During the 1970s and 1980s, however, a number of international reports elevated current population growth rates into a main stumbling block impeding the economic development of third world countries and threatening the survival of the whole world. The first of these, the Pearson Report, set the scene for future reports with its apocalyptic claim that 'No other phenomenon casts a darker shadow on the prospect of international development than the staggering growth of population' (Pearson, *et al.*, 1969, p. 55). The Club of Rome Reports, the Brandt Report, and other such reports adopted a similar line with a fair amount of statistical data of varying degrees of reliability. Others coined such phrases as 'population explosion', 'population crisis', 'population bomb', and so on to dramatise even more the imminent dangers of rapid population growth rates to the economy, the environment and the general survival of 'spaceship earth'. Not surprisingly, most of these 'danger signals' have come from people and groups in the affluent countries. Since it has now become a major issue, it is important to examine the various claims in some detail. After a brief review of world demographic trends, the relationship between population growth on the one hand, and poverty and economic growth on the other, is discussed in

Table 5.1   World population, 1930–2000

Year	World Population		EDCs' Population		LEDCs' Population	
	Millions	Per cent	Millions	Per cent	Millions	Per cent
1930	2044	100.0	759	37.1	1285	62.9
1950	2486	100.0	858	34.5	1628	65.5
1970	3621	100.0	1084	29.9	2537	70.1
1984	4524	100.0	1119	24.7	3405	75.3
2000	6407	100.0	1368	21.4	5039	78.6

Sources: World Bank, *Population Policies and Economic Development*, John
　　　　Hopkins University Press, 1974, table 1, p. 8.
　　　　For 1984, *World Development Report, 1985*, table A.1, p. 148.

some detail in terms of both theory and public policy.

Table 5.1 presents the main world demographic trends, and
shows that the rate of population growth in third world
countries is almost four times as high as that in affluent
countries. What is more, the difference in the rate of population growth between the two groups of countries has
widened during the last twenty years, largely because death
rates in third world countries have declined much faster than
they have done in rich countries. There is also room for very
much further reduction in death rates in third world countries
than there is in rich countries, with the result that differences in
population growth rates between the two groups of countries
will widen even further in the near future up to at least the year
2000.

The different population growth patterns in the two groups
of countries mean also that they have different age structures
in their populations. Third world countries have a much
younger population structure than rich countries or, to put it
differently, advanced industrial societies have a more ageing
population.

In 1980, 39 per cent of the population in the Third World
was below the age of fifteen; 57 per cent was aged fifteen to
sixty-four, and the remaining 4 per cent was aged sixty-five
and over. By contrast, the corresponding figures for all rich
countries were 23 per cent, 66 per cent and 11 per cent respectively (World Bank, 1984, table 4.2, p. 67). A very young age
population structure creates, among other things, a 'popu-

lation momentum', i.e. such considerable potential for population growth that population would continue to grow very fast indeed even after birth rates become about the same as death rates (Kegfitz, 1971).

The result of these demographic trends is that an increasing proportion of the world population lives in third world countries. Whereas in 1950, two thirds of the world's population lived in third world countries, by 1980 the proportion rose to three quarters and it is estimated that it will be slightly higher—78.6 per cent—by the year 2000 (World Bank, 1974, table 1, p. 8).

While there is general agreement that death rates in the Third World will continue to fall for the immediate future, no such agreement exists on the future trends of birth rates, simply because there is no agreement on the causes behind the current high birth rates. It is, of course, generally agreed that having children is the result of a complex web of factors involving economic, cultural and personal considerations. On the economic side, a child means both costs and benefits to its parents. In third world countries, the costs are low because children either do not go to school at all or leave school early. The benefits can be higher than the costs because through their work in the fields, in shops or in the streets, children can bring in some revenue to the family budget. Child labour and child exploitation are commonplace in third world countries. Children are also seen as a form of investment for old age—as an alternative to social security benefits. Surveys of parents' attitudes show that children are expected to support their parents in old age even though international cross-section studies disagree on the importance of the 'old-age security' motive to population growth (Nugent, 1985). More to the point, however, historical studies of individual countries show that the introduction of social security benefits for old people is statistically related to declines in birthrates (Nugent and Gillaspy, 1983). On balance, therefore, it appears that the economic insecurity of third world countries tends to encourage high rates of population growth.

The cultural base of high fertility rates in third world countries is generally acknowledged but difficult to assess. It is made up of a number of strands, all of which are related, to a greater or lesser degree, to the economic base of society. Early marriage for women is the cultural norm largely because of the lack of employment opportunities; having many children is considered by men as a sign of success—living proof of their virility; low education levels, particularly on the part of women, have an adverse effect on the use of birth control techniques; and the general low status of women in employment, education, at home, and elsewhere: all these encourage high birth rates (Boserup, 1985). The implication of all this is that a more industrial base in third world societies will have a restrictive effect on fertility rates. It will improve women's position, it will increase the costs and reduce the economic benefits of having many children and it will raise people's ambitions and aspirations in life—all factors which militate against high birth rates. The current decline in infant mortality rates results in high population growth rates, but historical evidence shows that it usually precedes a decline in birth rates even though there can be a considerable time lag between the two (Cassen, 1976).

The problem with the process of fertility decline resulting from industrialisation, claims the family planning lobby, is that it takes a great deal of time and it is not automatic because other variables such as religion or nationalism can intervene to lengthen the process. It is for this reason that international bodies such as WHO, World Bank, etc., have been actively encouraging governments of third world countries to introduce family planning services in order to reduce the current high birth rates as quickly as possible. They acknowledge the primary importance of industrialisation and economic growth, but they point to the example of several third world countries which reduced fertility rates through active family planning policies. China is the example most often cited, but China also illustrates that family planning policies have to be accompanied by improvements in income distribution and by the provision of other social services. The Brandt Report, which called for reduction of population growth through family planning services, also recognised that these services: 'are rarely effective unless they go hand in hand with community development, education, better chances for survival of infants and children, higher status for women, and other advances, which require general economic and social progress' (Brandt Report, 1980, p. 107).

Though there is no inherent conflict between economic development and family planning as methods of reducing fertility rates, the latter is ineffective without the former unless it is pursued using dictatorial methods that obliterate individual freedom. Such an approach, however, creates a great deal of personal unhappiness, health worries and even medical problems when the necessary medical services are in short supply, as they are in most third world countries.

Despite the general current high rates of population growth in developing countries, birth rates have declined in many of them in recent years, and in some they have actually declined faster than mortality rates. The very young age structure of developing countries, however, means that these declines in fertility will make very little difference to the size of world population in the next two decades, but they could be quite influential after that depending on how mortality rates develop. The general conclusion must be that the period of very high rates of world population growth is probably over and that world population will continue to grow at lower rates in the very near future. This appears to be the case for the two largest countries in the world—China and India—though the picture is one of continuing high rates of population growth for many low-income countries, particularly in Africa.

The fact, however, that rates of population growth in third world countries are high by European standards does not necessarily mean that they are either the main or even one of the causes of poverty. It is easy to make this quantum leap, as, indeed, it is also tempting if one wishes to blame the poor for their poverty. Over the years, population growth rates have been seen as responsible for poverty and famine in two ways: the direct Malthusian explanation and the indirect impediment to economic growth explanation. The Malthusian thesis postulates that since the population of any country has the potential of growing at a much faster rate than its food production, starvation and famine are inevitable unless population growth rates are checked. Either people learn to control their fertility, or nature, through famine and starvation, will control the size of the population.

At the national level, Malthus's thesis makes very little sense because the capacity of a country to feed its people does not depend on the amount of food it produces but on the strength of its economy. Switzerland, for example, does not produce all the food that it needs to feed its people but it has a strong enough economy to enable it to import the amount and type of food that its citizens want. Thus the Malthusian thesis has to be seen on a worldwide perspective. Does the world produce enough food to feed an expanding population? Historically, the answer has been in the positive: food production has not only kept pace with population growth but it has exceeded it. Table 5.2 shows that during the period 1960–80, only the Sub-Saharan countries as a group experienced negative per capita food production and that was only for one decade. This tendency for world population to grow more slowly than food production has always gone hand in hand with the opposite tendency experienced by some countries, but these are not necessarily the same countries that experience also famine and starvation. If historical trends lend no support to the Malthusian thesis, they do not corroborate either the claims of those who maintain that population growth comes first and that this stimulates increased food production (Boserup, 1965). The logic of this argument is that, faced with increased food demands, countries find ways of producing it. This, however, may be true for some countries but not for others. It will depend on a variety of factors ranging from population density to stage of technological development, political forces within the country and outside, and so on. There is no automatic relationship between rates of population growth and food production, either positive or negative.

Though there is now general agreement that the world today produces more than enough food to feed itself, fears still persist that this may not be the case in the twenty-first century and beyond, given current rates of population growth. If that were to happen, the proportion of the world's population starving would increase rather than remain stable, let alone decrease. We have noted above that the rates of world population growth are likely to slow down in the future. But this is only one side of the equation. What about the other side— future food production trends? As expected, there is a great

Table 5.2   Per Capita growth of food production by region

Region	Average percentage change per annum	
	1960–70	1970–80
1 World	0.8	0.5
2 Developing Countries	0.4	0.4
Low Income*	0.2	–0.3
Middle Income*	0.7	0.9
Sub-Saharan Africa	0.1	–1.1
East Asia	0.3	1.4
South Asia	0.1	0.0
Middle East and North Africa	0.1	0.2
Southern Europe	1.8	1.9
Latin America and the Caribbean	0.1	0.6
3 Industrialised Market Countries	1.3	1.1
4 Centrally Planned Economies	2.2	0.9

Source: S. Reutlinger and J. V. H. Pollekaan, *Poverty and Hunger*, World Bank, 1986, table B.1, p. 58.
Note: * Low income countries = less than $400 per capita in 1983; middle-income countries = more than $400 per capita in 1983.

deal of disagreement stemming from disagreements on the total acreage of world arable land and on maximum possible food productivity per acre. Estimates of future world arable land depend on the defintion of what constitutes arable land, on future trends in deforestation, desertification, reclamation of land for agriculture, and so on. Even estimates of currently existing arable land acreage disagree, let alone of what the position will be in some distant future. Current estimates of arable land today range from 3.4 billion hectares by the World Bank, to 7.7 billion hectares by the US President's Science Advisory Committee, and to 9.2 billion hectares by Colin Clark (Clark, 1985). Estimates of future maximum achievable food productivity per acre are even more complex and hence more uncertain because they have to take into account such diverse factors as technological innovations, availability of fertilisers, water supplies, land distribution, government policies, and so on.

Despite these legitimate differences of opinion, the general view is that there will be enough land, adequate supplies of fertilisers, sufficient technological innovations and other pre-requisites for the world to produce enough food for a modestly rising world population in the foreseeable future. It is the distribution of food between and within countries that will remain a problem, and as much a cause of starvation in the future as it is today. Indeed, the whole debate so far has been conducted on the implicit assumption that the consumption patterns prevailing in the rich countries are beyond reproach, and no change is necessary in that direction. The problem is seen as one of the Third World and the solution, therefore, must be found there. Yet any rational commentator on this issue cannot but remark that the amount of food consumed as well as wasted by people in rich countries is beyond belief. Americans, for example, make up only 6 per cent of the world's population but they consume, according to one estimate, 35 per cent of the world's resources. Looked at in another way, the population of all the third world countries makes up three quarters of the world's population, but consumes only about the same quantity of the world's resources as the United States (George and Paige, 1982, p. 68). The problem, therefore, may not be that the world does not produce enough food for all but that so much of the food produced is wastefully consumed by the small minority of the world's affluent population.

The argument that rapid population growth is a major indirect cause of poverty in the Third World because it holds back economic growth is just as unsustainable as the Malthusian thesis. This argument is based on three claims— rapid population growth reduces savings per person, the amount of capital invested per person declines, and efficiency in the national economy suffers (World Bank, 1984, p. 82). Savings are necessary in any country to assist investment in industry, agriculture, commerce and so on and hence to promote economic growth. But the amount of savings that can be secured from very poor families is always negligible since such families do not have enough money to pay even for their basic necessities. Even if they reduced the number of children that they have, the position in relation to savings would not change in third world countries. It would make more sense if it was argued that the wealthy groups in third world countries should be made to spend less and save more for investment in their countries, but this raises as many questions as it answers.

The second claim that rapid population growth reduces the amount of capital that can be invested per person and hence reduces economic growth appears self-evident but it is not so when examined more closely. High rates of population growth create labour surpluses which may be an attraction to overseas investors because wage costs can be kept low; in some countries, though not all, the extent of acreage used for agriculture can be increased as population increases by bringing more land under cultivation; and population increases may well encourage more efficient use of capital as well as provide larger markets (Simon, 1981). There is, however, some truth in the argument that high rates of population growth mean that such government services as education and health have to be spread more thinly with the result that human investment suffers and eventually economic growth suffers. This, however, does not mean that lower rates of population growth make improvements in these services possible. This is a mere assumption, for there is no empirical evidence showing that third world countries with low fertility rates spend more per person on education than other countries (Lee, 1985).

Finally, the contribution of education and health to economic growth must be seen in perspective—it is not as substantial as it is claimed and it must be seen as only a small part of a wider range of internal and external factors (George and Wilding, 1984, Chapter 4). In several third world countries, the proportion of young people enrolled in higher education is as high as that in affluent countries (World Bank, 1984, table 25, p. 266), while in others there is an exodus of educated people to rich countries. Education and health are important in themselves, and they contribute somewhat to economic growth, but they cannot be strictly linked to population growth and thus made responsible for the low rates of economic growth and poverty in the Third World.

As far as the third claim is concerned, i.e. that efficiency suffers when population growth is rapid, the evidence points mostly in the opposite direction, even though it is often no more than circumstantial evidence. Thus, Simon argues that population growth 'spurs the adoption of existing technology as well as the invention of new technology', and he also refers to the supporting evidence from Boserup's studies in agricultural development (Simon, *ibid.*, p. 199). It is difficult to accept the logic of the argument that population growth undermines efficiency, especially since the supporting 'evidence' put forward by the World Bank is of very dubious validity. It argues, for example, that high rates of population growth means an increase in youth unemployment, which, in turn, results in a rise in crime and hence in excessive government expenditure on the police force (World Bank, 1984, p. 90). It is not only the logic but the evidence, too, which is shaky for this argument. It assumes that if governments did not have to spend so much on the police, they would spend more on other services. This is a mere assumption and, as noted above, there is no comparative evidence in support of it. Moreover, it can be argued that the existence of high rates of juvenile crime may strengthen the forces within a country making for higher rates of public expenditure on education, training, and so on. Fear is often a more potent force for social policy legislation than reason, let alone altruism.

What can we conclude from this discussion on the relationship between rates of population growth and poverty? Historically and comparatively, size and density of population have been associated with both economic affluence and economic deprivation. It is impossible to tell from the available evidence whether there is an optimum population size or density for maximum rates of economic growth. High rates of population growth have always been the result of poverty—this was the case in the past for affluent societies and it is the case today for third world countries. The reduction of high rates of population growth follows, in most cases, rather than precedes the improvement of economic and social conditions in the country. It is, perhaps, possible for large-scale family planning programmes to reduce high rates of population growth, provided they are part of a wider growth-with-redistribution government policy. Such programmes, however, 'must be established as a measure of personal and family liberation rather than as an arm of state control' (Nelson, 1986). Family planning is desirable because it raises the health and status of women, men and children irrespective of any effects it may have on rates of economic growth. The inescapable conclusion must be that the impoverishment of third world countries cannot possibly be attributed to their high rates of population growth, even though these rates may at times exacerbate difficult situations. The world produces enough food to feed everyone adequately both now and in the foreseeable future, and though there is a strong case for reducing high rates of population growth, there is an even stronger case for reducing the scandalous wasteful consumption patterns of affluent societies which consume the greatest part of the world resources (Warnock, 1987).

The final internal explanation of poverty and low economic growth rates is the mistaken policies that have been pursued by governments in all third world countries since their independence. Initially, this was the explanation espoused by conservative economists but in recent years the IMF and the World Bank have also subscribed to it. In essence, this argument maintains that the central cause of third world impoverishment has been the policy of central planning pursued in varying degrees and in varying ways by all third world countries. Governments, with the help of outside financiers and policy advisers, attempted to plan and manage the economy of their countries—industry, agriculture and trade—by manipulating prices, interest rates, investment targets, exports and imports and such like economic levers. These government policies were, as Rimmer argues, mistaken both in concept and in the way they were implemented (Rimmer, 1984). Conceptually they were mistaken for they attempted to expand all sectors of the economy simultaneously on a scale that ignored one of the fundamentals of economic growth— the principle of comparative advantage. It was simply not possible for these countries to create and sustain industries that would compete with those of affluent societies. It would have been far better had they concentrated their efforts on one sector— agriculture or mining—where they could compete effectively in the international market. If the concept of development was mistaken, so too was the way it was executed. The driving force behind government policies was political rather than economic. Government policies were designed to satisfy the various groups of government supporters in the cities, in the civil service and, occasionally, in the rural areas. It was the only way that governments could secure and sustain power in countries where the art of government was at its early stages. It was government by public policy bribery.

A slight variant of this position has been put forward by Fieldhouse, who argues that these mistaken policies cannot, by themselves, explain the low rates of economic development— they have to be seen in conjunction with other factors and particularly the world economic recession of the late 1970s. Inefficient government policies slowed down economic growth but it was only when they combined with the world recession that their economic effects were catastrophic. 'Black Africa', he concludes, 'would undoubtedly have been better developed if it had been wisely governed; but in a recessionary world, even the best-run state was bound to lose momentum' (Fieldhouse, 1986, p. 238).

The solution to the economic problems of third world countries, maintain the conservative critics, lies in the dismantlement of central planning—the replacement of Keynesian by monetary economics. Nationalised industries should be dismantled, prices should be allowed to find their own levels, trade protectionism should be abolished, agriculture should be emphasised at the expense of industry, government spending should be reduced to levels that can be afforded without borrowing and generally the labour market should be allowed to run itself with as little government intervention as possible. This would stimulate private enterprise and initiative, it would reduce inefficiency in industry and agriculture, it would gradually cut down the amount of foreign debt with all its disastrous effects and in the end enable countries to develop mainly through their own efforts.

It goes without saying that all governments make mistakes and it can be even argued, though hard to prove, that governments of third world countries make more mistakes than others simply because of the enormity of the problems facing them and the scarcity of resources at their disposal for solving these problems. But it is hardly a convincing argument that poverty in the Third World is either solely or primarily due to these mistakes. After all, governments in advanced industrial societies make mistakes, too, but this has not had any noticeable effects on living standards. There is another angle to this issue: policy outcomes which can be considered a success from one perspective may well be judged as failures from another. An example of this is the rise in economic growth (a success) which had no effect on the reduction of inequalities and poverty (a failure)—in many countries.

Equally unconvincing is the argument that *laissez-faire* capitalism will be more successful than Keynesian managed capitalism or central planning. There are several examples where central planning has proved successful—China, Cuba—as well as examples where it has failed and the same applies to Keynesian managed economies over the years. Ironically, it was partly the influence of the World Bank that led many third world countries to adopt 'indicative planning' forms of development. It is difficult to see how governments in third world countries can avoid intervening on a large scale when they are faced with such national issues as deforestation, desertification, inadequate irrigation systems, and the like. Equally difficult to understand is the argument that if, say, the mines of a country were denationalised and passed over to private enterprise—mostly foreign dominated—the country would benefit as a result. Inevitably third world countries need major government intervention in their economies, though there must be legitimate debates about its extent and form. What the current anti-planning strategy does well, however, is to remind governments and the supporters of planning that the mere existence of government plans is no guarantee that they can either be carried out or that they will have the predicted effects only.

The new emphasis on agriculture is welcome as far as it does, but it has to be accompanied, where necessary, with land redistribution measures to reduce on one hand landlessness and on the other landlordism. There is no reason, either, why the development of agriculture and of industry should be treated as mutually exclusive, though resource problems set limits to the extent of development that is possible. For third world countries, however, not to develop any industries renders them totally dependent on industrial imports from the affluent societies, with all the problems that this entails. Moreover, overproduction of agricultural products that are destined for the markets of the affluent countries—such as tea, coffee, cocoa, bananas, etc.—can result in a fall in prices. Countries need, as far as possible, balanced forms of economic development, bearing in mind their natural wealth, geographical position, technological knowledge, and so on. Over-reliance on a very small number of products can be, as we shall see below, disastrous for people's living standards.

It is, therefore, not surprising that the World Bank's newly found commitment to privatisation and agriculture has been greeted with both scepticism and hostility from so many quarters in third world countries. No wonder that the Bank's World Development Report of 1986, where these policies are set out, was dubbed 'World Bank Bankruptcy' in an editorial of the Hindustani *Times of Delhi*, and treated in similar terms by other newspapers (Bhushan, 1986). These hostile sentiments stem not only from the World Bank's excessive emphasis on internal factors, but also from its virtual neglect of external obstacles to economic development in third world countries. It is to these factors that we now turn.

EXTERNAL FACTORS: TRADE, AID AND DEBT

Despite all the methodological problems involved in this area, the existing evidence suggests that the overall combined effect of the diverse and complex financial relationships between developed and developing countries is a reinforcement of existing world income inequalities. It goes without saying, however, that not all financial transactions between the two groups of countries are detrimental to the interests of third world countries, nor are all developing countries similarly affected. In this section we shall examine the three main transactions— trade, aid and debt—that have direct implications for the living standards and hence for the impoverishment of large sections of the population in third world countries. It is these transactions rather than internal factors that are the primary explanations of third world poverty. To emphasise the external factors, however, is not to dismiss the internal factors—rather it is to prioritise them. There is no way that poverty in third world countries can be abolished through merely internal policy changes; vice versa, however, improvement in the external factors has to be put to good use by the governments of individual countries if they are to benefit their citizens.

Trade between industrially developed and developing countries

Though we are not concerned here with the extensive theoretical literature on world trade, it is worth summarising very briefly the main positions, partly because they reflect the theoretical frameworks of development outlined in the first chapter and partly because they have strong policy implications. Three main schools of thought have dominated this field. The first, and by far the oldest tradition, claims that trade benefits all participating countries alike and it also reduces inequalities between them, since the prices of primary commodities *vis à vis* manufactures rise over the years. The policy implications are for maximum free trade between countries without internal or external barriers or government subsidies and with each country specialising in the export of goods that it can produce relatively cheaply. It is the classical theory of trade from Ricardo to Keynes and supported today by the major international bodies—IMF, World Bank, and so on. The second perspective, the structuralist theory of unequal trade is associated with the work of Prebisch and Singer in the early 1950s, and Myrdal in the late 1950s, and it is espoused today by third world governments. Under existing rules and practices, international trade between countries of unequal economic and political power increases rather than reduces income inequalities between countries. The prices of primary commodities *vis à vis* manufactures tend to fall for a variety of reasons, with the result that third world countries lose out to the industrialised world. Only if trade is conducted along different lines can it become a force for the reduction of world inequalities. The third, the Marxist tradition, holds that world trade is a structural component of the world capitalist system and it is inevitably a form of unequal exchange. So long as the world capitalist order exists, unequal exchange will persist, too, to the detriment of third world countries (Smith and Toye, 1979).

Despite the growth of manufactured goods for export in the small number of newly industrialising countries, developing countries rely overwhelmingly on primary products for their exports: about three quarters of exports from developing countries are primary products—foodstuffs and minerals. Heavy reliance on primary products for exports has a number of unfavourable economic implications for third world countries which can only be summarised briefly here. In the first place, it means that primary products are exported to advanced industrial countries at low prices to be processed or to be used for manufactured goods which are, in turn, exported to third world countries at high prices. Had these primary commodities been processed in third world countries, they would have added substantially to their national wealth. There are various estimates of this loss of income to third world countries, but an average estimate is that quoted by the Brandt Report that in 1975 'for ten commodities local semi-processing could provide the developing countries with gross additional export earnings of about $27 billion per year, more than one and a half times what these commodities now earn' (Brandt Report, 1980, p. 142). The amounts of money lost to third world countries are simply vast and there is an urgent need to rectify the situation as far as possible.

Second, since Prebisch's pioneering work in the early 1950s, it has come to be accepted that the price of primary commodities tends to deteriorate *vis à vis* the price of manufactured goods. Since third world countries rely on primary commodities for their exports, the result is that they lose out to industrialised countries from whom they import manufactured goods. Spraos's work shows this to be the case for the period 1950–79 (Spraos, 1982, UNCTAD Review, p. 110), while Thirlwall and Bergevin come to the same conclusion for the period 1954–82. They summarise their findings as follows: 'There is substantial and convincing evidence to support the view that, apart from minerals and crude petroleum, the terms of trade of primary commodities has deteriorated in the post-war years, continuing the long-run historical trend.'

Moreover, primary commodities from third world countries fared worse than those from industrialised countries (Thirlwall and Bergevin, 1985). The situation has deteriorated so badly in recent years that the IMF concluded that 'the real commodity prices in the third quarter of 1986 had fallen to a level not experienced since at least the 1930s' (IMF, 1986). Again, the financial loss to third world countries is very considerable. Todaro refers to one estimate which placed the financial loss to third world countries 'at over $2.5 billion per year during the last decade' (Todaro, 1985, p. 372). Looking at the same issue from the industrial countries' perspective, the United Nations estimated that 'perhaps as much as a fifth to a quarter of the growth of real output in the industrial countries during 1985 was due to gains in terms of trade' (United Nations, 1986, p. 13). One of the main reasons for this relative drop of third world primary commodity prices is overproduction and cut-throat competition among third world countries for the markets of industrialised countries. Despite all this over-production, the World Bank and the development agencies of various industrialised countries are funding projects in several third world countries for the production of such commodities as rubber, palm oil, cotton and other products whose prices have plummeted in recent years.

The situation is particularly difficult in those third world countries where one or two products dominate their exports— a situation which is not at all uncommon. Thus in 1981, according to UNCTAD, twenty of the thirty-five least developed countries relied on one product for 50 per cent of their exports and eleven countries relied on one product for 67 per cent of their exports. Several countries showed an even higher degree of concentration in their exports: coffee accounted for 60 per cent of the value of all exports in Ethiopia, 79 per cent in Burundi, 60 per cent in Rwanda, and 95 per cent in Uganda. Cotton accounted for 78 per cent of exports in Chad, 52 per cent in Mali, and 24 per cent in the Sudan (UNCTAD, 1984, table 15, pp. 16–18). Zambia relied for 94 per cent of its export earnings on copper, Cuba on sugar for 84 per cent of its export earnings, Mauritius on sugar for 90 per cent, Cambodia on groundnuts for 85 per cent, and so on. What is more, this reliance on a couple of products has not changed at all in the least developed countries, and changed only slightly in the larger groups of developing countries during the past twenty years.

Reliance on one or two primary commodities can play havoc with the economy of a country when prices fall sharply as a result of either world overproduction, a fall in the exchange rate of the country *vis à vis* the American dollar or other major currencies, substitution of the product by a synthetic product manufactured in the developed countries, or trade war directed against a particular country because of its political stance. Zambia's reliance on copper provides one of the most striking examples of the effects of price instability on the country's economy. Unlike industrialised countries, third world countries do not have the economic power to protect easily the prices of their products by regulating the levels of production—and yet they must do this if they are to place their products in a stronger bargaining position in the international markets.

Not only have the industrialised countries benefited massively in their trade transactions with third world countries, but they have also been fairly successful in protecting their industries and agriculture from competition by third world products through a series of tariff and non-tariff barriers. Existing tariff systems provide for duty-free treatment of industrial goods with the exception of 'sensitive' products (shoes, textiles and leather goods) but duty-free treatment is limited to only a few selected agricultural products. The result is that, as the UNCTAD report concluded 'potential benefits for the least developed countries ... are small and the effective benefits relatively insignificant' (UNCTAD, 1984).

Moreover, if tariff barriers prove insufficient, then various non-tariff measures can be used—quotas, prohibitions and discretionary licensing. Indeed, non-tariff barriers are becoming increasingly used, and they may affect exports from developing countries more severely than tariffs. It is true that these tariff and non-tariff barriers are used by industrial countries in relation to imports from other industrial countries, but some of the non-tariff barriers affect particularly those products which come from developing countries. Thus, in 1984, non-tariff barriers imposed by industrial countries affected 11.3 per cent of all imports from other industrial countries, but almost twice as high a proportion—20.6 per cent—of imports from developing countries. (World Development Report, 1986, *ibid.*, table 2.5, p. 23). The overall result of these various trade barriers has been to reduce the volume and range of exports from developing to developed countries, to reduce the earnings of developing countries from foreign trade, and hence to make economic development in third world countries more difficult.

All the evidence, therefore, shows that international trade has operated on terms that are disadvantageous to developing countries as a group. There are, however, several qualifications to this conclusion: producers of certain primary products have done considerably better either because of the nature of the product or the organisation of the producer countries. Oil has fared better than tin; coffee has done better than tea; hides have been more profitable than cotton; and so on. Moreover, larger countries have been able to withstand the trade disadvantages better than the smaller developing countries, and this is reflected in their higher rates of economic growth (United Nations, 1986, p. 13). Despite these trade disadvantages, there is no way that developing countries can either individually or collectively cut themselves off from the world trading system. What they can do, however, is to reduce their reliance on trade with industrialised countries and to increase trade and economic co-operation among themselves, as far as possible, financially and politically.

This massive trade loss has been one of the major reasons why the non-oil-producing developing countries have had to borrow from the industrialised world in order to expand their economies and to provide public services to meet the rising aspirations of their citizens. This has come to be known as 'aid' and it has taken various forms which we shall now proceed to examine in order to establish whether it has helped or hindered economic development and the alleviation of poverty.

Aid to developing countries
Financial flows from the rich to the poor countries are of two major types: first, lending which is made on purely commercial terms by banks and other financial institutions when interest rates are set at the prevailing commercial levels, repayment periods are fixed, and the ability of the borrower to repay the loan is a crucial consideration. Second, financial transactions which are made by governments or other official or voluntary bodies on non-commerical terms. These trans-

actions can be either grants which do not have to be paid back
or loans at low interest rates and with long repayment periods.
It is this second type of lending which constitutes aid (Official
Development Assistance) from the rich to the poor countries.
Our aim here is not to review the massive literature on the
subject but merely to assess the importance of aid to development and hence to the reduction or otherwise of poverty in
third world countries.

Table 5.3 shows several important trends in the composition
of financial flows to third world countries. First, a substantial
proportion of these flows has always been in the form of
commercial transactions. This proportion rises and falls in
accordance with the degree of profitability that is possible at
any one time and not according to the needs of developing
countries. When banks and governments in rich countries feel
that it is safe and profitable to lend to the governments of developing countries this proportion is high; at other
times they naturally lend less;. The same point emerges from
the fact that most of the financial flows—90 per cent in 1982—
to the poorest thirty-six of the developing countries is official
development assistance. There is no good commercial reason
for banks to lend vast sums of money to these countries
(UNCTAD, 1984, table 1.4, p. 24). Second, most of the ODA
comes from the seventeen rich capitalist countries directly in
the form of bilateral aid. All governments prefer bilateral aid
because it allows them freedom to decide which developing
countries 'to help' and for what purpose. Channelling aid
through such multilateral agencies as the World Bank, IMF,
ILO, WHO, FAO, UNICEF and so on reduces this freedom,
particularly for the smaller countries. Third, the proportion of
aid from voluntary agencies has always been small despite the
high profile of many of these agencies. Nevertheless, it is aid
which is used mostly for meeting basic needs directly and for
projects related to these needs.

The volume of ODA as a proportion of GNP of the donor
countries has declined over the years: for the DAC countries it
declined from 0.51 in 1960 to 0.36 in 1986; and for the OPEC
countries from 2.92 per cent in 1975 to 1.06 per cent in 1986. A
certain degree of 'aid fatigue' seems to have set in over the
years reflecting doubts about the effectiveness of aid to

development. Thus a public opinion study in the USA in 1979 found that '77 per cent of the correspondents were in favor of maintaining or increasing "aid to combat hunger" but support dropped to 49 per cent when put in terms of "economic aid" to developing countries' (Burki and Ayres, 1986). There are also substantial variations among countries in the proportion of GNP that they allocate to aid. If one uses the United Nations' aid target of 0.70 per cent of GNP, only five countries achieved it in 1986 among the DAC group and three of these were Scandinavian countries. Aid from the United States is crucial because of the country's international role: it has the second lowest figure among the DAC group, 0.23 per cent of GNP, though, in absolute terms, its contribution is by far the largest single country contribution.

Table 5.3 *Percentage composition of financial flows to developing countries 1960–85*

		1960	1970	1975	1980	1985
		%	%	%	%	%
I	Official development assistance	59	46	45	35	60
	1. DAC bilateral aid	48	28	14	14	28
	2. OPEC ,, ,,	—	2	10	7	3
	3. Multilateral aid	2	5	7	6	9
	4. Multilateral non-concessional lending	2	3	4	4	11
II	Export credits	14	13	10	13	4
III	Private flows	27	41	45	51	36
	1. Direct investment	19	18	20	9	10
	2. Bank sector	6	15	21	38	16
	3. Bonds	—	2	1	1	5
Total I, II and III		100	100	100	100	100

Source: OECD, 1986, p. 9.

The conditions attached to aid-giving are just as important as the amount of aid to both the donor and the recipient country. It can mean that the recipient country has to use aid for the purchase of goods from the donor country or for the payment of the salaries of experts from donor countries, or to send students to donor countries, and so on. As expected, bilateral aid is more likely to be tied to these conditions than multilateral aid, but in both cases the published figures of tied aid are underestimates. Official reports acknowledge both this fact as well as the detrimental effects of tied aid to developing countries which we shall discuss later. Thus the OECD report for 1984 acknowledged that though 'the untied percentage of bilateral aid as reported by DAC countries is still relatively high (53 per cent in 1982/83) this figure may underestimate the actual volume of tied aid because of the increasing number of informal arrangements to secure procurement' (OECD, 1984, p. 93).

The uses to which aid has been put have changed over the years reflecting not so much the changing needs of developing countries but rather the changing views of donor countries and the international agencies about the appropriate notion of development. In the 1950s and early 1960s most aid was used to build roads, power stations and railways with very little going to agriculture and even less to the expansion of the social services. This reflected the then prevailing notion of development through industrialisation but, as mentioned in Chapter 1, when this was replaced with the notion of development through 'basic needs', aid was diverted to agricultural and social services. Today most tied aid is for agricultural projects and for the development of education and health (OECD, 1984, table V1.4, p. 221). The preferences of donor countries are equally marked in the geographical allocation of their aid. France and the UK give most of their aid to their ex-colonies, the USA to countries of strategic importance to its world interests, Australia to its neighbouring countries, and so on.

All that has been said so far points to the fact that aid is given to promote the interests of the donor country at least as much as those of the recipient country. It is for this reason that aid is not given primarily to those developing countries with the lowest income per capita where the need is greatest. As Burki and Ayres, members of the World Bank Task Force on Aid, point out, 'low-income countries receive only about 40 per cent of ODA, with the remainder going to middle-income countries (if low-income countries are defined ... as those with GNP per capita of less than $400 in 1983)' (Burki and Ayres, 1986). Thus, during the decade 1973–83, the top four recipient countries, in terms of aid per capita, were Jordan, Israel,

Oman and Syria—all strategically important to the USA and the West. The USSR is no different in this, since most of its aid goes to Cuba, Angola and other third world countries that are strategically important to its political and economic interests. All this has been acknowledged by several government spokesmen in both the USA and the UK as the following quotation from an American government aid official amply shows:

> The biggest single misconception about the foreign aid program is that we send money abroad. We don't. Foreign aid consists of American equipment, raw materials, expert services, and food—all provided for specific development projects which we ourselves review and approve.... Ninety-three per cent of AID funds are spent directly in the United States to pay for these things. (Gaud, 1968)

Even the Word Bank, which is the main body of multilateral aid, acknowledges that self-interest and a modicum of humanitarianism are the main motives for aid-giving: 'Donors supply official assistance for many different reasons: to assist the economic development of the recipient; to further their own strategic, political and commercial interests; to maintain historical and cultural ties; and to express their humanitarian concern' (World Development Report, 1985, p. 100).

Motives influence but they do not necessarily determine the outcomes of a policy or programme. Evaluating the effects of aid is as important as it is difficult, and all we can do here is to review the research findings and the views of competing schools of thought on the subject. On a broad issue like this, findings are bound to be ambiguous and opinions are inevitably divided. Empirical studies of the effectiveness of aid in promoting economic growth and in reducing poverty are of two main types: macro-economic studies, which seek to establish whether the volume of aid given to specific countries is related to their rate of economic growth or to the reduction of poverty; and second, evaluation of the effectiveness of specific aid projects.

The general conclusion of macro-economic studies regarding the effects of aid on economic growth is, at best, neutral and, at worst, discouraging to the advocates of aid. Mosley's study covering the twenty-year period 1960–80 for aid to all developing countries, as well as for aid to developing countries arranged by continent, concluded that 'we cannot confirm for any continent or either decade' any significant and positive correlation between volume of aid and rate of economic growth (Mosley, 1986). More optimistically, a recent OECD report argues that some of the developing countries with the fastest rates of economic growth have also been major recipients of aid during the period 1970–82, but it also accepts that 'many low income countries which have received major amounts of financial and technical assistance have not made very significant progress'. It also points out that aid could not have been the decisive factor either for the high or the low performers (OECD, 1985, p. 280). The issue clearly is so complex that the findings of such statistical macro-economic studies need to be treated with caution—they depend on the methodology used, the countries included, the period covered, and so on.

Macro-studies of the effects of aid on the reduction of poverty are even more difficult for the definition of poverty is far more open to debate than the definition of economic growth. If by poverty one means the reduction in the proportion of people dying of malnutrition and famine, then aid must have had a positive effect. Similarly, if by poverty one means the improvement of health and education standards in general, then aid must have had a positive effect. If, however, by poverty one means the amount of income accruing to the lowest income groups in society, then the conclusions are pessimistic. Thus even the most optimistic assessment of the effectiveness of aid programmes on poverty reduction by Cassen for the Task Force on Concessional Flows concluded that, though the 'proportion of people in poverty seemed to be declining in several developing countries in the 1970s, progress has probably been halted by the global recession' (Cassen, 1986). Others are more forthright in rejecting aid as a medium for alleviating poverty. Griffin, for example, argues that the evidence suggests that despite all the aid 'the standard of living of many poor people, particularly those in the rural areas, has fallen substantially in the last 10 or 15 years' (Griffin, 1986). What we cannot tell is whether the incomes of the poor would have been relatively higher, lower, or no different without the volume of aid given to their governments.

If attempts to evaluate the effects of aid from a global macro-perspective have not been very illuminating, what of the evaluation studies of individual projects from a more micro-perspective? The general conclusion is far more optimistic at the project level, but rather uncertain with regard to the implications of project completion for either economic growth or poverty. The usual approach of these project evaluation studies is to attempt to establish the extent to which the project's stated aims have been achieved within a certain period of time. The period normally allowed for is six months after the completion of the project, with the result that, for some projects, this is a premature evaluation of their effects. The second weakness of this approach is that, though a project may have been completed successfully, it is hard to measure its effects on economic growth, let alone poverty. The extreme example is a project that involves the construction of a road: it may be successful six months after the road completion but may be a failure in five years' time if the road collapses either through lack of adequate maintenance or initial faulty con-struction. Moreover, it is hard to measure the effects of the road, even if successfully completed, on economic growth and poverty. These two qualifications need to be borne in mind when summarising the findings of the various project evalu-ation studies.

The World Bank claims that, out of almost one thousand of its projects completed during the ten year period up to 1985, the vast majority of projects were successful in varying degrees and 'only 14 per cent of the projects, accounting for 9 per cent of total investment, were judged at the time of audit to be unsatisfactory or uncertain in outcome' (World Development Report, 1985, p. 103). This is a very high rate of success though, as explained above, the definition of success is of limited value. A more extensive evaluation study financed by the Development Committee of the DAC countries and headed by Cassen, which examined the performance of all projects by Western countries, in Bangladesh, Colombia, India, Kenya, South Korea, Malawi, and Mali, reached equally optimistic conclusions: 'Between two thirds and three quarters of aid projects (and somewhat more in the case of the

World Bank) are judged satisfactory by rate-of-return or other criteria; a small percentage (less than 10 per cent) failed to produce any of the desired results' (Cassen, 1986a; see also Cassen, 1986).

Cassen also claims that aid had 'a substantial direct effect on poverty' despite the fact that very little aid 'had been directed at or had any effect (positive or negative) on the very poorest people'. In other words, poor people may have benefited through programmes directed at all sections of the community. Clearly this is a complex area and project evaluations cannot provide much more than indications of the possible effects of aid. Nevertheless, there seems to be a paradox: micro-studies suggest that most projects are successful and hence contribute to economic growth, while macro-studies suggest the opposite—i.e. they have no bearing on economic growth. Research has thus been unable to provide conclusive evidence that can settle the debate on the effectiveness of aid. It is, therefore, important to review briefly the debate.

Critics of aid to developing countries come from the right and the left wings of the political spectrum and their criticisms are both pragmatic and theoretical in nature. Here we shall concentrate on the main criticisms rather than look at the views of these groups of critics separately.

The first such criticism is that many of these aid projects are prestige projects and they have no bearing on economic development. Indeed, they are not only wasteful of foreign aid but they 'represent a drain also on domestic resources' (Bauer and Yamey, 1981). It is difficult to deny this, though there are legitimate differences of opinion on the magnitude of the problem.

Second, aid projects often lack co-ordination, with the result that they cause confusion and they also lose out in their effectiveness. The World Bank acknowledges this problem, though it does not seem to view it in the same serious way as its critics. It is a problem that can be sorted out rather than an inherent problem of aid that is not amenable to solution.

Third, many projects are based on ideas and values that are generally acceptable in the industrialised world but which are alien in many devleoping countries, particularly when they are introduced with little, if any, local consultation and participation. Again, this is a practical problem acknowledged by the World Bank but one which is amenable to change.

Fourth, when aid is tied it tends to benefit the donor countries more than the recipient in several ways: it results in the import of goods and services at inflated prices from the donor country and, claims Hayter, 'it can be used not only to open up new markets, but also to sell otherwise uncompetitive products' (Hayter, 1981, p. 84). The World Bank accepts some of this criticism and points out that tied aid 'reduces the value of development loans by about 15 to 20 per cent and in individual cases by much more' (World Bank, 1985, p. 101).

Fifth, most of the aid is used to pay the salaries of professionals and civil servants in both the donor and the recipient country, with the result that very little aid finds its way to the poor in developing societies. Moreover, it is difficult to see what can be done about this, bearing in mind the power structures of developing societies as well as the ability of professionals to manipulate situations to their advantage. All these five criticisms are shared in varying degrees by the critics of the left and right but they diverge from here on.

The sixth criticism, which is central to the right wing critique, is that aid does more harm than good to economic development because it undermines what little local initiative there is; it expands government activity; it makes people dependent on governments and it leads to inefficiency all round. Countries develop through the entrepreneurial efforts of their citizens and not through outside donations or government planning. It is a criticism very much in line with the modernisation thesis and the anti-collectivist view that governments should interfere as little as possible in economic affairs (Bauer, 1971).

The seventh criticism, that comes from the left and reflects the Marxist or dependency position, is that aid is used as a means of preserving the capitalist system on a world scale and it is inherently detrimental to the interests of third world countries. Hayter expresses this view most strongly in all her work, as the following quotation shows:

> Aid can be regarded as a concession by the imperialist powers to enable them to continue their exploitation of the semi-colonial countries; it is

similar in its effects to reform within capitalist countries, in the sense that the exploiting classes relinquish the minimum necessary in order to retain their essential interests' (Hayter, 1971, pp. 8–12; see also Hayter, and Watson, 1985)

Clearly, the contribution of aid to economic growth and to the reduction of poverty is strongly contested on both theoretical and pragmatic grounds, and the whole debate reflects the division of opinion on development and underdevelopment discussed in Chapter 1. Bauer and other right-wing critics follow through the logic of their thesis to argue for the abolition of official aid as it operates today. Instead, any aid given should be bilateral only, it should not be tied, it should be in the form of donations and it should be restricted solely to the 'relief of disaster' (Bauer and Yamey, 1981). On the other hand, Hayter feels that aid on a big scale is still necessary, particularly for the smaller developing countries, but it should not be tied, it should be in the form of grants and it should not be given in order to bolster right-wing regimes in third world countries.

What then can we conclude from all this heated debate on the usefulness of aid to economic development and the reduction of poverty? Clearly most aid is given primarily with the economic and political interests of the donor countries in mind. Only in the exceptional circumstances of famine relief is aid given for primarily humanitarian, altruistic reasons. Moreover, the effects of aid on development depend not only on the motives of its donors but also on the type of policies pursued by individual governments in third world countries. Thus the effectiveness of aid to third world development must vary from one country to another depending on the internal government policies, the type of aid being granted and how the country's exports fit into the prevailing world market. Because of all these constraints, the contribution of aid to economic growth and the reduction of poverty can only have been marginal over the years for the developing countries as a whole.

All this is not an argument for the reduction or abolition of aid, but rather for changes in the conditions attached to it and the ways in which projects are formulated and implemented. There is a need to reduce the extent of tied aid as it has operated over the years, though this does not necessarily mean that no conditions should be attached to aid. Rather the need is to attach conditions that aid should be used for basic needs projects rather than for the purchase of goods and services from the industrialised countries, as has so far been the case. Similarly, the need to involve the local population in the formulation and implementation of projects is now generally recognised. What is at issue is not so much the changes that need to be made if aid is to make a real contribution to third world development, but rather the political feasibility of such changes. Aid represents an unequal symbiotic relationship between two groups of countries—the givers and the receivers—which confers benefits to both sides and it is difficult to see why the stronger group would willingly give up its advantageous position in the relationship. Questions of aid are also, more than at any time before, connected with the question of third world debt to banks and governments in industrialised countries. What the industrialised world gives in aid to the third world it more than takes back in debt repayment instalments, as the following section shows.

DEBT OF DEVELOPING COUNTRIES

As we saw in the previous section, most of the lending to developing countries up to 1970 was in ODA, either in free grants or in low-interest loans. Lending by banks on purely commercial terms was of less importance. Yet by 1980, the situation was reversed, with commercial lending being more important than ODA. It is this increased commercial bank lending which is mainly responsible for the increased indebtedness of developing countries. While in 1970 the outstanding debt of all developing countries stood at $68 billion, by 1984 it reached $686 billion—a tenfold increase—despite the massive amounts of money that had been repaid during the period. The Third World was, and still is, as we shall see below, in the unenviable position of having to repay increasingly more every year in order to stand still in terms of the amount of debt it owed to the American, British, Swiss, Japanese and other banks.

It is generally agreed that the reasons for this heavy indebtedness are both external and internal to developing countries, though there is no doubt that the external factors are by far the most significant (Adedji, 1985). It is true that governments in developing countries overcommitted themselves and, for a variety of reasons, they increased public expenditure too far and too fast but this, in itself, would not have led to their present state of indebtedness. The rise in oil prices in 1973 and 1979 was the first major external reason for third world debt. This is shown by the fact that, while in 1973 the deficit on their current account as a group amounted to just 0.08 per cent of their GNP, it rose to 3.5 per cent in 1974 and 4.0 per cent in 1975.

The second major external reason was the sharp rise in interest rates in industrial countries, which meant that borrowing became more expensive at a time when the need for borrowing also increased. High interest rates obviously mean high profits for the lending banks but, they also mean cuts in living standards in third world countries. As the Archbishop of Sao Paolo graphically put it: 'Everytime the United States raises its interest rates, thousands die in the Third World because money that would be used for health care and food is sent outside these countries to repay the debt' (Arms, 1985).

The third and fourth external reasons for Third World debt were the decline in both the volume and the prices of exports—other than oil—to the industrialised countries as a result of the recession. Cline estimates that these four factors account for 85 per cent of the total rise in indebtedness by the non-oil developing countries during the period 1973–82 (Cline, 1983, quoted in Todaro, 1985, p. 558).

Moreover, the need for borrowing coincided with the growth in the revenues of the OPEC countries and the resultant problem of their utilisation. Bankers were more than pleased to act as mediators for the lending of funds to developing countries, confident that both the OPEC countries and their banks would do well out of the deal. As Allsopp and Joshi put it, 'there was little but praise and self-congratulation over the way the market system seemed to cope with redirecting OPEC savings to rapidly growing third world countries where the economic returns were high' (Allsopp and Joshi, 1986) Profit being the primary motive, most of the bank lending was directed at the middle-income group of developing countries rather than the low-income group. Thus seven middle-income countries—Brazil, Mexico, Argentina, Venezuela, Indonesia, South Korea and the Philippines— accounted for 44 per cent of the total non-concessional bank debt of all 123 indebted developing countries in 1984 (Lever and Huhne, 1985, p. 23).

The definition of 'debt crisis' is indicative of a lot of thinking in this area. The 'debt crisis' originated from Mexico's declaration in 1982 that it was no longer able to pay its debt. Thus the banking community of rich countries was faced with 'a crisis' of how to get debts owed to it paid. The 'crisis' was not the suffering caused to so many people in third world countries by endless massive debt payments, but rather the possibility that banks in the rich world might not be able to continue receiving these vast sums every year in repayment of the loans that they made to third world countries. The solution to the 'crisis' was therefore one which enabled the banks to continue receiving their repayment instalments. In order to implement this solution, the banks needed the assistance of the two major international finance institutions—the IMF and the World Bank—which was not slow in forthcoming.

The package, known as 'debt re-scheduling', consisted of three main interrelated policy strands: the banks would extend the period of debt repayment, the debtor countries would introduce austerity programmes and the IMF would provide some further financial help to debtor countries to enable them to repay their debts. The strategy has so far worked out fairly well as far as the banks and the industrialised world are concerned. Indeed, it has worked out better than first envisaged. Unexpectedly, 'the debtor countries have proved willing to tolerate bigger cuts in living standards and made more of their resources available for transfer to the industrialised world than most of their creditors thought possible in the immediate aftermath of the debt crisis' (Kaletsky, 1986, p. 3).

For the third world debtor countries, the policy has been disastrous, for it has resulted in vast sums of money being paid to the banks, with the result that they now pay far more than they receive in loans or aid from the industrialised world. The United Nations Economic Commission for Latin America and the Caribbean (ECLAC since 1985 but ECLA before then) has estimated that the region paid on average $25 billion a year more between 1982 and 1985 than it received from the industrialised countries, and that most of this negative net transfer of money went to the United States (Griffith-Jones, 1986). Despite all this, the amount of third world debt continues to grow, not because of increasing loans but because of increasing accumulated interest amounts.

Table 5.4 shows the seriousness of the debt problem and the extent to which all the debt indicators have worsened between 1970 and 1984. The relative size of the debt of a country is perhaps best expressed as a proportion of its GNP and, as table 5.4 shows, this ratio for all developing countries was 33.8 per cent in 1984. This average conceals a range of figures with twenty-seven countries having a debt/GNP ratio of 50 per cent and five countries a ratio of over 100 per cent. Perhaps the best guide to a country's ability to pay back its debt is the proportion of export earnings that have to be used up in order to pay both the interest on the debt and the instalment of the principal loan—the debt service ratio. This amounted to 19.7 per cent for all developing countries in 1984, but for nine countries it exceeded 30 per cent. These figures are likely to get worse if the present policies of debt repayment continue and if the world economic recession does not improve. It is no wonder that some —Peru for example—have insisted that they are not prepared to pay more than 10 per cent of their export earnings for debt repayments. High repayment ratios mean both a direct reduction in living standards—a mixture of lower real wages, greater taxation, less social services and more poverty—and a lower proportion of the country's income being invested for the development of its industry and agriculture, which, in turn, results in a reduced ability to pay the debt. Thus high debt ratios are counterproductive even for the banks and the industrialised countries. It is for this reason that Lever and Huhne conclude their assessment of the debt problem that the 'debt crisis' may have been smoothed over for the time being but it has not been resolved: 'The volcano of the debt crisis is dormant but far from extinct', they declare (Lever and Huhne, 1985, p. 144).

Broadly speaking there are two main alternative strategies to

Table 5.4   Debt indicators for developing countries

Debt indicator	1970	1984
Ratio of Debt to GNP	14.1	33.8
Ratio of Debt to Exports	108.9	135.4
Debt Service Ratio	14.7	19.7
Ratio of Interest Service to GNP	0.5	2.8
Total Debt outstanding and disbursed	$68 billion	$686 billion
Private Debt as percentage of total	50.9	65.0

Source: World Bank, *World Development Report, 1985*, Table 2.6, p. 24.

dealing with third world debt, apart from continuing as at present and creating even more hardship in third world countries. The first strategy consists of a series of measures that, on one hand, reduce both the amount of debt and the interest rates while, on the other, they extend the period of repayment as well as the financial help offered by the governments of industrialised countries. The aim of the strategy is to enable the banks to get as much as possible in repayment of their loans while not destroying the economies and undermining the political stability of third world countries. It is a strategy that may or may not work because the serviceability of debt even under these terms depends, as Faber argues, 'upon a host of other unknowns like future interest rates, the relative behaviour of commodity and other prices, the weakness of the dollar, and how tolerant populations in debtor countries will remain of their governments' willingness to transfer 4 per cent or 5 per cent of everything they produce to foreign creditor banks' (Faber, 1987). It is for these reasons that many commentators believe that an increasing number of developing countries will find it impossible to service their debts and will have no option but to resort to the second solution, i.e. repudiate their entire debt obligations.

This is clearly a prospect that banks and governments in the West and the IMF do not relish, and will do all in their power to avert. It is a solution that will only come about if several large indebted developing countries join together in a debtors' cartel to counteract the obvious financial and political pressures that will be directed at them. Once one large developing country manages to set a precedent without incurring retaliation or copes well with any retaliatory measures, other developing countries would follow its example (Devlin, 1984). The fact that no developing country has so far repudiated its debt is an indication of the fears of retaliation, as well as of the divisions of class interests within developing societies. The upper socio-economic groups within developing societies have an interest in finding compromise solutions to the debt problem so long as these solutions do not create an internal political situation that threatens the political stability of the country and hence their overthrow. There is, therefore, some truth in the claim by Hayter and Watson that the absence of any total debt repudiation so far is 'an illustration of the pre-eminence of class over national interests' though the position is more complicated than that (Hayter and Watson, 1985, p. 34).

It is not possible to measure precisely the adverse effects of debt servicing on living standards in developing countries. Yet if one uses incomes per capita as a rough yardstick of national economic standards, one finds that they have declined in most Latin American countries in recent years. Thus comparing the relevant figures for 1982 and 1985, incomes per capita expressed in American dollars dropped from 2240 to 1640 in Brazil; 2270 to 2080 in Mexico; 2520 to 2130 in Argentina; 2210 to 1430 in Chile; 2650 to 1650 in Uruguay; 1310 to 1160 in Peru, and so on (World Development Report, 1984, table 1, pp. 218–19 and World Development Report, 1987, table 1, pp. 202–3). Clearly, there are many other factors for this, such as the rise in population, the reduction in commodity prices and so on, but it is hard to believe that debt servicing on such a massive scale is unconnected with the sharp drop in living standards. The point, moreover, has been made several times in this book that during periods of economic recession, the living standards of the lower income groups drop more sharply than those of other groups in society.

CONCLUSION

All the evidence shows that the current complex network of financial transactions between advanced industrial and third world countries works to the advantage of the former. Obviously there are exceptions to this but, as a general statement, it stands. Contrary to the commonly held view in affluent countries that the West is giving aid to promote economic development in the Third World, the available evidence shows that the reverse is happening today—the Third World is subsidising the rich, affluent countries. This is the result of the massive debt interest repayments, the fall in commodity prices relative to the price of manufactured goods, the trade barriers created against imports of certain goods from developing countries and the conditions attached to part of the aid programme. The main source of subsidy from the West to third world countries is the untied, interest-free aid, granted bilaterally or multilaterally, and this in no way equals the amount of subsidy that flows in the opposite direction. Estimates of the exact amounts of net flows from third world countries to advanced industrial countries have to be treated with caution, but the figures are so substantial that a certain margin of error does not change the overall conclusion. Thus Salim Lane, editor-in-chief of the United Nations publication, *Africa Recovery*, estimates that in 1986 Africa 'received about $15 billion in assistance, an amount smaller than the $19 billion loss in commodity income, not to mention the $16 billion expended in debt service' (Lane, 1987). This is in addition to the ECLA estimate for Latin America, referred to earlier, supporting the same conclusion.

Within this unfavourable external economic climate, even the best governments with the most appropriate policies will fail. Where this unfavourable external economic climate is compounded by internal political factors or natural disasters, the result is catastrophic. Media attention in advanced industrial countries, however, has so often concentrated on the internal factors that the main reason—the unfavourable external economic climate—is lost sight of. Yet until this is recognised, there is no basis for a rational public discussion of the reasons and the solutions to third world poverty.

The abolition of subsistence poverty in third world countries depends first, on a substantial improvement in their economic fortunes so that there are sufficient economic resources to meet the basic needs of everyone; and second, on a more equal distribution of income so that the rising economic affluence 'trickles down' to the lower socio-economic groups. Bearing in mind the distribution of power at the world level and within individual countries, it is hard to see how the abolition of poverty in the Third World can be achieved in the immediate future. From the longer term point of view, the process of poverty alleviation will vary from one third world country to another. In some, subsistence poverty will be reduced through relatively peaceful political processes; in others a violent revolution may be the only way out; and in some others the problem may prove insuperable. The abolition of under-nutrition is, however, a more achievable goal for it does not demand the same amount of resources and it does not meet with the same degree of opposition as the abolition of subsistence poverty. The experience of the affluent advanced industrial societies is not irrelevant on this issue; undernutrition has been largely abolished but subsistence poverty still exists on a large scale. There is no reason to believe that those third world countries which gradually become more affluent will adopt forms of income distribution that are very different from those prevailing in advanced industrial societies of either the capitalist or the centrally planned type.

6 Conclusion

Despite the substantial economic growth that has taken place in all parts of the world during the post-war period, material inequalities between the industrialised and the third world countries remain very substantial. A small number of third world countries have managed to narrow the gap that separated them from the industrialised countries, but the majority have seen their relative position in the world either unchanged or worsened. Living standards have risen in all countries but they have risen faster in the industrialised world than in most parts of the Third World, with the result that the social stratification system of the world has changed very little.

A very similar process seems to have taken place in relation to the stratification systems of individual countries. In the industrialised world, wealth inequalities within countries have declined but most of the redistribution has been from the very rich to the rich. The bottom two thirds of the population have benefited very little from this redistribution. Income inequalities have also declined but, again, the redistribution has been confined mostly within the top third of income earners. The position is even less encouraging in the case of third world countries. Wealth and income inequalities are more extreme and, in most countries, they have either remained constant or even widened during the post-war period. In only a small number of third world countries have these inequalities narrowed. The experience of the centrally planned societies has been rather different: wealth inequalities have diminished as a result of the nationalisation of enterprises and sometimes of agriculture, but income inequalities have not narrowed as much. What is more, their economies have not expanded any faster than those of comparative capitalist societies, with the result that their more egalitarian income distribution patterns have reduced the risk of absolute poverty and starvation but they have failed to raise general living standards very much.

Poverty and inequality are related but they are two different concepts. Poverty is the lowest part of inequality which is generally considered unacceptable and which societies and governments attempt to reduce or abolish. It is a relative concept in the sense that the poverty level varies from one country to another depending on the prevailing living standards. Thus the living standards of the poor in the industrialised world are not only considerably higher than those of the poor in the Third World but also higher than those of the vast majority of people in the third world countries. For this reason, comparisons between the extent of poverty in the two groups of countries are, in essence, meaningless.

It is also relative in the sense that what is considered necessary for its abolition changes over time within any one country. At all times and in all countries, however, there is a core of basic necessities which is irreducible and which must be satisfied if people are not to be in poverty. Thus poverty consists of a core of basic necessities that is universal and timeless as well as a list of other necessities that change over time and place. We have seen that the extent of poverty in the industrialised countries has declined substantially since the end of the last world war as a result of the rise in real wages, the reduction in unemployment for most of the period, and the improvement in the social security benefit schemes. Nevertheless, poverty remains substantial, due partly to cost considerations and partly to the fears that measures to abolish it would undermine work incentives and hence economic growth and profits. There is no good economic or financial reason for the existence of poverty in these countries because they all have enough wealth to ensure that all their citizens achieve a minimum standard of living. On present evidence, however, it is most unlikely that governments will act to abolish poverty in the foreseeable future.

Poverty in the third world is both more widespread and

more physiological than it is in the industrialised world. Poverty means starvation of varying degrees, and it affects a very large section of the population of most third world countries. For some, no amount of internal redistribution can abolish poverty because they do not possess enough resources to meet the basic needs of all their citizens even at the lowest physiological level. Others are in a better economic position and they have the resources to abolish poverty, if they so choose. Some progress has taken place in some third world countries where the incidence of poverty has declined during the post-war period, but in most of them poverty has either remained unchanged or has increased. This is by far the most depressing and worrying feature of post-war economic development, and it does not auger at all well for the immediate future.

There has been no shortage of theories of development at the world level, or of theories of poverty within individual countries. All theories are policy packages, too, and as such they have obvious implications for the constituent parties, be they groups of individuals or countries. In this book we have attempted to relate theories of development at the international level to theories of poverty at the intranational level. The modernisation theory, that attempts to explain the poverty of nations, is very similar to the culture of poverty theory that purports to explain the poverty of individuals and families within countries. Both approaches see poverty as the result of individual inadequacies, be they the values or skills of individuals or those of entire nations. It has been the theory favoured by many governments and international official agencies, even though it is now rejected by most social scientists, particularly since it has been found wanting in practice. The orthodox Marxist explanation sees poverty at the individual and the country level as the inevitable result of exploitation that is inherent in capitalist systems. In the same way that the capitalist class exploits the working class within a country, the capitalist classes of the industrialised world collectively exploit the third world countries through an interlocking network of economic, political and cultural mechanisms. The orthodox Marxist position sees exploitation as an undesirable means to a desirable end—socialism—and it is fairly hopeful that progress is taking place in both the industrialised and third world countries. This total emphasis on class and the very optimistic outlook for economic growth, equality and socialism in third world countries are the Achilles heel of the orthodox Marxist theory. There is no evidence to support such optimism, whether it comes from the modernisers or from the orthodox Marxists. The neo-Marxist approach, however, is far more cautious about the possibilities of progress, particularly in third world countries, as well as more aware of the complexities of the stratification systems of third world countries. It is, therefore, more useful for analysing and understanding issues of development and underdevelopment in the Third World.

A variant of the Marxist position—the dependency thesis—takes a much more global view of wealth and poverty: they are both the result of a long chain of exploitative trade relationships starting at the financial centres of the industrialised world and running through the capitals of the Third World right down to the impoverished town dweller and the landless labourer of the countryside. Profit flows upwards, with the result that wealth is concentrated in the industrialised world and poverty is dominant in the Third World. There are no prospects of improvements at the national level in third world countries—only a world socialist revolution can initiate the changes that can lead to greater equality both between and within nations. The total pessimism and the virtual disregard of political processes within countries deprive the dependency theory of any meaningful analytical power. Finally, there is the structuralist explanation which stresses the unequal distribution of power as the main reason for poverty at both national and the world level. It considers wealth and poverty as two sides of the same coin, for they are both the result of unequal economic and political relationships. Its main difference from the neo-Marxist perspective centres around the issue of the sources of power: unlike the Marxist perspective, which makes class and class relations the main source of power and the main axis of conflict, the structuralist perspective sees class as one of a small number of sources of power—the others being race, religion, gender and occupational grouping. It is for this reason that the analysis presented in this book leans so heavily on the structuralist perspective.

Each theory has not only its own explanation of what has happened so far but also its own prediction for the future. These vary, as we saw, from the very optimistic views of the modernisation and orthodox Marxist position to the utter pessimism of the dependency thesis, and to the very cautious and uncertain approaches of the neo-Marxist and structuralist perspectives. The question of how successful impoverished countries, or impoverished groups within countries, will be in their efforts to improve their relative standards of living is as crucial as it is impossible to answer with any degree of confidence. There are, however, a number of general points that can be made that are relevant to the question. The first and obvious point is that the redistribution of income necessary for the abolition of poverty is a more likely possibility in industrialised than in third world countries partly because they possess the wealth to do it and partly because their political systems are more amenable to pressures for anti-poverty programmes. The second general point is that a great deal will depend on the future rates of economic growth and particularly on the types of policies pursued to achieve such growth. High rates of economic growth achieved through policies which provide employment for as many people as possible in third world countries within a favourable world trade system are most likely to reduce poverty levels in the Third World. This, however, is not happening at present: not only are rates of economic growth low but prices of primary commodities from third world countries are at a record low relative to prices of manufactured goods from industrialised countries. Within the rich countries themselves, current policies emphasise economic growth so much at present that their impoverished groups have suffered as a result.

Humanitarianism has always been a weak force in distributional issues at the national but particularly at the international level. At times of economic recession it is even more so, apart from emergency situations of famine and obvious starvation. It is partly for this reason that recent reports on world poverty, of which the Brandt Report is the best known example, have appealed to reason and self-interest to convince governments and the affluent sections of the public that solving the problem of world poverty makes sense for all concerned. The world possesses enough wealth, the rational argument claims, to feed, house and clothe all its people and it is surely in everyone's interest that this should happen. By enabling third world countries to raise their standards of living, industrialised countries also help themselves because they expand the markets for their own exports.

There is, or course, an element of truth in this, since grossly impoverished third world countries cannot afford the imports of manufactures from the industrialised world. But if the industrialised countries were, on the one hand, to pay the Third World realistic, i.e. relatively higher prices for their products and, on the other, charge third world countries realistic, i.e. relatively lower prices for the manufactures it exports to them, then the relative standard of living of their people *vis à vis* that of the Third World would decline. From a rational perspective this would be a desirable trend because most people in affluent countries consume far too much for their own physical and mental health. But voters, governments and corporations do not act in these objectively rational ways, otherwise the problem of poverty, at least within affluent societies themselves, would have been solved by now. Indeed, a similar argument has been used in relation to the reduction of poverty in affluent societies. The poor must be given adequate financial resources in order to stimulate their consumption and to improve their human capital so that the economy of the country can grow to the mutual benefit of all citizens. Its effect on government policies has been marginal but certainly greater than at the international level where the feeling of community does not exist at all.

Private profit at the national level and country profit at the international level govern economic relationships, with the result that the poverty of individuals and of countries is inevitable to a greater or lesser extent. This individualistic mechanism of income distribution has always been buttressed by the ideology of inequality and, more recently, by the ideology of constantly rising consumption—consumerism. It dominates the lives and the aspirations of most people as well as the entire private and public systems of affluent societies.It is propelled incessantly by an ever-expanding consumer technology and an all-embracing acquisitive ideology that is spreading beyond the shores of the affluent societies to the middle-income as well as the impoverished world. It is difficult to see a relaxation, let alone an end, to this disease of constantly rising consumerism, and so long as this exists the poor will be neglected as well as blamed for their condition. Yet a critical examination of consumerism shows that it is an impossible goal at a world level. It is most unlikely that the world possesses sufficient resources to raise the living standards of the Third World—which is the majority of the world's population—to those of the affluent societies. Logically, the only way that the Third World can approximate—let alone reach—the living standards of the affluent is through a reduction or perhaps a change in the consumption patterns of the industrialised world. The likelihood of this happening is, at present, negligible.

The conclusion that flows from all this is that third world countries cannot expect the rich world to help them at its own expense. They must help themselves by adopting policies that emphasise self-reliance as well as increased industrial and commercial co-operation among themselves. Greater emphasis on a South-South form of development, and less emphasis on a north-South approach stands a better chance of raising living standards in the Third World than current policies. There are several major problems in this approach, too, the most obvious of which is that the Third World is not a unified whole. It forms the largest section of the globe and it contains countries whose economic interests, political ambitions and religious ideologies are in conflict. It is equally obvious that the economies of many third world countries are dominated by the industrialised world and by multinational companies whose main interest is increased profits rather than reductions in levels of poverty. Thus the South-South approach emphasising co-operation among third world countries and greater self-reliance is full of difficulties but it, nevertheless, offers a little bit more hope than the current approaches.

The only realistic conclusion that can be drawn from the arguments and facts presented in this book is that, for the immediate future, say to around the year 2000, poverty in the affluent societies as well as starvation and famine in the Third World will be just as extensive as they are today, and they will co-exist with wealth and affluence in much the same exploitative pattern that they do today. There are, of course, some third world countries where the standards of living of the poor will improve, but there are also others where the opposite will happen. Similarly, the position of the poor will improve somewhat in some industrialised countries and will deteriorate somewhat in others. These minor changes will certainly take place but the general picture in the year 2000 will be substantially the same as that of today. From the longer term point of view, the picture can only be uncertain and variable. It is hard to believe, however, that impoverished groups of individuals within affluent countries will not be able eventually to extract the necessary concessions from their governments. At a world level, third world countries possess the economic potential to abolish famine and starvation in their midst and it is, again, hard to believe that they will not be able to achieve this modest goal at different times in the future. It is a gloomy scenario but not a hopeless one. Progress, unfortunately, occurs not in spectacular leaps and bounds but at an exasperating snail-like pace.

Bibliography

Abel-Smith, B., and Townsend, P., *The Poor and the Poorest*, Bell, 1965.

Adedeji, A., 'Foreign Debt and Prospects for Growth in Africa During the 1980s', *The Journal of Modern African Studies*, Vol. 23, *No. 1*, March, 1985.

Adelman, I., and Morris, C. T., *Economic Growth and Social Equity in Developing Countries*, Stanford University Press, 1973.

Ahluwalia, M. S., and Chenery, H. B., 'The Economic Framework, and A Model of Distribution and Growth', in Chenery, H. B. *et al.*, *Redistribution with Growth*, Oxford University Press, 1974.

————, Carter, N. G., and Chenery, H. B., *Growth and Poverty in Developing Countries*, World Bank, 1978.

————, 'Rural Poverty and Agricultural Performance in India', *Journal of Development Studies*, Vol. 14, *No. 3*, April, 1978.

Alavi, H., 'The State in Post-Colonial Societies', in Goulbourne, H. (ed.), *Politics and State in the Third World*, Macmillan, 1979.

Alber, J., 'Some Causes of Social Security Expenditure Development in Western Europe 1949–1977', in Loney, M., *et al.* (eds), *Social Policy and Social Welfare*, Open Univeristy Press, 1983.

Allen, E. A., *Poverty and Social Welfare in Brazil*, University of Glasgow, Institute of Latin American Studies, Occasional Paper No. 44, 1985.

Allsopp, C., and Joshi, V., 'The Assessment: The International Debt Crisis', *Oxford Review of Economic Policy*, Vol. 2, *No. 1*, Spring, 1986.

Altimir, O., 'Poverty in Latin America: a Review of Concepts and Data', *CEPAL Review*, No. 13, April, 1981.

Amin, S., 'Underdevelopment and Dependence in Black Africa: Origins and Contemporary Forms', *Journal of Modern African Studies*, vol. 10, *No. 4*, 1972.

215

————, *Accumulation on a World Scale, Vols. I and II*, Monthly Review Press, 1974.

————, *Unequal Development*, Harvester Press, 1976.

————, *Unequal Exchange*, Monthly Review Press, 1976.

————, *Imperialism and Unequal Development*, Monthly Review Press, 1977.

Anderson, M., *Approaches to the History of the Western Family, 1500–1914*, Macmillan, 1980.

Anstey, V., *The Economic Development of India*, Longman, 1936.

Arms, P. E., Archbishop of Sao Paolo, 'Abyss of Fear', The Guardian (UK), 2 August 1985.

Arrighi, G., and Saul, J., 'Socialism and Economic Development in Tropical Africa', *Journal of Modern African Studies*, Vol. 6, *No. 2*, 1968.

Ashby, P., *Social Security After Beveridge: What Next?* Bedford Square Press, 1984.

Atkins, G. L., 'The Economic Status of the Oldest Old', *Health and Society*, Vol. 63, *No. 2*, Spring, 1985.

Atkinson, A. B., *Unequal Shares*, Allen Lane, 1972.

————, *Income Maintenance and Social Insurance: A Survey*, Welfare State Programme Paper, No. 5, London School of Economics and Political Science, 1985.

Australian Government, *Commission of Enquiry into Poverty*, Vol. 1, 1975.

Baker, J., 'There is an Alternative: France's Single Parents', *Poverty*, No. 66, Spring, 1987.

Baran, P., *The Political Economy of Growth*, Monthly Review Press, 1957.

Bardhan, P. K., 'The Pattern of Income Distribution in India: a Review', in Srinivasan, T. N., and Bardhan, P. K., *Poverty and Income Distribution in India*, Statistical Publishing Society, Calcutta, 1974.

Baster, N., 'Development Indicators: an Introduction', *The Journal of Development Studies*, Vol. 8, *No. 3*, April, 1972.

Bauer, P., *Dissent on Development*, Weidenfeld and Nicolson, 1971.

————, and Yamey, B., 'The Political Economy of Foreign Aid', *Lloyd's Bank Review*, No. 142, October, 1981.

Beckerman, W., *Poverty and the Impact of Income Maintenance Programmes* International Labour Office, 1979.

————, 'How Large a Public Sector?' *Oxford Review of Economic Policy*, Vol. 2, *No. 2*, Summer, 1986.

Beeghley, L., *Living Poorly in America*, Praeger, 1984.

Beneria, L., (ed.), *Women and Development*, Praeger, 1982.

Bequele, A., and Van Der Hoeven, R., 'Poverty and Inequality in Sub-Saharan Africa', *International Labour Review*, Vol. 119, No. 3, May–June, 1980.

Bergmann, T., *Farm Policies in Socialist Countries*, Lexington Books, 1975.

Berry, A., and Urrutia, M., *Income Distribution in Colombia*, Yale University Press, 1976.

Berthoud, R., *The Disadvantages of Inequality*, MacDonald and Jane's Publications, 1976.

Bhushan, K., The Riches of the Poor Help the West, *Sunday Standard*, Nairobi, 24 August 1986.

Bigsten, A., *Income Distribution and Development Theory: Evidence and Policy*, Heinemann, 1983.

Blecher, M., 'Inequality and Socialism in Rural China: a Conceptual Note', *World Development* Vol. 13, No. 1, January, 1985.

Blomstrom, M., and Hettne, B., *Development Theory in Transition*, Zed Books, 1984.

Booth, D., 'Marxism and Development Sociology: Interpreting the Impasse', *World Development*, Vol. 13, No. 7, July, 1985.

Borowczyk, E., 'State Social Policy in Favour of the Family in East European Countries', *International Social Security Review*, Year XXXIX, No. 2, 1986.

Boserup, E., *The Conditions of Agricultural Growth*, Allen and Unwin, 1965.

——, 'Economic and Demographic Inter-relationships in Sub-Saharan Africa', *Population and Development Review*, Vol. 11, No. 3, September, 1985.

Bradford, C., 'Rise of the NICSs as Exporters on a Global Scale', in Turner, L., and McMullen, N. (eds), *The Newly Industrialising Countries: Trade and Adjustment*, Allen & Unwin, 1982.

Brandt, W. (Chairman). *North-South. a Programme for Survival*, the Report of the Independent Commission on International Development Issues under the Chairmanship of Willy Brandt, Pan Books, 1980.

——, (Chairman), *Common Crisis*, Second Brandt Report, Pan Books, 1983.

Brown, J. C. (ed.), *Anti-Poverty Policy in the European Community*, Policy Studies Institute, London, 1984.

Brown, M., and Madge, N., *Despite the Welfare State*, Heinemann, 1982.

Brundenius, C., *Economic Growth, Basic Needs and Income Distribution in Revolutionary Cuba*, University of Lund, 1981.

Burghes, L., and Lister, R. (eds), *Unemployment: Who Pays the Price?* Child Poverty Action Group, 1981.

Burki, S. J., and Ayres, R. L., 'A Fresh Look at Development Aid', *Finance and Development*, Vol. 23, *No. 1*, March, 1986.

Bussink, W. F., 'Reflections on Socio-Economic Development and Poverty in East Asia', *World Bank Staff Working Paper*, No. 406, 1980.

Byres, T., and Nolan, P., *Inequality: India and China Compared 1950–1970*, Open University Press, 1976.

Cardoso, F. H., and Faletto, E., *Dependency and Development in Latin America*, University of California Press, 1979.

——, Review of S. Morley's book, *Journal of Development Economics*, Vol. 13, 1983.

Cass, B., 'Income Support for Families with Children', *Social Security Review*, Paper No. 1, Australian Government Publishing Service, 1986.

——, and Loughlin, M. O., *Social Policies for Single-Parent Families in Australia*, Social Welfare Centre, University of New South Wales, 1984.

Cassen, R. H., 'Population and Development: a Survey', *World Development*, Vol. 4, *Nos 10/11*, October/November, 1976.

——, *Does Aid Work?* Oxford University Press, 1986.

——, 'The Effectiveness of Aid', *Finance and Development*, Vol. 23, *No. 1*, March, 1986(a).

Clark, C., Review of World Development Report, 1984, *Population and Development Review*, Vol. 11, *No. 1*, March, 1985.

Cline, W. R., 'International Debt and Stability of the World Economy', Institute for International Economics, Washington, 1983, quoted in Todaro, M., *Economic Development in the Third World*, Longman, 1985.

Cole, S., and Miles, I., *Worlds Apart*, Wheatsheaf Books, 1984.

Coleman, D., and Nixson, F., *Economics of Change in Less Developed Countries*, Allan Publishers, 1978.

Commission of the European Communities, *Final Report from the First Programme of Pilot Schemes and Studies to Combat Poverty*, Brussels, 1981.

——, *Social Europe*, special issue, 1983, Brussels, 1983.

Crystal, S., 'Measuring Income and Inequality Among the Elderly', *The Gerontologist*, Vol. 26, *No. 1*, February, 1986.

Cutler, P., 'The Measurement of Poverty: A Review of Attempts to Quantify the Poor with Special Reference to India', *World Development*, Vol. 12, *Nos 11/12*, November/December, 1984.

Dandekar, V., and Rath, N., 'Poverty in India', *Economic and Political Weekly*, Vol. 6, *No. 1*, 1971.

Dando, W. A., *The Geography of Famine*, Edward Arnold, 1980.
Davies, J. B., 'On the Size Distribution of Wealth in Canada', *Review of Income and Wealth*, Series 25, 1979.
Davis, K., and Moore, W., 'Some Principles of Stratification', *American Sociological Review*, Vol. 10, *No. 2*, April, 1945.
Dawson, A., 'In Defence of Food Aid: some Answers to its Critics', *International Labour Review*, Vol. 124, *No. 1*, January–February 1985.
Department of Health and Social Security, *Second Report of the Social Security Advisory Committee, 1982/83*, HMSO, 1983.
———, *Low Income Families 1983*, HMSO, 1986.
Devlin, R., 'The Burden of Debt and Crisis: is it Time for a Unilateral Solution?' *CEPAL Review*, No. 22, April, 1984.
Dilnot, A., *et al.*, *The Reform of Social Security*, Clarendon Press, 1984.
Duncan, G. J., *Years of Poverty, Years of Plenty*, The University of Michigan, 1984.
Dyson, T., and Moore, M., 'On Kinship Structure, Female Autonomy and Demographic Behaviour in India, *Population and Development Review*, Vol. 9, 1983.

Elliott, C., *The Development Debate*, SCM Press, 1971.
———, *Patterns of Poverty in the Third World: a Study of Social and Economic Stratification*, Praeger, 1975.
Estes, C. L., 'The Agin Enterprise: in Whose Interests?' *International Journal of Health Services*, Vol. 16, *No. 2*, 1986.

Fabner, M., 'How do you Write off $300 Million Debts?' *The Guardian* (UK), 6 June 1987.
Fagin, L., and Little, M., *The Forsaken Families*, Penguin, 1984.
Ferge, S., *A Society in the Making*, Penguin, 1979.
Fiegehen, G. C., *et al.*, *Poverty and Progress in Britain 1953–1983*, Cambridge University Press, 1977.
Fieldhouse, D., *Black Africa, 1945–1980*, Allen and Unwin, 1986.
Fields, G. S., *Poverty, Inequality and Development*, Cambridge University Press, 1980.
Finer Report, *Report of the Committee on One-Parent Families*, Cmnd. 5629, HMSO, 1974.
Fogelman, K., *Growing Up in Britain*, Macmillan, 1983.
Food and Agriculture Organisation, *Third World Food Survey*, Rome, 1963.
———/World Health Organisation, Report of a Joint FAO/WHO Expert Committee, *Energy and Protein Requirements*, World Health Organisation Technical Services Report Series, No. 522, Geneva, 1973.

220   *Wealth, Poverty and Starvation*

————, *Fourth World Food Survey*, Rome, 1977.
————, *The State of Food and Agriculture, 1981*, Rome, 1982.
————, *The State of Food and Agriculture*, Rome, 1984.
————, *The Fifth World Food Survey*, Rome, 1987.
Frank, A. G., *Capitalism and Development in Latin America*, Monthly Review Press, 1967.

Galbraith, K., *The Nature of Mass Poverty*, Penguin, 1980.
Gaud, W. S., 'Foreign Aid: What it is and how it Works; Why we Provide it', *Department of State Bulletin*, 59, *No. 1537*, 1968.
George, S., and Paige, N., *Food for Beginners*, Writers and Readers Publishing Co-operative Society, 1982.
————, *Ill Fares the Land*, Writers and Readers Publishing Co-operative Society, 1985.
George, V., and Wilding, P., *Motherless Families*, Routledge and Kegan Paul, 1972.
————, *Social Security and Society*, Routledge and Kegan Paul, 1973.
————, and Lawson, R. (eds), *Poverty and Inequality in Common Market Countries*, Routledge and Kegan Paul, 1980.
————, and Manning, N., *Socialism, Social Welfare and the Soviet Union*, Routledge and Kegan Paul, 1980.
————, and Wilding, P., *The Impact of Social Policy*, Routledge and Kegan Paul, 1984.
Ghai, D., and Radwan, S., (eds), *Agrarian Policies and Rural Poverty in Africa*, ILO, 1983.
Gilliand, P., 'Towards the Study of the Standard of Living of Old People in Switzerland', *International Social Security Review*, Vol. XXXV, *No. 4*, 1982.
Ginneken, Van, W., *Socio-economic Groups and Income Distribution in Mexico*, Croom Helm, 1980.
Golzen, G., 'Top Executives' Fringe Goodies Get Juicier Still', *Sunday Times*, 18.10.87.
Gorce, de la, P. M., *La France Pauvre*, Bernard Grassett, 1965.
Griffin, K., *Underdevelopment in Spanish America*, Allen and Unwin, 1969.
————, *Land Concentration and Rural Poverty*, Macmillan, 1976.
————, *International Inequality and National Poverty*, Macmillan, 1978.
————, 'World Hunger and the World Economy', in House of Commons Foreign Affairs Committee, *Famine in Africa*, House of Commons Report, 1985, No. 56.
————, 'Rural Development in an Arid Region: Xinjiang', *Third World Quarterly*, Vol. 18, *No. 3*, 1986.

————, 'Doubts About Aid', *IDS Bulletin*, Vol. 17, *No. 2*, April, 1986.

————, *World Hunger and the World Economy*, Macmillan, 1987.

Griffith-Jones, S., 'Ways Forward from the Debt Crisis', *Oxford Review of Economic Policy*, Vol. 2, *No. 1*, Spring, 1986.

Gulati, L., *Profiles in Female Poverty: a Study of Five Poor Working Women in Korala*, Pergamon Press, 1981.

Harbury, C., and McMahon, P., 'Inheritance and the Characteristics of Top Wealth Leavers in Britain', *Economic Journal*, Vol. 83, 1973.

Harrington, M., *The Other America*, Penguin, 1962.

Harrington, P., *Inside the Third World*, Penguin, 1979.

Harrinson, P., *The Greening of Africa*, Paladin, 1987.

Hayter, T., *Aid is Imperialism*, Penguin, 1971.

————, *The Creation of World Poverty*, Pluto Press, 1981.

————, and Watson, C., *Aid: Rhetoric and Reality*, Pluto Press, 1985.

Holman, R., *Poverty: Explanations of Social Deprivation*, Martin Robertson, 1978.

Hoselitz, B., *Sociological Aspects of Economic Growth*, Free Press, 1960.

House of Commons, Foreign Affairs Committee, Second Report, *Famine in Africa*, HMSO, 1985, HCP 1984–85, No. 56.

Independent Commission of International Humanitarian Issues, *Famine: a Man-made Diaster?* Pan Books, 1985.

International Labour Office, *Meeting Basic Needs. Strategies for Eradicating Mass Poverty and Unemployment*, Geneva, ILO, 1977.

————, 'Income Distribution in Selected Countries', *World Labour Report 1*, Statistical Annexe, 1984.

————, Social Security in the Highly Industrialised Countries, *World Labour Report, 1*, 1984.

International Monetary Fund, The Sharp Fall in Commodity Prices, 1984–86, *Finance and Development*, Vol. 23, *No. 4*, December, 1986.

Jackson, T., and Eade, D., *Against the Grain*, Oxfam, 1982.

Joseph, K., and Sumption, J., *Equality*, Murray, 1979.

Kaletsky, A., 'Debating Debt Default', in Gauher, R., (ed.), *Third World Affairs*, Third World Foundation, 1986.

Kamarck, A. M., *The Tropics and Economic Development*, Johns Hopkins University, 1976.

Kamerman, S., and Khan, A., 'Income Transfers and Mothers-only Families in Eight Countries', *Social Service Review*, Vol. 57, *No. 3*, September, 1983.

Kavalsky, B., 'Poverty and Human Development in the Middle East and North Africa', in *World Bank Staff Working Paper*, No. 406, 1980.

Kegfitz, N., 'On the Momentum of Population Growth', *Demography*, Vol. 8, *No. 1*, February, 1971.

Khan, A., 'Poverty and Inequality in Rural Bangladesh', in ILO *Poverty and Landlessness in Rural Asia*, Geneva, 1977.

Kirkpatrick, C., and Diakosavvas, D., 'Food Insecurity and Foreign Exchange Constraints in Sub-Saharan Africa', *Journal of Modern African Studies*, Vol. 23, *No. 2*, June, 1985.

Kravis, I. B., 'International Differences in the Distribution of Income', *Review of Economics and Statistics*, Vol. 42, November, 1960.

———, Heston, A., and Summers, R., *World Product and Income: International Comparisons of Real GDP*, Johns Hopkins University Press, 1982.

Krongkaew, M., 'Agricultural Development, Rural Poverty and Income Distribution in Thailand', *The Developing Economies*, Vol. XXIII, *No. 4*, December, 1985.

Kurian, C. T., 'Rural Poverty in Tamil Nadu', in ILO, *Poverty and Landlessness in Rural Asia*, Geneva, 1971.

Kuznets, S., 'Underdeveloped Countries and the Pre-industrial Phase in the Advanced Countries', in Agarwala, A. N., and Singh, S. P., (eds), *The Economics of Underdevelopment*, Oxford University Press, 1954.

———, 'Economic Growth and Income Inequality', *The American Economic Review*, Vol. XLV, *No. 1*, March, 1955.

Laclau, E., 'Feudalism and Capitalism in Latin America', *New Left Review*, No. 67, 1971.

Lall, S., 'Is "Dependence" a Useful Concept in Analysing Underdevelopment?' *World Development*, Vol. 3, *Nos 11 & 12*, November–December, 1975.

Lane, D., *The End of Social Inequality*, Allen and Unwin, 1982.

Lane, S., 'Debt Sinks the Hope of Africa', *The Guardian*, (UK), 18 July 1987.

Layard, R., *et al.*, *The Causes of Poverty*, HMSO, 1978.

Lecaillon *et al.*, *Income Distribution and Economic Development*, ILO, 1984.

Lee, R., Review of World Development Report, 1984, *Population and Development Review*, Vol. 11, *No. 1*, March, 1985.

Lenin, V., *The Development of Capitalism in Russia*, Progress Publishers, 1956.

——, *Imperialism: the Highest Stage of Capitalism*, Progress Publishers, 1966.

Lerner, D., *The Passing of Traditional Society*, Free Press, 1964.

Lever, H., and Huhne, C., *Debt and Danger: the World Financial Crisis*, Penguin, 1985.

Lewis, A., *Theory of Economic Growth*, Allen and Unwin, 1955.

——, 'Development and Distribution' in Cairncross, A., and Puri, M., (eds), *Employment, Income Distribution and Development Strategy*, Macmillan, 1976.

Lewis, O., *La Vida*, Random House, 1966.

Lisk, F., 'Conventional Development Strategies and Basic—needs Fulfilment: a Reassessment of Objectives and Policies', *International Labour Review*, Vol. 115, *No. 2*, March–April, 1977.

Loeff, J. W., The Level and Trend in Poverty, *Social Security Bulletin*, Vol. 49, *No. 4*, April, 1984.

Long, N., *An Introduction to the Sociology of Rural Development*, Tavistock, 1977.

Manley, M., and Brandt, W., *Global Challenge*, Pan Books, 1985.

Marx, K., *Capital, VOL I*, Penguin, 1976.

——, and Engels, F., *Communist Manifesto*.

McCauley, A., *Economic Welfare in the Soviet Union*, Allen and Unwin, 1979.

McLelland, D., *The Achieving Society*, Norstrand, 1961.

Midgley, J., *Social Security, Inequality and the Third World*, John Wiley and Sons, 1984.

——, 'Social Assistance: an Alternative Form of Social Protection in Developing Countries', *International Social Security Review*, Vol. XXXVII, *No. 3*, 1984.

Mitton, R. M., *et al.*, *Unemployment, Poverty and Social Policy in Europe*, Bedford Square Press, 1983.

Molina, S. S., 'Poverty: Description and Analysis of Policies for Overcoming it', *CEPAL Review*, No. 18, December, 1982.

Moore, B., Jr., *Social Origins of Dictatorship and Democracy*, Penguin, 1969.

Moore, W., *Social Change*, Prentice-Hall, 1963.

Morawitz, D., *Twenty-five Years of Economic Development 1950 to 1975*, The World Bank, 1977.

Morley, S., *Labor Markets and Inequitable Growth: the Case of Authoritarian Capitalism in Brazil*, Cambridge University Press, 1983.

Mosley, P., 'Aid-effectivness: the Micro-Macro Paradox', *IDS Bulletin*, Vol. 17, *No. 2*, April, 1986.

Mouton, D., *Social Security in Africa*, ILO, 1973.

Moylan, S., *et al.*, *For Richer for Poorer?* DHSS Cohort Study of Unemployed Men, DHSS, 1984.

Musgrove, P., 'Food Needs and Absolute Poverty in Urban South America', *Income and Wealth*, Series No. 1,March, 1985.

Myrdal, G., *Development and Underdevelopment*, Fiftieth Anniversary Commemoration Lectures, National Bank of Egypt, 1956.

――――, *Rich Lands and Poor*, Harper and Row, 1957.

――――, *The Challenge of World Poverty*, Penguin, 1970.

Naseem, S. M., 'Rural Poverty and Landlessness in Pakistan', in ILO' *Poverty and Landlessness in Rural Asia*, Geneva, 1977.

National Council of Welfare, *Poverty Profile, 1985*, Ottawa, 1985.

Navarro, V., 'The Limits of the World Systems Theory in Defining Capitalist and Socialist Formations, *Science and Society*, Vol. XLVI, *No. 1*, Spring, 1982.

Nayyar, R., 'Wages, Employment and Standard of Living of Agrticultural Labourers in Uttar Pradesh', in ILO, *Poverty and Landlessness in Rural Asia*, Geneva, 1977.

Ndegwa, P., *et al.*, *Development Options for Africa in the 1980s and Beyond*, Oxford University Press, 1985.

Nelson, D., 'Have we been Wrong about Family Planning?', *The Standard*, 3 September 1986 (Kenyan daily newspaper).

Neysmith, S. M., and Edward, J., 'Economic Dependence in the 1980s: its impact on Third World Elderly', *Ageing and Society*, Vol. 4, *No. 1*, 1984.

Nugent, J., 'The Old Age Security Motive for Fertility', *Population and Development Review*, Vol. 11, *No. 1*, March 1985.

――――, and Gillaspy, T., 'Old Age Pensions and Fertility in Rural Areas of Less Developed Countries: Some Evidence from Mexico', *Economic Development and Cultural Change*, Vol. 31, *No. 4*, July, 1983.

Nyerere, J., *The Arusha Declaration: Ten Years After*, Kenyan Government Printing Office, 1979.

Organisation for Economic Co-operation and Development, *Public Expenditure on Income Maintenance Programmes*, Paris, 1976.

――――, *Development Co-operation Review*, 1984.

――――, *Employment Outlook*, September, 1984.

――――, *Twenty-five Years of Development Co-operation: a Review*, Paris, 1985.

――――, *Financing and External Debt of Developing Countries: 1985*

Survey, Paris, 1986.

Orshansky, M., Counting the Poor, *Social Security Bulletin*, Vol. 28, *No. 1*, January, 1965.

Oxley, C., *Assistance for Families with Dependent Children–A Comparative Study*, Department of Social Security, Canberra, 1986.

Pacey, A., and Payne, P., (eds), *Agricultural Development and Nutrition*, Hutchinsoin, 1985.

Paddock, P., and Paddock, W., *Famine–1975, America's Decision: Who Will Survive?* Little Brown and Co., 1967.

Papanek, G. F., and Kyn, O., The Effect on Income Distribution of Development, the Growth Rate and Economic Strategy, *Journal of Development Economics*, Vol. 23, *No. 1*, September, 1986.

Parsons, T., *Towards a General Theory of Action*, Harvard University Press, 1951.

————, *Societies*, Prentice-Hall, 1966.

Pearce, D., The Feminisation of Poverty: Women, Work and Welfare, *Urban and Social Change Review*, Vol. 2, *Nos 1 and 2*, 1978.

Pearson, L. B., *et al.*, *Partners in Development*, Pall Mall Press, 1969.

Quan, N. T., and Koo, A. Y. C., 'Concentration of Land Holdings: an Empirical Exploration of Kuzents's Conjecture', *Journal of Development Economics*, Vol. 18, *No. 1*, May–June, 1985.

Quin, J. F., 'The Economic Status of the Elderly: Beware of the Mean', *The Review of Income and Wealth*, Series 33, *No. 1*, March, 1987.

Rai, L. *England's Debt to India*, Huebsch, 1917.

Rajaraman, I., 'Growth and Poverty in the Rural Areas of the Indian State of Punjab, 1960–61 to 1970–71', in ILO, *Poverty and Landlessness in Rural Areas*, Geneva, 1977.

Randall, V., and Theobald, R., *Political Change and Underdevelopment*, Macmillan, 1985.

Rao, V. V., Bhanoji. 'Measurement of Deprivation and Poverty Based on the Proportion Spent on Food: An Exploratory Exercise', *World Development*, Vol. 9, *No. 4*, 1981.

Reutlinger, S., and Pellekaan, van Holst, J., *Poverty and Hunger*, World Bank, 1986.

Reynolds, L. G., *Economic Growth in the Third World*, Yale University Press, 1986.

Rimmer, D., *Economies of West Africa*, Weidenfeld and Nicolson, 1984.

Rodney, W., *How Europe Underdeveloped Africa*, Bogle-L'Overture Publications, 1972.

Rostow, W., *The Stages of Economic Growth*, Cambridge University Press, 1962.

Rowntree, B. S., *Poverty: a Study of Town Life*, Macmillan, 1901.

Roxborough, I., *Theories of Underdevelopment*, Macmillan, 1979.

Royal Commission on the Distribution of Income and Wealth, *Report No. 5*, Cmnd. 6999, HMSO, 1977.

Rutter, M., and Madge, N., *Cycles of Deprivation*, Heinemann, 1976.

Saith, A., 'Development and Distribution: a Critique of the Cross-Country U-Hypothesis', *Journal of Development Economics*, Vol. 13, 1983.

Sarvasy, W., and Allen, J. V., Fighting the Feminisation of Poverty: Socialist-Feminist Analysis and Strategy, *Review of Radical Political Economics*, Vol. 16, *No. 4*, 1984.

Schofield, S., 'Seasonal Factors Affecting Nutrition in Different Age Groups', *Journal of Development Studies*, Vol. 11, 1974.

Seabrook, J., *Landscapes of Poverty*, Blackwell, 1985.

Seers, D. 'What are we Trying to Measure?' *The Journal Development Studies*, Vol. 8, *No. 3*, 1972.

Sen, A., 'Poverty, Inequality and Unemployment', in Srinivasan, T., and Bardham, P., *Poverty and Income Distribution in India*, Calcutta, Statistical Publishing Society, 1974.

————, *Poverty and Famines*, Clarendon Press, 1981.

————, and Senqupta, S., Malnutrition of Rural Children and Sex Bias, *Economic and Political Weekly*, Annual Number, May, 1983.

————, The Food Problem: Theory and Policy, *Third World Quarterly*, Vol. 4, *No. 3*, July, 1983.

Shaw, B. G., *Man and Superman, The Works of George Bernard Shaw, Vol. 20*, Constable, 1930.

Simon, J., *The Ultimate Resource*, Robertson, 1981.

Sinfield, A., *What Unemployment Means*, Martin Robertson, 1981.

Sinha, R., *et al.*, *Income Distribution, Growth and Basic Needs in India*, Croom Helm, 1979.

Smith, D. S., *Where the Grass is Greener*, Penguin, 1977.

Smith, S., and Toye, J., 'Three Stories about Trade and Poor Economies', *Journal of Development Studies*, Vol. 15, *No. 3*, April, 1979.

Spraos, J., Deteriorating Terms of Trade and Beyond, *Trade and Development*, No. 4, Winter, 1982.

Sukhatme. P. V., Measurement of Undernutrition, *Economic and*

Political Weekly, XVII, *No. 50*, December 11, 1982.

Sutcliffe, B., Industry and Underdevelopment Re-examined, *Journal of Development Studies*, Vol. 21, *No. 1*, October, 1984.

Thirlwall, A. P., and Bergevin, J., 'Trends, Cycles and Asymmetries in the Terms of Trade of Primary Commodities from Developed and Less Developed Countries', *World Development*, Vol. 13, *No. 7*, July, 1985.

Todaro, M. P., *Economics for a Developing World*, Longman, 1977.

———, *Economic Development in the Third World*, Longman, 1985.

Townsend, P., *Poverty in the United Kingdom*, Penguin, 1979.

———, 'A Theory of Poverty and the Role of Social Policy', in Loney, M., *et al.* (eds), *Social Policy and Social Welfare*, Open University Press, 1983.

Trescott, P., 'Incentives Versus Equality: What does China's Recent Experience Show?' *World Development*, Vol. 13, *No. 2*, February, 1985.

Tumin, M., 'Some Principles of Stratification. a Critical Analysis', *American Sociological Review*, Vol. 18, 1953.

United Nations International Children's Education Fund, *The State of the World's Children 1985*, Oxford University Press, 1985.

United Nations Organisation, United Nations Report of the Secretary General, *Effective Mobilisation of Women in Development*, United Nations/A/33/238, 1978.

———, UNCTAD, *The Least Developed Countries, 1984*, Report, Vol. II, 1984.

———, *World Economic Survey, 1986*, New York, 1986.

———, 'Economic and Social Commission for Asia and the Pacific', *Economic and Social Survey of Asia and the Pacific*, 1986, Bangkok, 1987.

United States Department of Health and Human Resources, Social Security Administration, *Social Security Bulletin, Annual Statistical Supplement, 1986*, Washington, 1987.

Van Ginneken, W., *Rural and Urban Inequalities in Indonesia, Mexico, Pakistan, Tanzania and Tunisia*, ILO, 1976.

———, *Socio-economic Groups and Income Distribution in Mexico*, Croom Helm, 1980.

Walker, R., Lawson, R., and Townsend, P., (eds), *Responses to Poverty: Lessons from Europe*, Heinemann, 1984.

Wallerstein, I., *The Modern World System*, Academic Press, 1974a.

———, 'The Rise and Future Demise of the World Capitalist

System', *Comparative Studies in Society and History*, Vol. 16, *No. 4*, 1974.

——, *The Capitalist World Economy*, Cambridge University Press, 1980.

Warnock, J. W., *The Politics of Hunger*, Methuen, 1987.

Warren, B., *Imperialism, Pioneer of Capitalism*, New Left Books, 1980.

Winyard, S., *Fair Remuneration*, Low Pay Unit, 1982.

Woodham-Smith, C., *The Great Hunger: Ireland 1845-9*, Hamish Hamilton, 1962.

World Bank, *Population Policies and Economic Development*, Johns Hopkins University Press, 1974.

——, *World Development Report*, Washington, 1978.

——, *World Development Report*, Oxford University Press, 1980.

——, *Accelerated Development in Sub-Saharan Africa*, Washington, 1981.

——, *World Development Report*, Oxford University Press, 1984.

——, *World Development Report*, Oxford University Press, 1985.

——, *World Development Report*, Oxford University Press, 1986.

——, *World Development Report*, Oxford University Press, 1987.

Wright, C. L., 'Income Inequality and Economic Growth: Examining the Evidence', *The Journal of Developing Areas*, Vol. 13, *No. 1*, October, 1978.

Index